RESEARCH IN TESTING

This volume is published by the Center for Research in Accounting Education, School of Accounting, James Madison University, directed by Dr. Ralph L. Benke, Jr.

All rights reserved. This book or any part thereof may not be reproduced without written permission of the authors.
Copyright 1990.

RESEARCH IN TESTING

Edited by:

Donna L. Street
Ashton C. Bishop
Ralph L. Benke, Jr.

Published by Center for Research in Accounting Education, School of Accounting, James Madison University, Harrisonburg, VA. Copyright 1990.

TABLE OF CONTENTS

Section I The Process of Testing 1
    Fundamental Issues in Educational Measurement--
        Hartwell C. Herring III 3

Section II Testing Formats 17
    Testing with Multiple-Choice Items--Lewis R. Aiken 19

    The Role of Difficulty and Discrimination in
        Constructing Multiple-Choice Examinations:
        With Guidelines for Practice Applications--
        Bruce A. Baldwin 47

    The Relative Merits of Multiple True-False
        Achievement Tests--David A. Frisbee and
        Daryl C. Sweeney 59

    Measuring Higher Level Learning Outcomes--
        Donna L. Street 67

    Improving Essay Tests--Donald R. Coker,
        Rosemarie K. Kolstad and Alonzo H. Sosa 85

Section III Testing and Test Construction 91
    Implications for Altering the Context in Which Test
        Items Appear: A Historical Perspective on an
        Immediate Concern--Linda F. Leary
        and Neil J. Dorans 93

    College Student Performance Under Repeated Testing
        and Cumulative Testing Conditions: Report on
        Five Studies--Rosalie H. Rohm, Frank J. Sparzo,
        and Carson M. Bennett 125

    On the Benefits of Cumulative Exams: An Experimental
        Study--Thomas P. Edmonds 137

Section IV Test Anxiety 149
    Correlates, Causes, Effects and Treatment of Test
        Anxiety--Ray Hembree 151

Secion V Computerized Testing 181
    On-Line Computer Testing: Implementation and
        Endorsement--John Gwinn and Loretta Beal 183

PREFACE

One of the most important aspects of the educational process is the evaluation of student performance through testing. Despite the importance of student assessment, most college and university faculty have received little, if any, training in testing and test construction.

The purpose of this book is to bring together a collection of papers covering key testing issues. These papers have appeared as articles in professional journals such as *Accounting Review, Journal of Accounting Education, Journal of Education Research, Journal of Educational Measurement, Journal of Research and Development in Education*, and *Review of Educational Measurement*.

Section I of the book is an introduction to the fundamental issues of educational measurement. This paper [Herring], previously unpublished, was written especially for this book. The paper includes a discussion of the importance of testing as a form of educational assessment and the objectives of educational measurement. Test reliability and validity are also defined and explained; the discussion centers around valuable illustrations which hopefully will clarify these key concepts for the reader.

Section II serves as an introduction to various testing formats. Two papers in this section address the multiple choice test format. One of these papers [Aiken] is a critical review of research conducted on multiple choice tests of achievement and aptitude and emphasizes the design and use of this testing format.

The second paper [Baldwin] explores some of the concepts of testing and measurement theory that underlie the development of high quality multiple choice questions. In addition, specific guidelines are developed for use in generating high quality multiple choice questions.

Another paper [Frisbee and Sweeney] explores the merits of multiple true false achievement tests. The results of the study indicate that multiple true false questions compare favorably with multiple choice questions, and support the theoretical expectation that multiple true false questions may be superior to multiple choice items.

In another previously unpublished paper [Street], the education literature concerning the relationship between test format and the types of knowledge, skills, and abilities which are measured is reviewed. This research suggests that most classroom examinations fail to adequately measure important higher level learning outcomes. The paper also discusses the types of knowledge, skills, and abilities that can be measured using the following question types: true false, multiple choice, the interpretative exercise, numerical problem solving--objective format versus free response, and essay. The advantages and limitations of these question types are also discussed.

The final paper [Coker, et al.] in this section provides guidelines for constructing essay examinations.

Section III addresses various aspects of testing and test construction. This section begins with a paper [Leary and Dorans] which reviews the education literature on question arrangement. Included in the review are studies which investigated: 1) the main effect of question order on test performance, 2) the interactions between question order and factors of examinees; psychological and biological characteristics, and 3) effects of question order on the stability of question parameters. The literature indicates that context effects (hard to easy, easy to hard, random order, order in which items were covered, etc.) do exist but does not provide evidence that the effects are sufficiently strong to invalidate test theory or practice.

Another paper in this section [Rohm, Sparzo, and Bennett] explores the benefits of cumulative examinations. This study analyzes the effect of two types of cumulative examinations. One strategy involves the use of randomly selected review questions on each cumulative examination. The other strategy involves cumulative examinations where special review questions are designed for each student which emphasize topics missed by that student on previous examinations. A control group, which did not take cumulative examinations, was also included in the study. The findings indicate that the random review cumulative examination was the more efficient strategy. Concluding this section is a paper [Edmonds] which examines the effect of repeated testing and cumulative testing on student performance. The results of the study indicate that repeated testing led to better performance than cumulative testing under every-other-week but not weekly conditions. However, repeated cumulative tests promoted better achievement than either non-repeated cumulative or repeated single-unit tests (incorporate only content that is currently under study) when tests were administered weekly.

Text anxiety is the subject of Section IV. This section is comprised of a single paper [Hembree] which uses meta-analysis to integrate the results of 562 studies addressing test anxiety. Based on the results of the meta-analysis, the author makes the following conclusions: test anxiety causes poor performance; test anxiety relates inversely to a student's self esteem and directly to fear of negative evaluation, defensiveness, and other forms of anxiety; causes of test anxiety include ability, gender, and school grade level; a variety of treatments are effective in reducing test anxiety; and improved test performance and grade point average consistently accompany test anxiety reduction.

Section V addresses computerized testing. The paper in this section [Gwinn and Beal] describes an interactive computer testing and record keeping system which was implemented for a large self-paced university course. In addition, the results of a study on student preference for on-line testing, test anxiety, attitude, and achievement are presented. Strengths and weaknesses of on-line testing for faculty and students are discussed. The results of the study indicate that over time there was a slight reduction in realistic computer attitudes and a slight increase in test anxiety. Overall, the authors found no major educational or economic drawbacks in the use of on-line computer testing.

The editors hope that *Research in Testing* will strengthen the interest of college and university faculty in the area of testing and test construction. In addition, we hope that the book will stimulate further research in this important area and enhance the quality of teaching and student evaluation.

We thank the authors and copyright holders of the selections included in this book. Special thanks to Lori McFall for doing the laborious and essential production work associated with this endeavor.

>Donna L. Street
>Ashton C. Bishop
>Ralph L. Benke, Jr.

SECTION I

The Process of Testing

FUNDAMENTAL ISSUES IN EDUCATIONAL MEASUREMENT

Hartwell C. Herring III
University of Tennessee

This article is an introductory reading for the other articles in this book. The purpose of the article is to review the basic concepts of developing good achievement tests. These concepts include specification of testing objectives and test reliability and validity.

SPECIFICATION OF TESTING OBJECTIVES

Testing for achievement

Testing for selection and testing for achievement are *distinctly* different activities with different objectives. Selection tests are used in college and graduate school admission decisions. These tests emphasize particular types of verbal and quantitative skills. The skills are considered by proponents of these tests to be fundamental to achievement in virtually all areas of learning. While some objections have been stated about the limitations of these tests, empirical evidence strongly supports their validity. (Ebel, 1972, 539-541.)

In contrast, testing for achievement is concerned with whether the learning process has had an impact upon an important educational outcome. Objections to the concept of achievement tests have been raised by some writers. However, educational psychologists are in general agreement that educational outcomes are measurable and that achievement tests are indispensable in the measurement process. While it may be possible to teach without giving tests, one cannot teach without evaluating the learning process. Testing remains the most efficient and dependable means of evaluation yet devised (Ebel, 1972, p. 36-42).

The objectives of educational measurement

To assess changes in important educational outcomes by testing, these outcomes must be specified. One way to identify educational outcomes is for the teacher to formalize the educational objectives of the material to be covered.

Educational objectives can be categorized into at least two basic groups. One basic group has global goals. These objectives are concerned with the development of a student's self image, citizenship, values, and social responsibility. All educational programs and curricula, including technical college courses, should implicitly have these objectives. Failure to incorporate global goals into the development and teaching of a course deprives the course of its moral significance.

A second set of objectives consists of one or more levels of specific behaviors or performance levels that students are expected to attain (Krathwohl & Payne, 1971, pp. 17-23). Omission of this set of objectives from a course contributes to a lack of organization. It also opens the pathway to emphasis upon unimportant issues to the exclusion of essential material.

For example, multiple choice examinations often stress the learning of isolated facts as learning objectives, even though the professors who prepare these questions believe that their test items require the employment of complex cognitive skills (Milton, Pollio, & Eison, 1986, pp. 19-23). Strong evidence repeatedly emphasizes that the type of test given will affect what students learn. If tests emphasize surface level mental processes and memorization, those are the processes the students will use. If tests emphasize trivia, students will learn trivia (Milton, 1982; Frederiksen, 1984). The failure of teachers to consider carefully the specific learning objectives of their courses contributes to the construction of tests which discourage the development and use of analytical skills.

Most accounting teachers probably take the time to conceptualize in some form both types of objectives for their classes. Many accounting textbooks begin each chapter with statements of the objectives or purposes of the chapter. A few books provide a formal list of specific objectives at the beginning of each chapter. Some faculty also provide a statement of course objectives in course syllabi. The extent to which current practice is adequate is an empirical question. Anecdotal evidence, however, produces a skeptical view of the adequacy of current practice.

If professors wish to emphasize important educational outcomes in their achievement tests, they should begin by basing their courses on carefully stated objectives. When these objectives are formalized in textbooks, syllabi, handouts, or lectures, the probability that tests will be related to objectives is increased. Elementary and secondary school teachers have long recognized the importance of this process. Standard textbooks on the subject of educational measurement provide detailed discussions of the process (Gronlund, 1976; Ebel, 1972; Ebel & Frisbee, 1986). The complexity of subject matter makes specification of educational objectives for college courses more difficult than for elementary school courses. However, this complexity does not make well stated objectives any less helpful.

TEST RELIABILITY

Test scores have important statistical properties. We are sometimes tempted to interpret test scores without considering these properties, but this temptation should be avoided. Both a mean and a variance can be computed for a test, and, when the number of students exceeds 20 or so, several other important statistics can be computed. Because of the importance of these statistics for understanding test reliability and validity, several issues related to them will be discussed.

An important statistical property of test scores is the correlation coefficient. It can be used to compare the relationship between two sets of test scores and assess test reliability. Reliability is the extent to which a test consistently measures whatever it measures.

Normally, the correlation between the scores on two tests (over the same material) given to a single class will be high because both tests measure the same thing. Correlations of less than .85 to .90 raise questions about the reliability of the test.[1]

The correlation between two sets of test scores is affected by the variability of the distribution of scores. As the variability of the test scores declines, so does the correlation. The explanation for this circumstance lies in test theory. As the correlation declines, the reliability of the test declines.

Test score variability is composed of two elements, a true element resulting from real differences in student performance and an error element. As individual student abilities converge (or narrow), a larger and larger portion of total test score variability is composed of error variation. Since error variability exhibits a random pattern from one test to another, correlation between scores on different tests will fall. This factor poses a potential problem for assessing the reliability of tests given to groups of students whose ability levels do not vary much (Stanley, 1971, p. 362).

Test score distributions are also likely to be affected by the types of tests given. Objective (multiple-choice) tests can be consistently scored, and this consistency contributes to the reliability of the test. But, objective tests are difficult to write and frequently fail to test complex cognitive skills. Another problem with multiple-choice tests is that better students often find some right in the wrong choices and some wrong in the right choices.

By comparison, essay or problem tests are much more difficult to score consistently. Furthermore, essay questions are frequently misinterpreted by the students answering them. While essay tests offer the potential for assessing more complex mental constructs and abilities, they may not necessarily do so (Green, 1981, p. 1002).

---

[1] One would also expect that the correlation between a set of test scores and criterion variables, such as grade point average, will be moderately high (Green, 1981, p. 1002). Criterion variables like GPA have factors underlying them that are not reflected in any particular test score. Therefore, their correlation with a test score will normally be lower than the correlation between test scores.

Assessing test reliability

For a test to be of any value, it must be *reliable*. Reliability is a statistical property of a test and does not address the additional issue of whether the content of the test is appropriate. Unless a test is reliable, no consideration can be made of the appropriateness of its content.

Reliability estimation techniques. In theory, test reliability can be assessed by comparing the results of a test with a second equivalent test. This approach has clear practical and cost-benefit limitations. A better approach is to divide the test into equal halves and compare the results of the two halves using the Spearman-Brown formula (Ebel & Frisbee, 1986, pp. 76-77; Green, 1981, p. 1005). This formula calculates test reliability, R, from the correlations of the two halves:

$$R = 2r/(1 + r)$$

Where: r = correlation coefficient of the two halves

For example, assume the odd-even correlation for the two halves of a test is .74. Total reliability calculated by the Spearman-Brown formula is 2(.74)/(1 + .74) or .85. Recall that a correlation of less than .85 raises questions about the reliability of the test.

A useful principle of test reliability is illustrated by the above application of the Spearman-Brown formula; the reliability of a test can be increased by lengthening it. The above formula can be used to determine how much reliability will increase when the length of the test is doubled. An underlying assumption of the formula is that the test is lengthened by adding items like those already in the test.

The explanation for the above relationship is that doubling the test length using the split halves approach doubles the true score element while minimizing the error score elements. The error score elements tend to cancel each other out (due to random variation), resulting in increased reliability for the longer test. One practical way of splitting a test into halves is to employ an odd-even scheme which correlates the odd numbered items with the even numbered ones.

Another simple means of estimating test reliability is the Kuder-Richardson (KR) formulas 20 and 21 (Ebel & Frisbee, 1986, pp. 77-79). The KR formulas assess reliability from the intercorrelations of the individual test questions. Each question is treated as if it is a separate test with a true and error element. In theory, the errors are not correlated, thus the question intercorrelations are based only on the true component (Green, 1981, p. 1005).

TABLE 1
EXAMPLE OF RELIABILITY ESTIMATES USING THE
KUDER-RICHARDSON FORMULAS 20 AND 21

Test item	Proportion of Correct Responses (p)	Proportion of Incorrect Responses (q)
1	85	15
2	70	30
3	53	47
4	70	30
5	76	24
6	89	11
7	47	53
8	59	41
9	87	13
10	77	23
11	74	26
12	66	34
13	85	15
14	83	17
15	96	04
16	59	41
17	74	26
18	70	30
19	72	28
20	76	24

Number of items   20

Number of Students   47

Mean score ($\bar{X}$)   14.68

Variance (s^2)   13.37

Σpq 3.61

Reliability: KR_{20} = 20/19 [1 - 3.61/13.37]
                       = .768

Reliability: KR_{21} = 20/19 [1 - $\frac{14.68 (20 - 14.68)}{20 \times 13.37}$]
                       = .745

Where test questions vary in difficulty, the KR formula 20 should be used:

$$R = k/(k - 1) [1 - \Sigma pq/s^2]$$

where: R = overall test reliability
k = number of questions on the test
p = proportion of questions answered correctly
q = proportion of questions answered incorrectly
s^2 = variance of test scores

The data in Table 1 provide an example of this calculation based on a 20 item multiple choice test. The KR formula 20 requires that questions be scored one point for a correct answer and zero for an incorrect answer. Should more complex grading schemes which adjust for guessing be used, other, more complex KR formulas must be employed (Ebel & Frisbee, 1986, p. 77).

If all test questions are of relatively equal difficulty, a simpler estimation of reliability can be made using the KR formula 21. This simpler estimation makes use of the test mean rather than the individual correct and incorrect proportions. The KR 21 formula is:

$$R = k/(k - 1) [1 - \frac{\bar{X}(k - \bar{X})}{ks^2}]$$

where: R = overall test reliability

k = number of test questions

$\bar{X}$ = mean of the test scores

s^2 = variance of the test scores

Table 1 also provides an example of the KR formula 21 calculations using the same data as in the KR formula 20. In Table 1, the assumption of relatively equal difficulty is generally satisfied since 16 of the 20 questions have 50% to 85% correct responses. Thus the KR 21 estimate is only slightly smaller (.745) than the KR 20 estimate (.768). The KR 21 may underestimate reliability considerably if the variation in difficulty of the individual items is large (Ebel & Frisbee, 1986, p. 78).

The KR formulas 20 and 21 are designed to be used with objective questions. A KR formula is also available for subjectively graded test questions where students answer several questions, or it can be applied to a single question with multiple graders (Ebel & Frisbee, 1986, p. 79):

$$R = k/(k-1)\,[1 - (\Sigma s_i^2 / s_t^2)]$$

where:
- k = number of questions or ratings
- s_i^2 = variance of student scores on question i or from a particular rater
- Σs_i^2 = sum of question or rater variances for all items
- s_t^2 = variance of total scores or sum of ratings from all raters

An example of this calculation is shown in Table 2. The example shows the reliability calculation for a 4 item test for 5 students. The relatively high reliability results from the high variability of the total scores and the similarity of the within student scores.

TABLE 2
EXAMPLE OF RELIABILITY ESTIMATES OF SUBJECTIVE TESTS

STUDENT	1	2	3	4	TOTAL SCORE
A	10	8	9	9	36
B	4	6	4	5	19
C	6	9	6	5	26
D	9	9	9	9	36
E	2	4	4	5	15
TOTAL	31	36	32	33	132
MEAN	6.2	7.2	6.4	6.6	26.4
VARIANCE	8.96	3.76	5.04	3.84	73.84

SUM OF QUESTION VARIANCES = 21.60

RELIABILITY = 4/3 [1 - (21.60/73.84)]

= .943

Evaluating the Reliability. An important question is whether the reliability of the test scores is high or low. There are two benchmarks which may be used to evaluate a reliability coefficient [Gronlund, 1982 p. 135]. The first benchmark compares the reliability coefficient with the extreme degrees of reliability that it is possible to obtain. A coefficient of .00 indicates a complete lack of reliability, while a coefficient of +1 indicates perfect positive reliability.

The second benchmark compares the reliability coefficient with those usually obtained for achievement tests. For standard achievement tests, the reported reliabilities are frequently over .90 when the Kuder-Richardson formulas are used. Reliability coefficients between .60 and .80 are typical of classroom tests (Diederich, 1973).

Causes of score variation. While test reliability is a statistical property, the underlying causes of test variation which affect reliability come from a wide variety of specific causes. It is not possible to attribute mathematical aspects of reliability to these causes, but the major causes of test variation can be identified. Faced with a problem of test reliability, a teacher could do much in the way of rectifying the problem simply by being familiar with these causes. In addition, knowledge of these issues can do much to develop an understanding of the factors that affect individual performance.

Thorndike (1951) and Stanley (1971) have identified six major sources of test variation. Two of these are concerned with permanent or lasting characteristics of the individual student. Two more describe temporary characteristics. A fifth source consists of factors associated with administration or grading of tests. A sixth source is chance--variation due to momentary distraction or luck.

Permanent characteristics of individual students include general characteristics related to the student's ability, specific abilities related to tests in general, and to the particular test in question. The largest factor affecting a test score is a student's ability in verbal and quantitative skills. These factors affect test taking, and understanding instruction. Empirical studies in accounting have strongly supported this relationship, demonstrating that general abilities measured by ACT are important predictive variables in models forecasting accounting student performance (Ingram & Petersen, 1987; Eckel & Johnson, 1983).

In addition to these general abilities, test performance is also affected by specific individual characteristics which relate to the test or to certain test items. For example, students may vary in ability with respect to specific test formats. In addition, a certain amount of test score variation can arise as a result of sampling error.

Temporary individual characteristics include general factors associated with the student's state of mind at a particular time. Some of the general factors are health, motivation, mental stress, and the external conditions in the test area. Temporary factors more specific to a particular test or test question may also cause variation in test scores. These factors include the student's knowledge of particular problem skills or techniques needed to complete the test, the student's level of practice on those skills, and psychological factors related to fluctuation in memory and attentiveness.

Important factors related to test administration and grading may also cause test score variation. Foremost among these are test conditions. Examples are time limits (speed tests), the existence of superfluous distractions, and the clarity of instructions.

Timed examinations are frequently used. Instructors must be aware that excessive time pressure may cause statistical estimates of reliability to be spuriously high. Reliability estimates of speed tests require that speed be controlled to avoid confounding ability with speed. If the split-halves or Kuder-Richardson methods are used to estimate reliability and the test halves or individual questions are not timed separately, the estimates of speed on the test parts will appear to be identical. This will inflate the reliability estimate based on the confounded variables (Ebel & Frisbee, 1986, p. 86-87).

In addition to test conditions, score variation may result from grading bias. This problem is much more likely to occur in problem or essay tests than on objective tests.

Ways of improving reliability. Teachers wishing to improve test reliability should concentrate their efforts on five basic areas (Ebel & Frisbee, 1986, pp. 82-83):

    1. Lengthening the test
    2. Increasing the homogeneity of questions
    3. Increasing the number of discriminating questions
    4. Increasing the number of questions of moderate difficulty
    5. Having students with broad ability ranges as opposed to narrow ability ranges

If all other factors are equal, a longer test will be more reliable than a shorter test. However, the relationship between length and reliability is not linear. For example, a 20 item test with a reliability of .50 must be increased 4 times to 80 items to reach a reliability of .80. The reliability of a lengthened test may be calculated using an adaptation of the Spearman-Brown formula (Ebel & Frisbee, 1986, p. 76):

$$r_n = \frac{n(r)}{(n-1)r + 1}$$

where n = number of times the test is lengthened
              r = reliability coefficient of the original test
              r_n = reliability coefficient of the lengthened test

Thus for the above data:

$$r_n = \frac{4(.5)}{3(.5)+1}$$

$$= .80$$

Increasing the homogeneity of test items makes it easier to write questions with high discriminating value. These questions will differentiate students according to ability and knowledge of the subject. Since accounting courses are relatively homogeneous, this goal is achievable. The ability to write good discriminators is a product of common sense and experience. Test questions should be based on good ideas which are clearly expressed.

Related to discrimination is the need to have a high number of questions of moderate difficulty. Test questions which all students miss or all students answer correctly contribute literally nothing to reliability because the items cause no variation in the scores.

Finally, if students have a narrow ability range, their scores are not likely to vary as much as if they have a wide ability range. A wide range of student abilities makes assessing test reliability easier. Unfortunately, this condition is generally beyond the control of the classroom instructor. However, knowledge of its impact on reliability is essential in test evaluation.

TEST VALIDITY

There are at least 10 terms and definitions for types of test validity (Cronbach, 1971; Ebel, 1986). However, for achievement tests (as opposed to psychological tests and placement tests), two essential concepts are central. First, a test which is not *reliable* cannot be *valid* (Ebel, 1972, p. 408). Thus, reliability is a necessary but not a sufficient condition for validity. "If a test does not correlate with itself, it cannot correlate with anything else." (Green, 1981, p. 1006).

The second feature of a valid test is relevance. An achievement test that is both reliable and relevant is valid. This association brings us to the question of what aspects of validity produce relevance in a test?

Content validity. The most essential feature of test validity involves the issue of whether the test is a representative sample of relevant knowledge and skills (Cronbach, 1971, p. 446). The test must both *sample fairly* and sample from a population of *relevant subject matter.*

Ebel (1972, pp. 436-438) includes content validity in a broader set of concepts which he calls direct or primary validity. Primary validity must be built into a test by reference to the goals and objectives which the teacher has previously established. The extent to which a test has primary validity is essentially a question answered by critical evaluation and not by empirical analysis.

To some extent there is a conflict between the content validity and the reliability of tests (Messick, 1975, p. 957). For example, many fundamental concepts in accounting might make appropriate test subjects from a content validity perspective. However, if these are concepts which most students have mastered, the resulting high correct response rate will lower score variability and thus lower test reliability. The same is true of questions which many students answer incorrectly.

A practical solution is for test writers to avoid the use of questions which are on the extremes of easy and difficult and concentrate on the use of questions in the middle ranges of difficulty. Questions on any subject in the extreme zones of easy and difficult provide little information to the teacher. While this approach may tend to lower overall scores, particularly when "gift" questions are avoided, this result should not pose a problem for the teacher. The whole theory of test reliability is based on concepts of relative relationships and of evaluation based on relative standing.

Construct validity. Construct validity is concerned with whether a test measures the attributes that it purports to measure (Cronbach, 1971, p. 446). To a large extent this question is empirical. However, assessing the construct validity of a classroom test requires that it be compared with some external variable. Few, if any, such variables are available.

Student grades can be used. But, grades are based on many factors other than the skills tested in a particular course. It is circular evaluation to use test scores to calculate grades and use grades to assess test validity. Conceptual difficulties such as this one cause Ebel (1972, p. 439) to conclude that construct validity, predictive validity, and other so called derived validities are much less important than direct validity, including content validity, in evaluating achievement tests.

It should be noted, however, that construct validity can be crucial to overall test validity. A teacher's knowledge of construct validity constitutes an important safeguard in the process of writing relevant tests. "A low score on a given examination tells the teacher that the student *did not* perform certain tasks. If the examination possesses adequate construct validity, we can also infer that the student *could not* perform those tasks" (Williams, et. al., 1988, p. 101-102).

Most teachers have heard students complain about tests that are excessively vague or confusing. Certainly students must have verbal skills, and it is appropriate to expect them to use those skills on accounting tests. However, classroom tests should not be more a test of reading skills or of reading speed than of the specific subject constructs covered in the class.

CONCLUSION

Construction of reliable, valid tests is perhaps the most difficult aspect of teaching. This difficulty may be far more apparent to the individual teacher than the reasons why the difficulty exists. This review of test theory leads to three rather straightforward suggestions. Teachers should derive their test questions from the goals and objectives of the courses they teach. The more formal the process, the more likely tests will reflect those goals and objectives.

Second, test reliability is an observable statistical property of tests. Teachers should adhere to the distinct principles of test construction that directly affect it.

Finally, the validity of classroom tests is a function of both test reliability and adherence to the principle of writing items which constitute a representative sample of important educational outcomes. Teachers should strive to write questions which conform to this principle.

References

Cronbach, N. (1971). Test Validation, in Thorndike, R., ed. *Educational Measurement*, second ed. Washington, DC: American Council on Education, 443-507.

Diederich, P. B., *Short-Cut Statistics for Teacher-Made Tests* (Princeton, N.J.: Educational Testing Service, 1973).

Ebel, R. (1972). *Essentials of Educational Measurement*. Englewood Cliffs, NJ: Prentice-Hall.

Ebel, R. & Frisbee, D. (1986). *Essentials of Educational Measurement*, 4th ed. Englewood Cliffs, NJ: Prentice-Hall.

Eckel, N. & Johnson, W. (1983). A Model for Screening and Classifying Potential Accounting Majors. *Journal of Accounting Education*. Fall, 57-65.

Frederiksen, N. (1984). The Real Test Bias: Influence of Testing on Teaching and Learning. *American Psychologist*, March, 193-202.

Green, B. (1981). A Primer of Testing. *American Psychologist*, October, 1001-1011.

Gronlund, N. E. *Constructing Achievement Tests*, 3rd ediction, Prentice Hall, Inc., Englewood Cliffs, NJ, 1982.

Gronlund, N. (1976). *Measurement and Evaluation in Teaching*. New York: Collier Macmillan.

Herring III, H., Scheiner, J., & Williams, J. (1989, forthcoming). The Development of Education Research in Accounting. *Issues in Accounting Education*. Spring.

Ingram, R. & Petersen, R. (1987). An Evaluation of AICPA Tests for Predicting the Performance of Accounting Majors. *The Accounting Review*. January, 215-223.

Krathwohl, D. & Payne, D. (1971). Defining and Assessing Educational Objectives, in Thorndike, R., ed. *Educational Measurement*, second ed. Washington, DC: American Council on Education, 17-45.

Messick, S. (1975). The Standard Problem: Meaning and Values in Measurement and Evaluation. *American Psychologist*, October, 955-966.

Milton, O. (1982). *Will That Be on the Final?* Springfield ILL: Charles C. Thomas.

Milton, O., Pollio, H., & Eison, J. (1986). *Making Sense of College Grades*. San Francisco: Jossey-Bass.

Stanley, J. (1971). Reliability, in Thorndike, R., ed. *Educational Measurement*, second ed. Washington, DC: American Council on Education, 356-442.

Thorndike, R. (1951). Reliability, in Lindquist, E., ed. *Educational Measurement*, Washington, DC: American Council on Education, 560-620.

Williams, J., Tiller, M., Herring III, H., & Scheiner, J. (1988). *A Framework for the Development of Accounting Education Research*. Sarasota, FL: American Accounting Association.

SECTION II

Testing Formats

TESTING WITH MULTIPLE-CHOICE ITEMS

Lewis R. Aiken
Pepperdine University

ABSTRACT. Because of their content and efficiency of administration and scoring, multiple-choice tests have become one of the most popular of all forms of evaluation in educational and other organizational contexts. However, may of the advantages and disadvantages of multiple-choice tests, as well as procedures for constructing, administering, scoring, and analyzing them, have not been adequately investigated. This paper is a critical review of research conducted during the past 20 years or so on multiple-choice tests of achievement and aptitude. The design and use of multiple-choice tests is emphasized, but information concerning the socioeducational implications of relying on tests having this format is also included.

In terms of their popularity as measures of academic achievement and other abilities, multiple-choice items undoubtedly surpass all other objective item formats and probably essay items as well. Numerous textbooks on testing concur that multiple-choice items have the advantage of:

1. versatility, in that they can measure both simple and complex objectives at almost all grade levels and in all subject areas;
2. more adequate sampling, in that they can sample the domain of abilities more satisfactorily than essay items and almost all other objective items;
3. less susceptibility than true-false items to both guessing and response sets;
4. objectivity of scoring, in that they can be scored accurately and rapidly by a clerk;
5. ease and objectivity of item analysis;
6. the provision of diagnostic information by an analysis of responses to item distracters;
7. greater reliability than other test items, because they are both objective and less susceptible to guessing effects.

Unfortunately, not all is well with multiple-choice items. Among their disadvantages or shortcomings are: (a) good items, especially items measuring higher-order objectives and having an adequate number of parallel options, are difficult to construct; (b) they require greater response time than true-false items and may sample the domain of knowledge less adequately in the time available; (c) they emphasize recognition of the correct answer rather than recall and organization (construction) of information. The third criticism is related to Hoffman's (1962) allegation that multiple-choice items are concerned only with the answer and not the quality of thought behind it or the

---

Reprinted by permission of the Journal of Research and Development, Vol. 20, No. 4 (1987): 44-58.

skill with which it is expressed. Hoffman also maintained that multiple-choice items favor the shrewd, nimble-witted, rapid reader, but penalize the subtle, creative, more profound individual.

Recognizing the fact that even skilled item writers make mistakes and that these mistakes are multiplied by beginners, textbooks on educational testing usually provide a set of recommendations or guidelines designed to improve the effectiveness of multiple-choice items as measures of subject-matter knowledge and ability. A list of 14 such guideline gleaned from several textbooks is presented in Table 1. Following these recommendations does not guarantee good item-writing, because the "art" of test-item preparation depends primarily on knowledge of the subject matter, an understanding of what students should know and are not likely to know about the subject, and skill in asking and writing items. Furthermore, the guidelines are primarily the products of experience and reasoning rather than empirical research.

ITEM CONSTRUCTION

Despite their reasonableness, violation of one or more of the item-writing guidelines listed in Table 1 does not invariably affect examinees' responses (Green, 1984; Weiten, 1984). The existence of "flaws" or "faults" (e.g. a resemblance or grammatical inconsistency between the stem and the correct option and making the correct option longer or phrased differently than the others) can cause items to be easier in some circumstances (Chase, 1964; McMorris Brown, Snyder, & Pruzek, 1972). However, multiple-choice items appear to be fairly "robust" in their ability to measure the examinee's knowledge of the subject-matter, even when item-writing guidelines are not followed precisely.

Number of Options

Although the probability of guessing the correct answer increases as the number of options decreases, items with three choices are frequently just as good as those having four or five choices (Costin, 1970, 1972; Neidemeyer & Sullivan, 1972). For example, Costin (1972) changed four-choice items to three-choice items by randomly discarding distracters, with the result that there was a marked reduction in testing time but no decline in the effectiveness of the test from a statistical viewpoint. Similarly, Straton and Catts (1980) reported that the reliability and standard error of measurement of three-choice item tests were equal or superior to those of four- or two-choice item tests, even when testing time was taken into account.

The advantages of three-choice items are seen especially in the case of complex items where parallel options are difficult to write and when

Table 1 Guidelines for Writing Multiple Choice Items

1. Either a question or an incomplete statement may be used as the stem for a multiple choice item, but the question format is preferred. Place blanks in an incomplete statement stem at the end.
2. State the specific problem of the question or incomplete statement clearly in the stem and at a reading level appropriate for the examinees, but avoid taking questions or statements verbatim from a textbook.
3. Place as much of the item as possible in the stem. It is inefficient to repeat the same words in every option, and examinees have less difficulty with shorter options.
4. Employ questions of opinion sparingly, but when they are used cite the authority or source of the opinion.
5. Four or five options are typical on multiple-choice items, but good items having only two or three options can also be written. Three options are preferable to four or five with students in the lower grades.
6. If the options have a natural order, such as dates or ages, it is advisable to arrange them accordingly; otherwise, arrange the options in random or alphabetical order (if alphabetizing does not give clues to the correct answer).
7. Make all options approximately equal in length, grammatically correct, and appropriate in relation to the stem. However, do not let the stem give away the correct option by verbal associations or other clues.
8. Make all options plausible to examinees who do not know the correct answer, but make only one option correct or "best." Popular misconceptions or statements that are only partially correct make good distracters.
9. Avoid, or at least minimize, the use of negative expressions (e.g. "not") in either the stem or options.
10. Although a certain amount of novelty, and even humor, is appropriate and may serve to interest and motivate examinees, ambiguous or "tricky" stems and options should not be used.
11. Use "none of the above," "all of the above," or "more than one of the above" as options sparingly. Also avoid specific determiners such as "always" or "never."
12. Put the options in stacked (paragraph) rather than tandem (back to back) format, using numbers for items and letters for options.
13. Prepare the right number of items for the grade or age group to be tested, making each item independent (not "interlocking" or associated) with other items.
14. Make the difficulty levels of items such that the percentage of examinees getting the item right is approximately halfway between the chance (random guessing) percentage and 100%.

examinees are of below-average ability (Reynolds, 1979). Furthermore, as pointed out by Lord (1977), there is an interaction between the number of options per item and the number of items on a test. Lord (1977) found that increasing the number of items while decreasing the number of options per item increased a test's efficiency with high-ability examinees but decreased its efficiency with low-ability examinees. The *efficiency* of a test refers to how accurately the test scores estimate the examinee's true ability.

Complex Items

Multiple-choice items may be made more complex in a variety of ways. Options such as "all of the above," "none of the above," "two of the above," "all but one of the above," etc, can make the task more difficult. In addition, all choices may be correct and the examinee directed to select the best choice, or all choices but one may be correct and the examinee required to select the incorrect choice. Finally, a variable number of choices may be correct, and the examinee asked either to select the correct choices (if any) or eliminate the incorrect choices (if any). Unfortunately, such multiple answer items may take too much time to answer and may be difficult to score.

The examinee's task can also be made more complex by requiring him or her to select an answer (whether right or wrong) and improve upon it. Another approach, useful on problem-solving tasks, is to have the examinee identify the correct "set up" (e.g. method of solution or equation). Six other types of complex multiple-choice items are listed in Table 2 (Aiken, 1982), and the reader will undoubtedly be able to think of additional ways of manipulating the stem or options to make the examinee's task more challenging.

Table 2
Some Complex Multiple-Choice Item Forms

---

1. <u>Multiple Premises.</u> Two or more conditions or statements are listed in the stem, and the examinee indicates whether one, all, or none is correct.
2. <u>Classification.</u> Examinee must classify a person, object, or condition into one of several categories designated in the stem.
3. <u>Oddity.</u> Examinee indicates which of a series of options does not belong with the others, according to some ascertained rule or principle.
4. <u>Relations and Correlates.</u> Concept 1 is to Concept 2 as Concept 3 is to Concept a, b, c, or d? Examinee must determine the relationship between concepts 1 and 2 and indicate which concept (a, b, c, or d) is related to Concept 3 in the same way.
5. <u>If-Then Conditions.</u> If conditions a, b, c, . . . are present (or correct), then which option is the right answer?

As might be expected, both elementary and secondary students prefer the conventional multiple-choice format in which there is one right (or best) answer to more complex varieties (Forsyth & Spratt, 1980; Rodgers, 1966). Consistent with this preference is the fact that items having less complex formats, as well as items requiring the selection of the correct answer, yield higher scores than more complex items or those requiring the selection of the incorrect answer (AbuSayf, 1979a).

Distracter Selection

It has been said that the primary factor in determining the effectiveness of multiple-choice items as measures of ability is selection of the distracters (Weitzman & MaNamara, 1946). The selection of distracters for the conventional (one right answer) multiple-choice item may be done either rationally or empirically. The rational method entails personal judgments by the test constructor of what distracters are reasonable, whereas the empirical method involves selecting distracters by the frequency of responses given to open-ended (stem) questions. Rimland and Zwerski (1962) reported evidence justifying the use of the open-ended format in determining distracters, but Owen, Hanna, and Coppedge (1970) found no differences in scores when distracters were selected by judgement, frequency of responses to open-ended statements, or discrimination methods. Hanna and Johnson (1978), who compared the reliability and validity of scores on tests produced by various item-construction procedures, concluded that individual judgment is a better procedure than selecting distracters by the frequency with which various options are chosen as correct on a pretest.

ITEM ARRANGEMENT

Among the principles traditionally recommended in arranging objective test items are to: (a) arrange the items so the answers follow no set pattern; (b) place all multiple-choice items in the same section of the test; (c) group items concerned with the same topic together. Another procedure that has been advocated is to (d) arrange items in order of difficulty from easiest to most difficult.

Position Preferences and Item Grouping

Concerning the first recommendation for item arrangement, it is plausible that, since examinee may have preferences or "sets" for selecting a distracter in a particular position (say "b" or "c"), the position of the correct option should be randomized or at least placed in the several (k) positions an equal number of times. However, the evidence does not support this contention (Jessell & Sullins, 1975; Marcus, 1963; Wilbur, 1970). Examinees may respond to options in a random manner when they do not know the correct answers (Wood, 1977), but preference for a particular option is usually not significant.

With respect to recommendations 2 and 3, placing items of the same type or having the same content in the same section of the test would seem to facilitate the examinee's task. Although there is no evidence that examinees are necessarily benefited by this arrangement, it may make the test easier to score.

Arranging Items by Difficulty Level

A large number of research studies have been conducted on the fourth recommendation--whether arranging test items in order of difficulty makes a difference. It might be assumed that an easy to difficult order would, by creating positive anticipations of success, motivate examinees to do better and, by improving performance, increase test reliability. But the evidence in this case is mixed. Aiken (1964) found that the same "critical" items were more likely to be left blank when included on more difficult tests than on easier tests, but that the position of a "critical" item (first, second, or last third section of the test) did not affect whether or not it was attempted. In a related investigation, Huck and Bowers (1972) reported that whether or not an item was answered correctly was unaffected by the difficulty level of the immediately preceding item. Although Gerow (1980) found that an occasional easy item improved performance on subsequent items, in general arranging items in order of difficulty appears to have little or no effect on scores on multiple-choice classroom achievement tests (Allison, 1984; Klimko, 1984; Lafitte, 1984).

In almost all of the studies referred to above, the tests were the "power" type, without stringent time limits. On these tests, the examinees presumably had ample time to skip more difficult items and return to them later for further deliberation. Students are usually well aware of the fact, sometimes included in the test's instructions, that it is advisable to skip over more difficult items and complete easier items (e.g., the ones they know) first--wherever those items may be located on the test. In any event, the results of a number of studies reveal that scores on speeded tests tend to be higher when items are arranged in easy to difficult order (Kleinke, 1980; Mollenkopf, 1950; Plake, Ansorge, Parker, & Lowry, 1982). An effect of difficulty order has also been obtained on more difficult tests (Green, 1984; Hodson, 1984; Savitz, 1985). Thus, when time limits are short or the test is rather difficult, examinees have less time to spend on harder items. In such cases it may improve scores to place the hardest items at the end of the test. Of course, the difficulty of a test also varies with the ability level and other personal characteristics of examinees.

The general implication of the research findings appears to be that, in the case of tests of easy to moderate difficulty, test constructors would do well to be less concerned with the way in which test items are arranged and more concerned that the items are well written and measure what they are supposed to measure (Gerow, 1980). But when a test is very difficult, examinees' knowledge of the subject-matter is quite limited, or the test is quite speeded, an easy-to-difficult item arrangement may improve motivation and result in higher scores.

PREPARING FOR AND TAKING A TEST

A frequently-cited recommendation concerning examinee-preparation is that unannounced tests or "pop quizzes" are not good educational practice: students should be told in advance when they are going to have a test, what it will cover, and what kind of test it will be. Informing examinees well in advance allows them ample time to prepare, both intellectually and emotionally, for the test. In addition, although there appears to be little or no relationship between scores and time to finish the test when time limits are not restrictive (Nevo & Spector, 1979), on most classroom tests it is recommended that enough time be provided so that at least 90% of the students complete the test.

Test Announced vs. Test Administered

The above recommendations appear to be sound, but announcing the type of test (recall, multiple-choice, etc.) in advance does not always affect test scores. In a study by Kumar, Rabinsky, and Pandey (1979), one group of students was told to expect a recall test, another group a multiple-choice test, and a third group a retention test on a passage of reading material provided to them. Regardless of what type of test they were told to expect, half the students in each group received either a recall or recognition test. It might seem that students would do better if they were administered the same type of test they were told to expect, but the mean scores of the several groups were not significantly different. On further reflection, however, it could be argued that group differences should not be expected with the limited material to which all students were exposed in a fixed time in this investigation. Only if students have a chance to choose what and how to study might one expect differences between means on recall and recognition tests.

In another investigation (Balota & Neely, 1980), students were first led to expect a recall or recognition test and then asked to remember a critical list consisting of high-frequency and low-frequency words. Then they received an expected or unexpected recall or recognition test. Those who expected a recall test did better on both the recall and recognition tests but to a much greater degree on high frequency than low frequency words. The high frequency words were recalled better but recognized more poorly than the low frequency words. From the results of this study, it would seem that students do better when a recall test is expected, regardless of what type of test--recall or recognition--is actually administered. Furthermore, the type of test interacts with the difficulty of the test material in affecting scores.

Instructions Concerning Guessing

In addition to requesting identifying data (name, etc.) and providing information on how answers should be marked and how the test is to be scored, instructions for multiple-choice tests frequently include directions about whether to omit an item or guess when in doubt about the answer. Guessing, which creates less of a problem in inflating scores on multiple choice than on true false items, is more likely to occur when items are difficult or wordy (Choppin, 1975). Typical instructions concerning guessing recommend that examinees not guess randomly but only if they can eliminate one or more options or have some idea what the answer is. In addition, the instructions may state that random guessing will be penalized by subtracting a portion of the items answered incorrectly from those answered correctly.

Research findings have usually demonstrated that examinees guess less when advised that they will be penalized for guessing than when instructed to guess when uncertain about an answer or when no instructions concerning guessing are provided (e.g., Bauer, 1971; Taylor, 1966). Similar findings of an increase in omitted items when guessing is penalized were reported by Waters and Waters (1971) and Traub and Hambleton (1973). However, these investigators also found that promising a bonus or a small reward for omitted items tended to encourage the omission of items. Furthermore, in the Waters and Waters (1971) study, examinees preferred the bonus for omitted items to the penalty for wrong answers.

Understandably, not all examinees follow or even read the test directions carefully, and those who read every word may interpret and react differently to the directions. For example, Bauer (1971) and Choppin (1975) cite evidence of pronounced individual and group differences regarding instructions concerning guessing. As with risk-taking behavior in other contexts, some examinees are more willing than others to guess on test items. The tendency to guess does not appear to be related to mental ability (Croker & Benson, 1976), but guessers have been found to differ from nonguessers in introversiveness and self-esteem (Wood, 1976; Cross & Frary, 1977). Guessing has also been shown to vary with demographic variables (sex, nationality, type of school attended, etc.) (Choppin, 1975), but it would be premature to generalize from the results of this one study.

Some years ago, Lord (1975) suggested that, when given appropriate directions, "the difference between an answer sheet obtained under formula-scoring directions . . . and the same answer sheet obtained under number right scoring directions . . . is only that omitted responses, if any, on the formula answer sheet were replaced by random guesses" (p. 8). If confirmed, Lord's assertion would tend to support the use of correction-for-guessing formula scoring. However, several researchers (e.g. Bliss, 1980; Cross & Frary, 1977; Guereshi, 1974), have failed to substantiate the assertion. It has been found that, when formula scoring directions are given, examinees frequently omit items which they had a better than chance probability of guessing correctly. In one study (Guereshi, 1974), the penalty for guessing resulted in a significant decrease in number right and increases in both the number of omissions and the number wrong. These and related findings have led to serious questioning of the wisdom of discouraging guessing on multiple choice tests, since such guessing is usually based on at least partial knowledge of the item and therefore contributes to the measurement of ability in the subject (Wood, 1976; 1977; Cross & Frary, 1977). It has been shown that when informed, rather than random, guessing is encouraged, there are typically small improvements in test reliability (Frary, Cross & Lowry, 1977).

How Are Test Items Answered?

Examinees often use quite different methods in selecting the correct option than intended by the test item writer. Observations and interviews of students taking multiple-choice tests indicate that although they sometimes answer an item simply by eliminating obviously incorrect choices, the more common procedure is to make comparative judgments among the various options. After administering a few tests, it becomes clear that not all examinees read the directions carefully, and on individual items they often fail to make use of all the information in the item stem (Williams & Jones, 1974).

Preston (1964) found that college students can often recognize the correct answer to a multiple choice item without even reading the passage on which the question is based. Apparently they are able in may instances to identify the correct answer intuitively--by a process of elimination in some cases, by noting that an option is too broad or too narrow to be correct, or even that an option is worded incorrectly.

Knowledge of a particular test constructor's (e.g. teacher's) idiosyncracies is also an aspect of test wiseness. Test wiseness, which appears to be a non-general, cue-specific ability (Evans, 1984), tends to develop as students pass through the grades and share information on test-taking skills (Slakter, Koehler, & Hampton, 1970). Preston (1964) found boys to be better at this process than girls, and Rowley (1974) observed that verbal items were more susceptible to test wiseness than numerical items. Some aspects of test-wiseness, or "test sophistication," can also be explicitly taught, as seen in the principles described by Millman and Pauk (1969) and The American College (1978).

A number of other factors, such as option length, technicality, and exoticness (Chase, 1964; Strang, 1980; Tidwell; 1980) can also affect which item options examinees select and consequently how well they perform on multiple-choice tests. The type of answer form used (Miller & Minor, 1963) can also affect response selection, and with elementary school children marking the test answers on a separate answer sheet rather than in a test booklet can lower test scores. For example, Muller, Calhoun, and Orling (1972) found that the use of separate answer sheets by samples of third-, fourth-, and sixth-graders resulted in more response errors and lower test reliability than when answers were marked on the same pages as the items appear.

Variations from the Conventional Test-Taking Format

In the conventional multiple-choice format, there is one correct (or best option) per item; examinees receive a score of 1 if they select the keyed option and 0 if they select any other option. One variation on the conventional format is for examinees to continue selecting options until they find the correct one. Then item scores are calculated as a inverse function of the number of responses required to get the item right (find the correct option). Gilman and Ferry (1972) and Hanna (1975) found that this answer-until-correct (AUC) procedure resulted in higher reliability than the conventional format, but Kane and Maloney (1978) disagreed. The procedure obviously takes more time, and the resulting scores are not necessarily more valid than those derived from the conventional procedure. In addition, it deprives examinees of the opportunity to reconsider their answer choices on items which they have already answered.

Another approach to answering and scoring both multiple-choice and true-false items is a confidence-weighting procedure in which examinees assign an integer or percentage to each option to indicate their degree of certainty that the option is correct. Whereas Stokes (1966) maintained that both students and teachers benefit from such confidence-weighting of answers, Hendrickson (1971) found the technique to be slightly poorer than conventional single-choice testing. Similarly, Krauft and Beggs (1973), who had students assign four points among four alternatives, found no statistically significant differences between confidence-weighted and conventional procedures in score means or reliabilities. With respect to validity, Hanna and Owens (1973) found that greater validity was attained by lengthening a conventional multiple-choice test than by using a confidence-weighting procedure.

Changing Answers

Another issue when taking a multiple-choice test is whether or not examinees should change their initial responses to items. It would seem reasonable to assume that answer-changing is related to uncertainty or anxiety about the test and one's answers to it. Payne (1984) found that, in an eighth-grade group of black and white, male and female students, test anxiety scores were higher for blacks and females. The black students also changed their answers to a science test, both from wrongs to rights and from rights to wrongs, more frequently than whites and made significantly lower mean test scores than whites. However, answer-changing was significantly related, in a positive direction, only for the white males. But test anxiety for all groups combined had a significant negative correlation (-.40) with overall scores on the science test.

One frequently hears both students and teachers state that it is unprofitable to go back over a test and change answers that have already been deliberated upon. However, the findings of studies on a wide range of students and subject-matter (Archer & Pippert, 1962; Copeland, 1972; Mueller & Shwedel, 1975; Payne, 1984; Reiling & Taylor, 1972; Smith, White, & Coop, 1979; Stoffer, Davis & Brown, 1977; Vidler & Hansen, 1980) indicate that test scores tend to be higher when examinees reconsider tests (Pascale, 1974) and with higher-scoring students (Copeland, 1972; Mueller & Wasser, 1977). Pascale (1974) also found that males did better than females when changing answers.

Among the characteristics of answer-changing is that answers are more likely to be changed from wrong to right than from right to wrong (Vidler & Hansen, 1980) and that the actual number of changed answers is relatively small (Skinner, 1983). Discussing the latter findings, Skinner (1983) maintains that the low rate of answer changing is due to the fact that examinees are reluctant to change their initial answers because they believe them correct and will change only when highly confident that the changed answers are correct. Thus, Skinner argues, the folk admonition against changing answers may have some support in actual fact. In any case, whether they change answers or not, no one can deny that examinees frequently make errors in reading, understanding, and marking the first time through a test. Consequently, they would be wise to check their answers when time permits, without painstakingly deliberating on them for too long and praying for sudden insight.

Response Feedback

A time-honored principle of learning and instruction is that people (and other animals) usually retain learned responses better when provided with fairly immediate feedback as to the correctness of those responses. In testing, the procedure referred to earlier provides immediate item-by-item feedback to the examinee. Various investigators (Arkin & Schumann, 1984; Fisher, Williams, & Roth, 1981; Fulmer & Rollings, 1976; Hanna, 1976, 1977; Yelvington & Brady, 1979) have found that the AUC or corrective feedback procedure has both affective and cognitive advantages: by a combination of information and reinforcement, it reduces anxiety, increases motivation, and promotes learning. Hanna (1977) also found that the AUC procedure yielded more internally consistent scores than the conventional (single response) testing procedure. Such immediate feedback is usually implemented by the use of special answer sheets (Fulmer & Rollings, 1976; Golman, 1982) or computer-assisted procedures (Fisher et al., 1981).

The need for special answer sheets or machines is one of the problems associated with an AUC procedure. Other problems include increased testing time, cumbersome scoring, the possibility that knowledge of the correct answer to one item might give away all or part of the answer to a subsequent item, the negative effects of immediate knowledge of failure, and possibly lower test reliability. Despite these shortcomings, the researchers referred to above concluded that the advantages of immediate item-by-item feedback outweigh its disadvantages.

Response feedback need not, of course, be provided after each item is attempted. Some teachers wait until students have completed the entire test and then give them a key showing all correct answers (O'Neill, Fasor, & Bartz, 1976). Students may then correct the items they missed, followed perhaps by a class discussion of the test. Because of its greater effects on retention of test material, O'Neill et al. (1976) favor this approach over item-by-item feedback. They also concluded that if item-by-item feedback is employed, two attempts are sufficient because continued searching for the correct answer overexposes examinees to incorrect answers and lowers their motivation.

The psychological literature on learning contains many examples of improved task performance, without further practice, after a time delay following an initial test on the task. This phenomenon, referred to as reminiscence and observed more often in motor than verbal learning, is thought to be due to a decrease in fatigue and interference effects during the initial test-final test interval. A similar effect was noted by Kulhavy and Anderson (1972) in comparing the effects of immediate (same day) and delayed (one day later) feedback on retention of the correct answers to an introductory psychology test. In short, the delayed feedback groups performed better than the immediate feedback groups. The researchers concluded that this delay-retention effect was due primarily to the forgetting of interference-producing errors during the delay interval and secondarily to the increased attention given to test feedback after the delay interval. Therefore, it can be argued that, especially when students have not mastered the test material thoroughly, it is better to wait a day or two after the test is administered before providing examinees with feedback on their test performance.

SCORING AND SCORE ANALYSIS

Correction for Guessing Formulas

The simplest and most popular procedure for scoring multiple choice tests is to count the number of items answered correctly, score = number right ($s = r$). It is widely recognized, however, that scores computed in this way are inflated by guessing, a bias which is greater on items having fewer options (Reid, 1977). Furthermore, not all examinees are equally well-served by the formulas: examinees who are more likely to guess at the answer when in doubt tend to score higher than those who leave more answers blank. Consequently, various formulas for "correcting" test scores for chance success have been proposed. The most popular of these is $s = r - w/(k - 1)$, where r is the number of items answered right, w the number answered wrong, and k the number of options per item. This formula, which is based on the questionable assumption of random or uninformed guessing, has been criticized as yielding overcorrected scores when examinees are less familiar with the test material and undercorrected scores when they are more familiar with it (Little, 1962, 1966).

Among the alternative formulas designed to provide a more accurate correction for guessing are those proposed by Little (1962) and Reid (1977). Little (1962) recommended that the correction-for-guessing formula be abandoned or at least modified to $s = r - w/[2(k - 1)]$. The formula proposed by Reid (1977) can be expressed as $s = (n + r)(kr - n)/[2r(k - 1)]$, where n is the total number of items on the test. Note that Reid's formula does not include the number of wrong answers, and it yields even higher scores than the conventional $s = r$ formula under certain circumstances.

Response Weighted Scoring

The conventional number right and correction-for-guessing formulas are not the only procedures proposed for scoring multiple-choice items. Because it seems reasonable that the number of points assigned to an item response should vary with the kind of item and the quality of the response, a priori weighting of options on multiple-choice items, such as giving partial credit to options that are not absolutely correct, has been advocated by a number of researchers (Arnold & Arnold, 1970; Bejar & Weiss, 1977; Bernhardson, 1966; Davis, 1967; Hambleton, Roberts & Traub, 1970). On multiple-response items several or all options on a given item may be scored as correct or partially correct. A number of investigators (e.g. Hsu, Moss & Khampalikit, 1984; Serlin & Kaiser, 1978; Willson, 1982) have concluded that a prior weighing of responses to items is more discriminating and reliable than conventional scoring, but Kansup and Hakstian (1975) concluded that the cost and time required for scoring differentially weighted item alternatives are not justified by the advantages of the technique.

Another scoring procedure in which options are numerically weighted is confidence weighting. In this procedure the score on an item consists of the number of points of confidence assigned to the keyed alternative. Confidence weighting may result in higher test reliability (Michael, 1968), but its effects on test validity have not been encouraging (Diamond, 1975; Hakstian & Kansup, 1975; Hanna & Owens, 1973; Koehler, 1974). The findings of Abu-Sayf (1975; 1979a, 1979c) are also negative with respect to confidence weighting: the technique was not superior to conventional scoring in terms of time required, clarity, or reliability. In certain circumstances when confidence weighting produces small increases in reliability, similar increases can also be obtained merely by lengthening the test and scoring it by the conventional number right formula (Hakstian & Kansup, 1975).

Elimination Scoring

In elimination scoring, examinees respond by indicating which options are wrong rather than marking only the one best answer. One variation of the elimination technique is to score correct and incorrect options separately and give equal importance to the resulting scores in the calculation of the final score (Edouard & Harris, 1983).

Concerning the effectiveness of elimination scoring, Collet (1971) concluded that it results in more reliable and valid scores than either corrected-for-guessing or item-weighted scores. However, Hakstian and Kansup (1975) maintained that, when compared with conventional scoring, neither reliability nor validity was consistently increased by using either elimination scoring or confidence weighting procedures. All things considered, then, it would appear that the conventional number right formula is the best overall approach to scoring multiple choice tests.

Item Analysis

After a test has been scored, it is customary to analyze the pattern of responses to each item to determine if the item is functioning properly. In addition to yielding data for making decisions on what items need discarding or revising, an item analysis can provide information on the differential strengths and weaknesses of examinees in the areas or abilities covered by the test.

Subjective procedures, such as having students evaluate items (Lueptow, Early, & Garland, 1976), have not proven to be a very effective approach to item analysis. Rather, the usual item analysis procedure is to compute indexes of the difficulty and discrimination power of each item and then examine the pattern of responses to the various item options of high-and low-scoring groups on the test as a whole. The difficulty index (p) is computed either as the proportion of all examinees who answer the item correctly or the proportion of those in the upper 27% and the lower 27% on total test score who get the item right. An optimum difficulty index for the items constituting a test, in the sense that it tends to result in a test composed of items with high discrimination indexes, may be computed as $(k + 1)/2k$ (see Sax, 1980). From this formula, it can be seen that the optimum difficulty index decreases as the number of options increases. Lord (1952) maintained, however, that $(k + 1)/2k$ underestimates the optimum item difficulty by a value of approximately .10.

When a test item is evaluated against an external criterion, the item discrimination index is usually computed as a point-biserial correlation between item scores (0 or 1) and scores on the criterion variable. In the case of classroom achievement tests, however, the criterion is an internal one--total test scores. Then the item discrimination index is computed as the difference between the proportion of examinees in a high-scoring group (upper 27%) and the proportion in a low-scoring group (lower 27%) on total test scores who get the item right.

Acceptable values of the item discrimination index may be as low as .20, depending on the number of high-scoring and low-scoring examinees (on total test score), the item difficulty index, and the desired statistical significance level (Aiken, 1979). Aiken (1968) also demonstrated that the item discrimination index and an index of the uniformity of the distribution of distracters provide useful information about the relative effectiveness of the distracters.

In addition to computing numerical indexes of difficulty, discrimination, and uniformity, it is advisable to examine the pattern of wrong answers given to an item. Wrong answers frequently contain information about sources of misunderstanding or lack of knowledge that is not included in right answers.

More sophisticated item analysis procedures involve drawing an item response (characteristic) curve, which is a graph of the proportion of correct responses plotted against total test scores or other criterion scores, for each item. Then the item difficulty index is computed as the value of the criterion variable at which 50 percent of the examinees pass the item, and the discrimination index is the linear slope of the item response curve. In the various approaches of item response theory (latent trait theory, Rasch model, etc.), item response curves may also be constructed by plotting the percentage passing the item against estimates of ability derived from a specified mathematical function (Hulin, Drasgow, & Parsons, 1983).

In general, it has been found that item analysis results can lead to significant improvements in the quality of multiple-choice tests (Bodner, 1980). The item discrimination index in particular is a fairly good measure of the quality of an item (Pyrczdk, 1973), and it, along with the difficulty index, can serve as a warning that something is wrong with an item. For example, Dudycha and Carpenter (1973) investigated the effects on item statistics of violating three item construction rules: item stem orientation--positive/negative, item structure--open/closed, and the presence of inclusive alternatives. All three of these variables were found to affect item difficulty: open stem items were more difficult than closed, negative items were more difficult than positive, and items with inclusive options were more difficult than items on which all options were specific. The item discrimination index was also affected by the use of an inclusive option, and there was a significant interaction between item orientation and item structure in their effects on item discrimination.

COMPARISONS AND CRITICISMS

As noted in the beginning of this paper, multiple-choice tests have both advantages and limitations. Discussions of the relative merits of these types of tests span a wide range of concerns, some of which have been discussed already. They include methods of construction, ease of administration and scoring, reliability and validity, and the educational and social effects of relying on multiple-choice items to measure school achievement and other abilities.

Comparisons With Other Types of Items

Compared with true-false or other double-choice tests, multiple-choice tests tend to be more reliable (Frisbie, 1973, 1974; Oosterhof & Glasnapp, 1974), although this is not invariably the case (e.g., Green, 1979). However, it is usually easier to write true-false than multiple-choice items, and more of the former can be answered during a given testing period. Consequently, one would expect a true-false test to cover a domain of content more thoroughly than a multiple-choice test. Some researchers have also noted advantages in a multiple true-false format, in which examinees respond to each of the several options on a multiple-choice item as separate true-false statements (Frisbie & Sweeney, 1982).

Investigations of the relative merits of multiple-choice compared with other types of items--completion or short answer, essay, and matching--are also noteworthy. Multiple-choice tests almost always yield higher scores than short answer or completion tests and are considered more versatile and resilient than these tests (Heim & Watts, 1967; Storey, 1968). However, the reliability of multiple-choice tests is not invariably higher than that of either completion or matching tests (Panackal & Heft, 1978; Zimmerman, Williams, & Symons, 1984). In comparing multiple-choice with cloze tests, Panackel and Heft (1978) found the former to be less reliable but more valid than the latter. But, as with any short-answer or completion test, a cloze test has the disadvantage of requiring more scoring time than a comparable multiple-choice test.

Despite the criticisms that they are more difficult to score and seemingly measure only knowledge of specific facts, short-answer or completion items may be more effective than multiple-choice items for certain purposes. Gay (1980) found that a short-answer test resulted in greater retention of concepts learned in an educational research course than a multiple-choice test when the retention test consisted of short-answer items. When retention was measured using a multiple-choice test, there was no difference between the mean scores of students who had initially taken the short-answer test and those who had taken the multiple-choice test. Thus, in this instance short-answer testing yielded equal or superior retention to multiple-choice testing.

It is often maintained that overuse of objective, compared to essay, tests is one reason why today's students cannot read and write as effectively as their counterparts of yesteryear (e.g., David, 1981). Whatever the cause of this reported condition may be, the great popularity of multiple-choice and other objective tests has undoubtedly been at the expense of essay (and oral) testing. Essay tests, although perhaps easier to construct, are obviously more difficult to score than objective tests. Furthermore, marks on essay tests tend to be lower and are frequently of questionable reliability. In any event, many students believe that in taking an essay test quantity will compensate for quality in answering and that they can "bluff" their way through the test (Warren, 1979). Despite these short-comings, essay tests do measure abilities and expose weaknesses that are not tapped by most teacher-made multiple-choice tests. Consequently, a good maxim in educational evaluation is to use a mixture of objective and essay items rather than relying exclusively on one type of item to measure the attainment of instructional objectives.

One factor that has received wide attention in the educational research literature but is less frequently considered in classroom testing is test anxiety. Any type of test induces a certain amount of anxiety in almost anyone, but certain types of tests, depending undoubtedly on how much and what kinds of experiences the examinee has had with them, appear to create greater anxiety than others. For example, a significant majority of the undergraduate students responding to a survey by Aiken & Romen (1984) stated that they were made more anxious by essay than multiple-choice tests, and preferred the multiple-choice format to other types of items--essay or objective. On the other hand, the high school students in Shaha's (1984) study, who took parallel matching and multiple-choice tests on the same topic, preferred matching to multiple-choice. These students also scored higher on the matching than the multiple-choice test and reported experiencing less debilitation anxiety on the former than the latter.

Socioeducational Effects of Multiple-Choice Testing

Over 20 years ago, Banesh Hoffman (1962, 1967) made a series of attacks on the use of multiple-choice tests. Hoffman's complaints, which were referred to at the beginning of this paper, were directed mainly at standardized tests such as the Scholastic Aptitude Test. One of his major criticisms was that such tests penalize the more subtle, creative, profound person, while favoring the shrewd, nimble-witted, rapid reader. Hoffman's criticisms were challenged by a number of professionals in the testing community (e.g., Chauncey & Dobbin, 1963; Dunnette, 1963) and gave rise to considerable self-examination by the College Entrance Examination Board and Educational Testing Service. In addition, empirical studies were conducted to determine the merit of these criticisms.

After reviewing earlier attempts to examine the criticism that multiple-choice tests reward less able and penalize more able students, Alker, Carlson, and Herman (1969) described the results of a study of 108 undergraduate males. The results, which were concerned with the relationships between scores on multiple-choice tests and the traits of creativity, nonconformity, ability to recognize ambiguity, preference for complexity, and test wiseness, were mixed, in that they neither completely confirmed nor disconfirmed the critics' assertions. As the critics alleged, test-wiseness was positively related to scores on multiple-choice tests of aptitude and achievement, but contrary to another allegation the ability to recognize ambiguity was also positively correlated with scores on the tests. Furthermore, preference for verbal complexity and an emphasis on achievement via independence instead of conformity were positively rather than negatively related to the multiple-choice test scores. Finally, creativity (divergent thinking) scores were not significantly correlated with scores on the SAT-V or other measures of verbal ability.

Alker et al.'s (1969) study, did not, of course, examine all criticisms of multiple-choice tests, and its findings are certainly not the last word on the criticism that it did examine. For example, Preston (1965) had earlier found that the act of responding to multiple-choice items can condition examinees to the ensuing response, even when the response is incorrect, and that more intelligent examinees tend to be more susceptible to such conditioning.

Some years ago, McClelland (1973) published a widely-read paper in which he argued against the use of all paper-and-pencil multiple-choice tests of what one already knows as a way of proving one's capabilities. As an alternative, McClelland advocated the development of other types of measures, such as those that assess the capacity to learn quickly. Even more recently, Nairn and Associates (1980) have criticized the SAT and other standardized tests distributed by Educational Testing Service as helping to preserve the status quo is higher education by their use in denying educational opportunities to lower-class students.

Another criticism of multiple-choice tests that is difficult to prove or disprove but has wide educational and social ramifications is that scores on such tests are not only poor measures of ability and achievement but that their use encourages inferior teaching and improper study habits. Consequently, the statement by the National Assessment of Educational Progress that standardized tests requiring brief answers are an important factor in the superficiality of students' reading skills demands attention by the educational community. The 1981 NEAP report called for teachers to beware of excessive reliance on objective tests and reinstate the traditional essay, which requires students to explain and support their answers (David, 1981).

The effective use of essay items requires, of course, that scorers evaluate not only the content of answers but also the style or skill with which the answer is expressed. Simply writing out an answer does not improve the ability to express oneself in writing unless constructive feedback is provided on the form of that expression.

Despite the continuing criticism of standardized and teacher-made multiple-choice tests, it is reasonable to expect that their use will increase rather than decrease in the foreseeable future. Recognizing their shortcomings, but also the need for efficient, economical methods of evaluation, perhaps we must simply learn to live with the fact that multiple-choice tests are substantially less than perfect measures of ability and achievement. However, this does not mean that the search for more valid measures, and ones that make a greater contribution to the realization of educational and other societal objectives, should be abandoned. And even if the decision is made to continue using the multiple-choice format in many situations, an awareness of the shortcomings and techniques of constructing more effective items of this type should be instilled in those who prepare, distribute, and administer educational and psychological tests.

References

Abu-Sayf, F. K. (1975). Relative effectiveness of the conventional formula score. *Journal of Educational Research, 69,* 160-162.
Abu-Sayf, F. K. (1979a). Scoring of multiple-choice tests: A closer look. *Educational Technology, 19,* 5-15.
Abu-Sayf, F. K. (1979b). Does multiple-choice item form affect students assessment results in science? *Journal of Research in Science Teaching, 16,* 359-362.
Abu-Sayf, F. K. (1979c). Recent developments in the scoring of multiple-choice items. *Educational Review, 31,* multiple-choice 269-279.
Aiken, L. R. (1964). Item context and position effects on multiple-choice tests. *The Journal of Psychology, 58,* 369-373.
Aiken, L. R. (1968). Discrimination and uniformity of test item distracters. *Psychological Reports, 23,* 301-302.
Aiken, L. R. (1979). Relationships between item difficulty and discrimination indexes. *Educational and Psychological Measurement, 39,* 821-824.
Aiken, L. R. (1982). Writing multiple-choice items to measure higher-order educational objectives. *Educational and Psychological Measurement, 42,* 803-806.
Aiken, L. R., & Romen, L. (1984). *Attitudes and experiences concerning psychological and educational testing.* (ERIC Document Reproduction Service NO. ED 247 322)
Alker, H. A., Carlson, J. A., & Herman, M. G. (1969). Multiple-choice questions and students' characteristics. *Journal of Educational Psychology, 60,* 231-243.
Allison, D. E. (1984). The effect of item-difficulty sequence, intelligence, and sex on test performance, reliability, and item difficulty and discrimination. *Measurement and Evaluation in Guidance, 16,* 211-217.
The American College (1978). *Test wiseness: Test taking skills for adults.* New York: McGraw-Hill.
Archer, N. S., & Pipper, R. (1962). Don't change the answer! *Clearing House, 37,* 39-41.
Arkin, R. M., & Schumann, D. W. (1984). Effects of corrective testing: An extension. *Journal of Educational Psychology, 76,* 835-843.
Arnold, J. C., & Arnold, P. L. (1970). On scoring multiple-choice exams allowing for partial knowledge. *Journal of Experimental Education. 39,* 8-13.
Balota, D. A., & Neely, J. H. (1980). Test-expectancy and word-frequency effects in recall and recognition. *Journal of Experimental Psychology: Human Learning and Memory, 6,* 576-587.

Bauer, D. H. (1971). Effect of test instructions, test anxiety, defensiveness, and confidence in judgment on guessing behavior in multiple-choice test situations. *Psychology in the Schools, 8,* 208-215.

Bejar, I. I., & Weiss, D. J. (1977). Comparison of empirical differential option weighting scoring procedures as a function of inter-item correlation. *Educational and Psychological Measurement, 37,* 335-340.

Bernhardson, C. S. (1966). Determination of the chance score on the three-decision multiple-choice test. *Psychological Reports, 19,* 559-562.

Bliss, L. B. (1980). Test of Lord's assumption regarding examinee guessing behavior on multiple-choice tests using elementary school students. *Journal of Educational Measurement, 17,* 147-153.

Bodner, G. M. (1980). Statistical analysis of multiple-choice exams. *Journal of Chemical Education, 57,* 188-190.

Chase, C. I. (1964). Relative length of option and response set in multiple-choice items. *Educational and Psychological Measurement, 24,* 861-866.

Chauncey, H., & Dobbin, J. E. (1963). *Testing: Its place in education today.* New York: Harper & Row.

Choppin, B. (1975). Guessing the answer on objective tests. *British Journal of Educational Psychology, 45,* 206-213.

Collet, L. S. (1971). Elimination scoring: An empirical evaluation. *Journal of Educational Measurement, 8,* 209-214.

Copeland, D. A. (1972). Should chemistry students change answers on multiple-choice tests? *Journal of Chemical Education, 49,* 258.

Costin, F. (1970). Optimal number of alternatives in multiple-choice achievement tests: Some empirical evidence for a mathematical proof. *Educational and Psychological Measurement, 30,* 353-358.

Costin, F. (1972). Three-choice versus four-choice items: Implications for reliability and validity of objective achievement tests. *Educational and Psychological Measurement, 32,* 1035-1038.

Crocker, J., & Benson, J. (1976). Achievement, guessing, and risk-taking under norm referenced and criterion referenced testing conditions. *American Education Research Journal, 13,* 207-215.

Cross, L. H., & Frary, R. B. (1977). Empirical test of Lord's theoretical results regarding formula scoring of multiple-choice tests. *Journal of Educational Measurement, 14,* 313-321.

David, P. (1981, November 27). Multiple-choice under fire: United States. *Times Education Supplement,* p. 11.

Davis, F. B. (1967). Note on the correction for chance success. *Journal of Experimental Education, 35,* 42-47.

Diamond, J. J. (1975). A preliminary study of the reliability and validity of a scoring procedure based upon confidence and partial information. *Journal of Educational Measurement, 12,* 129-134.

Dudycha, A. L., & Carpenter, J. B. (1973). Effects of item format on item discrimination and difficulty. *Journal of Applied Psychology, 58,* 116-121.

Dunnette, M. D. (1963). Critics of psychological tests: Basic assumptions; how good? *Psychology in the Schools, 1,* 63-69.

Edouard, L. J., & Harris, F. T. C. (1983). Multiple-choice questions: Fact, fallacy and fancy. *International Journal of Mathematical Education in Science and Technology, 14,* 685-691.

Evans, W. (1984). Test wiseness: An examination of cue-using strategies. *Journal of Experimental Education, 52,* 141-144.

Fisher, K., Williams, S., & Roth, J. (1981). Qualitative and quantitative differences in learning associated with multiple-choice testing. *Journal of Research in Science Teaching, 18,* 449-464.

Forsyth, R. A., & Spratt, K. F. (1980). Measuring problem solving ability in mathematics with multiple-choice items: The effect of item format on selected item and test characteristics. *Journal of Educational Measurement, 17,* 31-43.

Frary, R. B., Cross, L. H., & Lowry, S. R. (1977). Random guessing, correction for guessing and reliability of multiple-choice test scores. *Journal of Experimental Education, 46,* 9-15.

Frisbie, D. A. (1973). Multiple-choice versus true-false: A comparison of reliabilities and concurrent validities. *Journal of Educational Measurement, 10,* 297-304.

Frisbie, D. A. (1974). Effect of item format on reliability and validity. A study of multiple-choice and true-false achievement tests. *Educational and Psychological Measurement, 34,* 885-892.

Frisbie, D. A., & Sweeney, D. C. (1982). Relative merits of multiple true-false achievement tests. *Journal of Educational Measurement, 19,* 29-35.

Fulmer, R. S., & Rollings, H. E. (1976). Item-by-item feedback and multiple-choice test performance. *Journal of Experimental Education, 44,* 30-32.

Gay, L. R. (1980). Comparative effects of multiple-choice versus short-answer tests on retention. *Journal of Educational Measurement, 17,* 45-50.

Gerow, J. R. (1980). Performance on achievement tests as a function of the order of item difficulty. *Teaching of Psychology, 7,* 93-94.

Gilman, D. A., & Ferry, P. (1972). Increasing test reliability through self-scoring procedures. *Journal of Educational Measurement, 9,* 205-207.

Golmon, M. E. (1982). Immediate feedback testing technique. *Journal of College Science Teaching, 11,* 173-174.

Green, K. (1979). Multiple-choice and true-false: Reliability and validity compared. *Journal of Experimental Education, 48,* 42-44.

Green, K. (1984). Effects of item characteristics on multiple-choice item difficulty. *Educational and Psychological Measurement, 44,* 551-561.

Guereshi, M. Y. (1974). Performance on multiple-choice tests and penalty for guessing. *Journal of Experimental Education, 42,* 74-77.

Hakstian, A. R., & Kansup, W. (1975). Comparison of several methods of assessing partial knowledge in multiple-choice tests: Testing procedures. *Journal of Educational Measurement, 12,* 231-239.

Hambleton, R. K., Roberts, D. M., & Traub, R. (1970). Comparison of the reliability and validity of two methods for assessing partial knowledge on a multiple-choice test. *Journal of Educational Measurement, 7,* 75-82.

Hanna, G. S. (1975). Incremental reliability and validity of multiple-choice tests with an answer-until-correct procedure. *Journal of Educational Measurement, 12,* 175-178.

Hanna, G. S. (1976). Effects of total and partial feedback in multiple-choice testing upon learning. *Journal of Educational Research, 69,* 202-205.

Hanna, G. S. (1977). Study of reliability and validity effects of total and partial immediate feedback in multiple-choice testing. *Journal of Educational Measurement, 14,* 1-7.

Hanna, G. S., & Johnson, F. R. (1978). Reliability and validity of multiple-choice tests developed by four distractor selection procedures. *Journal of Education Research, 71,* 203-206.

Hanna, G. S., & Owens, R. E. (1973). Incremental validity of confidence weighting of items. *California Journal of Education Research, 24,* 165-168.

Heim, A. W., & Watts, K. P. (1967). Experiment on multiple-choice versus open-ended answering in a vocabulary test. *British Journal of Educational Psychology, 37,* 339-346.

Hendrickson, G. F. (1971). Effect of differential option weighting on multiple-choice objective tests. *Journal of Educational Measurement, 8,* 291-296.

Hodson, D. (1984). The effects of changes in item sequence on student performance in a multiple-choice chemistry test. *Journal of Research in Science Teaching, 21,* 489-495.

Hoffman, B. (1962). *The tyranny of testing.* New York: Crowell-Colliet.

Hoffman, B. (1971). Psychometric scientism. *Phi Delta Kappan, 48,* 381-386.

Hsu, T. C., Moss, P. A., & Khampalikit, C. (1984). The merits of multiple-choice items as evaluated by using six scoring formulas. *Journal of Experimental Education, 52,* 152-158.

Huck, S. W., & Bowers, N. D. (1972). Item difficulty level and sequence effects in multiple-choice achievement tests. *Journal of Educational Measurement, 9,* 105-111.

Hulin, C. L., Drasgow, F., & Parsons, C. K. (1983). *Item response theory,* Homewood, IL: Dow Jones-Irwin.

Jessell, J. C., & Sullins, W. L. (1975). Effect of keyed response sequencing of multiple-choice items on performance and reliability. *Journal of Educational Measurement, 12,* 45-48.

Kane, M., & Maloney, J. (1978). The effect of guessing on item reliability under answer-until-correct scoring. *Applied Psychological Measurement, 2,* 41-49.

Kansup, W., & Hakstian, A. R. (1975). Comparison of several methods of assessing partial knowledge in multiple-choice tests: Scoring procedures. *Journal of Educational Measurement, 12,* 219-230.

Kleinke, D. J. (1980). Item order, response location and examinee sex and handedness and performance on a multiple-choice test. *Journal of Educational Research, 73,* 225-229.

Klimko, I. P. (1984). Item arrangement, cognitive entry characteristics, sex, and test anxiety as predictors of achievement examination performance. *Journal of Experimental Education, 52,* 214-219.

Koehler, R. A. (1974). Overconfidence on probabilistic tests. *Journal of Educational Measurement, 11,* 101-108.

Krauft, C. C., & Beggs, D. L. (1973). Test-taking procedure, risk taking, and multiple-choice test scores. *Journal of Experimental Education, 41,* 74-77.

Kulhavy, R. W., & Anderson, R. C. (1972). Delay-retention effect with multiple-choice tests. *Journal of Educational Psychology, 63,* 505-512.

Kumar, V. F., Rabinsky, L., & Pandey, T. N. (1979). Test mode, test instructions, and retention. *Contemporary Educational Psychology, 4,* 211-218.

Lafitte, R. G. (1984). Effects of item order on achievement test scores and students' perception of test difficulty. *Teaching of Psychology, 11,* 212-213.

Little, E. B. (1962). Overcorrection for guessing in multiple-choice test scoring. *Journal of Educational Research, 55,* 245-252.

Little, E. B. (1966). Overcorrection and undercorrection in multiple-choice test scoring. *Journal of Experimental Education, 35,* 44-47.

Lord, F. M. (1952). The relationship of the reliability of multiple-choice tests to the distribution of item difficulties. *Psychometrika, 17*(2), 181-194.

Lord, F. M. (1975). Formula scoring and number right scoring. *Journal of Educational Measurement, 12,* 7-12.

Lord, F. M. (1977). Optimal number of choices per item: A comparison of four approaches. *Journal of Educational Measurement, 14,* 33-38.

Lueptow, L. B., Early, K., & Garland, T. N. (1976). Validity of student evaluations of objective test items. *Educational and Psychological Measurement, 36,* 939-944.

McClelland, D. (1973). Testing for competence rather than for "intelligence." *American Psychologist, 28,* 1-14.

McMorris, R. F., Brown, J. A., Snyder, G. W., & Pruzek, R. M. (1972). Effects of violating item construction principles. *Journal of Educational Measurement, 9,* 287-295.

Marcus, A. (1963). Effect of correct response location on the difficulty level of multiple-choice questions. *Journal of Applied Psychology, 47,* 48-51.

Michael, J. J. (1968). The reliability of multiple-choice examination under various test-taking instructions. *Journal of Educational Measurement, 5,* 307-314.

Miller, I., & Minor, F. J. (1963). Influence of multiple-choice answer form design on answer-making performance. *Journal of Applied Psychology, 47,* 374-379.

Millman, J., & Pauk, W. (1969). *How to take tests.* New York: McGraw-Hill.

Mollenkopf, W. G. (1950). An experimental study of the effects of item analysis data on changing item placement and test time limit. *Psychometrika, 15,* 291-317.

Mueller, D. J., & Shwedel, A. (1975). Some correlates of net gain from answer changing on objective test items. *Journal of Educational Measurement, 12,* 251-254.

Mueller, D. J., & Wasser, V. (1977). Implications of changing answers on objective test items. *Journal of Educational Measurement, 9,* 321-324.

Muller, D., Calhoun, E., & Orling, R. (1972). Test reliability as a function of answer sheet mode. *Journal of Educational Measurement, 9,* 321-324.

Nairn, A., & Associates (1980). *The reign of ETS: The corporation that makes up minds.* Washington, DC: Learning Research Project.

Nevo, B., & Spector, A. (1979). Personal tempo in taking tests of the multiple-choice type. *Journal of Educational Research, 73,* 75-78.

Niedermeyer, F. C., & Sullivan, H. J. (1972). Differential effects of individual and group testing strategies in an objectives-based instructional program. *Journal of Educational Measurement, 9,* 199-204.

O'Neill, M., Rasor, R. A., & Bartz, W. R. (1976). Immediate retention of objective test answers as a function of feedback complexity. *Journal of Educational Research, 70,* 72-75.

Oosterhof, A. C., & Glasnapp, D. R. (1974). Comparative reliabilities and difficulties of the multiple-choice and true-false formats. *Journal of Experimental Education, 42,* 62-64.

Owens, R. E., Hanna, G. S., & Coppedge, F. L. (1970). Comparison of multiple-choice tests using different types of distractor selection techniques. *Journal of Educational Measurement, 7,* 87-90.

Panackal, A. A., & Heft, C. S. (1978). Cloze technique and multiple choice technique: Reliability and validity. *Educational and Psychological Measurement, 38,* 917-932.

Pascale, P. J. (1974). Changing initial answers on multiple-choice achievement tests. *Measurement and Evaluation in Guidance, 16,* 236-238.

Payne, B. D. (1984). The relationship of test anxiety and answer-changing behavior: An analysis by race and sex. *Measurement and Evaluation in Guidance, 16,* 205-210.

Plake, B. S., Ansorge, C. J., Parker, C. S., & Lowry, S. R. (1982). Effects of item arrangement, knowledge of arrangement, test anxiety and sex on test performance. *Journal of Educational Measurement, 19,* 49-57.

Preston, R. C. (1964). Ability of students to identify correct responses before reading. *Journal of Educational Research, 58,* 181-183.

Preston, R. C. (1965). Multiple-choice test as an instrument in perpetuating false concepts. *Educational and Psychological Measurement, 25,* 111-116.

Pyrczak, F. (1973). Validity of the discrimination index as a measure of item quality. *Journal of Educational Measurement, 10,* 227-231.

Reid, F. (1977). Alternative scoring formula for multiple-choice and true-false tests. *Journal of Educational Research, 70,* 335-339.

Reiling, E., & Taylor, R. (1972). New approach to the problem of changing initial responses to multiple-choice questions. *Journal of Educational Measurement, 9,* 67-70.

Reynolds, W. M. (1979). Utility of multiple-choice test formats with mildly retarded adolescents. *Educational and Psychological Measurement, 39,* 325-331.

Rimland, B., & Zwerski, E. (1962). Use of open-end data as an aid in writing multiple-choice distracters: An evaluation with arithmetic reasoning and computation items. *Journal of Applied Psychology, 46,* 31-33.

Rodgers, F. A. (1966). Test-item format preferences of elementary school pupils. *Elementary School Journal, 67,* 45-49.

Rowley, G. L. (1974). Which examinees are most favoured by the use of multiple-choice test? *Journal of Educational Measurement, 11,* 15-23.

Savitz, F. R. (1985). Effects of easy examination questions placed at the beginning of science multiple-choice examinations. *Journal of Instructional Psychology, 12,* 6-10.

Sax, G. (1980). *Principles of educational and psychological measurement and evaluation.* Belmont, CA: Wadsworth.

Serlin, R. C., & Kaiser, H. F. (1978). Method for increasing the reliability of a short multiple-choice test. *Educational and Psychological Measurement, 38,* 337-340.

Shaha, S. H. (1984). Matching tests: Reduced anxiety and increased test effectiveness. *Educational and Psychological Measurement, 44,* 869-881.

Skinner, N. F. (1983). Switching answers on multiple-choice questions: Shrewdness or shibboleth? *Teaching of Psychology, 10,* 220-222.

Slakter, M. J., Koehler, R. A., & Hampton, S. H. (1970). Grade level, sex, and selected aspects of test-wiseness. *Journal of Educational Measurement, 7,* 119-122.

Smith, M., White, K. P., & Coop, R. H. (1979). The effect of item type on the consequences of changing answers on multiple-choice tests. *Journal of Educational Measurement, 16,* 203-208.

Stoffer, G. R., Davis, K. E., & Brown, J. B. (1977). The consequences of changing initial answers on objective tests: A stable effect and a stable misconception. *Journal of Educational Research, 70,* 272-277.

Stokes, R. R. (1966). Split-responses technique: Suggestions to increase the utility of multiple-choice tests. *Phi Delta Kappan, 47,* 271-272.

Storey, A. G. (1968). Versatile multiple-choice item. *Journal of Educational Research, 62,* 169-172.

Strang, H. R. (1980). Effect of technically worded options on multiple-choice test performance. *Journal of Educational Research, 73,* 262-265.

Straton, R. G., Catts, R. M. (1980). Comparison of two, three and four-choice item tests given a fixed total number of choices. *Educational and Psychological Measurement, 40,* 357-365.

Taylor, P. H. (1966). Study of the effects of instructions in a multiple-choice mathematics test. *British Journal of Educational Psychology, 36,* 1-6.

Tidwell, R. (1980). Biasing potential of multiple-choice test distractors. *Journal of Negro Education, 49,* 289-296.

Traub, R. E., & Hambleton, R. K. (1973). The effect of scoring instructions and degree of speededness on the validity and reliability of multiple-choice tests. *Educational and Psychological Measurement, 32,* 737-758; *33,* 877-878.

Vidler, D., & Hansen, R. (1980). Answer changing on multiple-choice tests. *Journal of Experimental Education, 49,* 18-20.

Warren, G. (1979). Essay versus multiple-choice tests. *Journal of Research in Science Teaching, 16,* 563-567.

Waters, C. W., & Waters, L. K. (1971). Validity and likability ratings for three scoring instructions for a multiple-choice vocabulary test. *Educational and Psychological Measurement, 31,* 935-938.

Weiten, W. (1984). Violation of selected item construction principles in educational measurement. *Journal of Experimental Education, 52,* 174-178.

Weitzman, E., & McNamara, W. J. (1946). Apt use of the inept choice in multiple-choice testing. *Journal of Educational Research, 39,* 517-522.

Wilbur, P. H. (1970). Positional response set among high school students on multiple-choice tests. *Journal of Educational Measurement, 7,* 161-163.

Williams, S. I., & Jones, C. O. (1974). Multiple-choice mathematics questions: How students attempt to solve them. *Mathematics Teacher, 67,* 34-40.

Willson, V. L. (1982). Maximizing reliability in multiple-choice questions. *Educational and Psychological Measurement, 42,* 69-72.

Wood, R. (1976). Inhibiting blind guessing: The effect of instructions. *Journal of Educational Measurement, 13,* 297-307.

Wood, R. (1977). Multiple choice: A state of the art report. *Evaluation in Education, 1,* 191-280.

Yelvington, J. Y., & Brady, R. C. (1979). Corrective feedback testing. *Educational Technology, 19,* 36-37.

Zimmerman, D. W., Williams, R. H., & Symons, D. L. (1984). Empirical estimates of the comparative reliability of matching tests and multiple-choice tests. *Journal of Experimental Education, 52,* 179-182.

THE ROLE OF DIFFICULTY AND DISCRIMINATION IN CONSTRUCTING MULTIPLE-CHOICE EXAMINATIONS: WITH GUIDELINES FOR PRACTICAL APPLICATION

Bruce A. Baldwin
Arizona State University

ABSTRACT: A task common to all accounting professors is that of constructing examinations; frequently containing multiple-choice questions. This paper explores some of the concepts from testing and measurement theory that underly the development of high quality multiple-choice questions.

First, the examination is conceptualized as a measurement device to assess the degree of student learning. Then the concepts of difficulty and discrimination are developed and applied to the testing process. Here convergent and discriminant validity are discussed. Finally, specific guidelines are developed for use in generating high-quality multiple-choice questions.

A task common to all accounting professors is that of constructing examinations. With large class sizes, a conventional practice is to dedicate a significant portion of an exam (if not the entire exam) to multiple-choice questions. It is well established in the testing and measurement literature that such questions can achieve coverage of broad content areas quite efficiently. Further, most professors are well aware of alternative sources of such questions; from Test Banks provided by publishers to questions borrowed from prior professional examinations. Unfortunately, the quality and useability of test items from these sources varies widely. While items from prior professional examinations tend to be of fairly high quality, their number tends to be relatively small. Also these questions are usually publicly available to the students being examined. Test bank items, on the other hand, tend to be plentiful in number but frequently of low quality. For several reasons, then, instructors are often forced to develop some or all of their own test questions. The purpose of this paper is to explore some of the concepts from testing and measurement theory that underly the creation of high quality multiple-choice questions. Further, practical guidelines are presented for implementing those concepts.

THE FUNCTION OF THE EXAM

What constitutes a high-quality question, however, depends upon what function the instructor wishes the exam to achieve. Currently, two views

---

Reprinted by permission of the Center for Research in Accounting Education from the Journal of Accounting Education, Vol. 2, No. 1 (Spring 1984): 19-28.

dominate the testing process. First, some view the examination as the culminative step in the learning process. That is, it is considered the last of many activities designed to help the student learn. Inherent in this philosophy is the belief that the examination is a learning device; students should learn from the exam and while taking the exam. The other dominant view is that examinations are measurement devices. That is, their function is *not* to help students learn, but rather to assess what degree of mastery of a topic a student has achieved. In this approach, examinations are summative evaluations as described by Frakes and Foran [1978] and Airasian and Madaus [1972]. Examinations are not designed to help students learn, but rather to measure their learning. This paper assumes this latter position; that is, examinations are measurement devices.

It can usually be assumed that all students have learned something, and further, that the variation in learning achievement is rather great. That is, examinations are not measurements with zero-one outcomes. Rather, the degree of learning is represented by a continuum of possible outcomes. The purpose of the examination is to place (measure) student performance along that continuum. After a series of measurements (exams), the net results are used to categorize student performance into grading groups such as A, B, C, D, and F.

MEASUREMENT CONCEPTS UNDERLYING THE EXAMINATION PROCESS

Two interrelated concepts, difficulty and discrimination, are basic to writing useful test questions that will result in students being categorized into the correct grade groupings. Difficulty refers to the proportion of students that answer a question correctly. Testing and measurement specialists routinely calculate the Difficulty Index (DI) for each test item [Helmstadter, 1964]. The DI is the percentage of students answering the question correctly. (Conceptually, however, it should probably be referred to as the Easiness Index since the higher the index number the easier the question).

A question can be too difficult or too easy with the result that the test item yields no (or very little) information to the examiner. Take the extreme case of a question that no one answers correctly. Such a test item is of no utility since it generates no information that will help categorize the student into the correct grade grouping. No information is obtained to help differentiate between the student that has done a good job of mastering course materials and the student that has done a poor job. The same is true of a question with a Difficulty Index of 100; it provides no information that differentiates between levels of mastery. While it may be interesting to know that all students mastered a particular concept, the measurement device has failed. It is similar to having a household thermometer that is accurate only to the nearest 100°. It tells an interesting story, perhaps, but it is rather useless for its intended function.

Clearly, then, test items at the extremes of the Difficulty Index are not very useful. Educational psychologists argue that the best test question is one that 50% of the students answer correctly [Womer, 1968; Nunnally, 1970]. The following intuitive proof describes "information content." First, "bits" of information is defined as the percent of students answering correctly times the percent of students answering incorrectly. If a question is answered correctly by all students, you have separated the class into two groups; 100% in one group, 0% in the other. Bits of information, then, equals:

$$(100) \times (0) = 0 \text{ bits of information}$$

If, instead, only 80% of the class responds correctly the amount of information obtained is:

$$(80) \times (20) = 1600 \text{ bits of information}$$

Similarly, observe the effect of the following levels of difficulty on the amount of information obtained from a test question.

Difficulty	Computation	Bits of Information
100	100 x 0	-0-
90	90 x 10	900
80	80 x 20	1600
70	70 x 30	2100
60	60 x 40	2400
50	50 x 50	2500
40	40 x 60	2400
30	30 x 70	2100
20	20 x 80	1600
10	10 x 90	900
0	0 x 100	-0-

Maximum information is derived from a question with a Difficulty Index of 50. By logical extension, then, maximum information is derived from an examination consisting of individual items with difficulties of 50. Such an exam, therefore, would also have a mean of 50 percent. In accounting education practice, however, it is common for many instructors to establish a "straight scale" for grading purposes such as A = 90%, B = 80%, C = 70%, D = 60%, and F = less than 60%. Such a scale implicitly assumes a mean score of approximately 75% (i.e. middle of the C range). It appears from the prior analysis of difficulty that accounting exams could be better measurement devices if they were made more rigorous.

Difficulty does not by itself, however, result in high-quality test questions. Also involved is the second basic concept: item discrimination. In fact, item discrimination is the more important of the two. Not only does the examiner want to split the class 50-50 on each question, but he (she) wants to insure that the groups are composed of the "right" students. For example, it may be relatively easy to write a question about contingent liabilities that has a Difficulty Index of 50, but the examiner wants to make sure that the 50% answering correctly is the 50% that comprehended the concept most fully. It is not just a question of splitting the class 50-50, but of getting the correct 50% in each group.

Testing and measurement specialists commonly prepare a Discrimination Index for each of the possible answers to a multiple-choice question [Lemke and Wiersma, 1976; Krus and Ney, 1978]. A Discrimination Index is a point biserial correlation of an alternative answer with the total exam score[1] (see Appendix 1). This correlation is computed for the correct answer and for each of the distractors (incorrect answers). The correct answer should have high positive correlation with the total exam score. That is, persons scoring well on the individual questions should score well on the entire exam. This is referred to as convergent validity. At the same time, distractors should show discriminant validity (i.e., they should have high negative correlations with total scores).

As examples, consider the following two questions that appeared recently on an Introductory Financial Accounting exam given to 300 students. One question was useful, the other was not.

1. A pending lawsuit at the end of the accounting period would:[2]
    a. be reported by a note to the Balance Sheet.
    b. be reported in the Balance Sheet as a current liability.
    c. be reported in the Income Statement as an expense.
    d. not be reported at all since the outcome is not known.

---

[1] While point biserial correlation is conceptually simple, its computation becomes quite tedious as the number of students increases. Such analysis is usually performed with the aid of a computer. A good discussion and illustration of point biserial correlation is provided by Ferguson [1976, pp. 415-418].

[2] Students were advised to select the one best answer. Although answer C is possible under some circumstances, answer A (especially in an introductory course) is the best answer.

2. The lower of cost of market basis of inventory valuation is a departure from which important accounting principle?
   a. exception principle
   b. matching principle
   c. cost principle
   d. consistency principle

Results of the item analysis were as follows:

Question	Correct Answer	Type of Analysis	A	B	C	D
1	A	Difficulty Index	.51	.12	.02	.35
		Discrimination Index	.56	-.22	-.20	-.38
2	C	Difficulty Index	.14	.16	.57	.13
		Discrimination Index	.06	-.11	.12	-.19

While both questions demonstrate an acceptable level of difficulty, notice that question #1 shows high positive correlation for the correct response (A = .56) and strong negative correlation on the incorrect responses (B = -.22, C = -.20, D = -.38). The students who understood the concept of a contingent liability and its accounting treatment tended to be students who scored well on the entire exam. Students selecting an incorrect answer tended not to do well on the rest of the exam either. There was convergent validity on the correct answer, and discriminant validity on the distractors.

For question #2, however, the results are not nearly as favorable. First, there is not very good convergent validity on the correct answer. That is, while the point biserial correlation is positive (.12), it is rather low and does not signal an effective question. A greater number of "better" students answered the question correctly than did "poorer" students; but not many. Further problems appear with the distractors. One of them (A) doesn't even have the expected negative correlation; it is positive at .06. What this means is that a greater number of better students were drawn to this incorrect response than weaker students. The distractor is not functioning properly. Good students should answer the question correctly, and poor students should answer it incorrectly. The other distractors (B and D) are at least negative, but only D is what might be called "adequately" so. Question #2, then, is not an effective test item and should be discarded or rewritten before subsequent reuse. Perhaps the problem is that some good students are misinterpreting the question as asking for what principle is involved when LCM is used. For that question, the correct response would be A.

PRACTICAL GUIDELINES FOR GENERATING EXAM QUESTIONS

In any event, difficulty and discrimination are the basic components from which useful multiple-choice questions are derived. Following are a series of practical guidelines for developing high quality questions:

1. Each question should test (measure) a specific principle, topic, concept, procedure, or combination thereof. That is, the exam must be planned before starting to write specific items. Conceptualize the exam as a sampling process, recognizing that a question cannot be asked on every topic. First determine the topics to be included in the exam and then prepare a specific item to test each one. When a question is completed, one should be able to analyze it and determine how it is that a student having mastered the concept will automatically be drawn to the correct answer (convergent validity). Similarly, one should be able to show how a student confused about "aspect X" of the concept or "aspect Y" will be drawn to a specific distractor (discriminant validity).
2. Avoid "gimme" questions; ones that you expect everyone to answer correctly. They contribute no information and only take up time and space on an exam. At the same time, it is equally fruitless to use a question that is too difficult. Shorten the exam (number of questions) if you must. It is better to have fewer good questions than many poorer ones. Most research also shows there is no benefit in starting an exam off with an easy question to build student confidence [Barcikowski and Olsen, 1975; Munz and Smouse, 1968; Howe and Baldwin, 1983].
3. Avoid lengthy, wordy questions and (more importantly) answers. Typically, the short direct question gets right to the concept being tested most efficiently. For example, the examiner may want to know if students have mastered the concept that dividends are not expenses, but rather are a distribution of earnings. The following short, direct, explicit question might be asked:

Dividends are
    a. always expensed
    b. never expensed
    c. sometimes expensed
    d. frequently expensed

If the student understands the concept, there is no question as to the correct answer (B). If the student is not clear about the concept, the question offers four equally unattractive choices. (Another interesting

aspect of this question is that in order to answer it correctly, the student is forced to violate the commonly repeated maxim of not selecting multiple-choice answers that include the words "always" or "never.")
4. Use a variety of conceptual questions (such as the dividends question above) as well as the numerical problem-type. A common fault or misconception of multiple-choice exams is that they (can) test only recall or recognition material. This is not accurate, as almost any concept, principle, or procedure can be tested in a multiple-choice format. A quick but careful perusal of any recent CPA Exam should confirm the point. A mixture of about half conceptual and half problem-type questions is generally suitable.
5. Use simple numbers wherever possible so as to test concepts and procedures rather than how well calculators work. For example, if knowledge of the Cost of Goods Sold formula (Cost of Goods Sold = Beginning Inventory + Net Purchases - Ending Inventory) is important, an exam question might give the following information and ask for the calculation of cost of goods sold.

	Usual Data in This Kind of Problem	Simple Numbers	Simpler Numbers
Purchases	$95,000	$70	$9
Beginning Inventory	30,000	20	4
Transportation-In	1,500	3	1
Ending Inventory	28,300	30	6
Purchase Returns	11,000	8	3

By using the simple (or preferably the simpler) numbers, a concept or formula is being tested and not computational skill. While there may be circumstances in which computational skill should be tested, it is typically not appropriate to do so in every test item.
6. Carefully choose the distractors. This is perhaps where most poor questions originate; the correct answer is often carefully determined but then three (or four) distractors are hastily or haphazardly generated to complete the question. The best indicator of this type of question building is the inordinate use of distractors such as "none of the above," "all of the above," "two of the above," "(a) and (c) above," etc. Frequent use of these types of alternatives usually indicates a poorly thought out question. They are easy to construct but seldom generate discriminant validity. Distractors (incorrect answers) should be responses that are plausible to the student that has not mastered the concept. Specifically, numerical distractors should be derived from incorrect combinations of data given in the problem. This principle is frequently violated with the result that a question does a poor job of measuring concept mastery. Consider

the following question regarding the year end adjusting entry for Bad Debt Expense:

Carvic Corporation uses the Balance Sheet method of determining Bad Debt Expense. The appropriate rate is 10%. Prior to year end adjusting entries, Carvic has the following account balances: Accounts Receivable, $5000 (debit) and Allowance for Doubtful Accounts, $200 (debit). The necessary adjusting entry will include a debit to Bad Debt Expense in the amount of:

    a. $600
    b. $700
    c. $800
    d. $900

Any reasonably intelligent student should be able to determine that "B" is the correct answer, even if they don't have the slightest mastery of accounting for receivables. Given the data, response B ($700) is the only suggested answer one can possible derive. None of the other answers can be derived from the data given. The result is that students *not* mastering the topic are measured as if they had. Such students are then categorized improperly for grading purposes. The question would be much improved by substituting the following set of responses:

    a. $300
    b. $500
    c. $520
    d. $700

All of these answers can be derived from the data. The student without mastery of receivables accounting is reduced to guessing.
    Concept question distractors should be opposites of the correct answer, common misconceptions, or applications of concepts not involved in the question. Further, they should be as lengthy (or short) as the correct answer. Whether there are four or five possible answers is usually unimportant.
7. Spread out the correct responses. Make a conscious effort to have a uniform distribution of correct responses spread out over the A, B, C, D and E alternatives. There is an unconscious tendency by most question writers to make the correct answer C or D. All test writers have probably heard the familiar conventional wisdom of "when in doubt mark C," but continue to have a preponderance of questions

with that answer. Spread the answers around to all alternatives so as to improve overall question discrimination.
8. Avoid the "unfortunate coincidence"; [Davidson, Stickney and Weil, 1980]. That is, don't allow the student to accidentally get to the correct solution via the wrong logic or sloppy thinking. A common example of the "unfortunate coincidence" is use of a 50% tax rate in problems involving tax effects. The student may be unable to conceptually differentiate between the amount of tax effect versus the amount of after-tax cost, yet answer the question correctly because they are "coincidentally" the same. Here again, such a question fails to measure appropriately. This "unfortunate coincidence," however, can be simply solved by using a tax rate different than 50%. This small change will greatly improve the quality of the question.

SUMMARY

Use of the preceding practical guidelines will enable instructors to design more effective measurement instruments. A secondary benefit of many of these suggestions is that the resulting questions become less ambiguous (or vague) and the number of student complaints about the examination are therefore reduced. On a properly constructed exam consisting of items with good convergent and discriminant validity, the student reaction is typically that the exam was "tough but fair." The student (as well as the professor) can look at an incorrectly answered question and see exactly where the student went wrong. Use of these principles will give the professor and student greater confidence in the grading process and increase student satisfaction with it.

APPENDIX 1

The purpose of this appendix is to describe the computation of the Discrimination Index presented in this paper. The Discrimination Index is a point biserial correlation that provides a measure of the relation between a continuous variable (exam score) and a dichotomous variable (whether or not a student chose a particular multiple-choice answer). Usually it is computed for both the correct answer and for each of the distractors. It is quite time consuming and is usually done by computer. Assuming that an exam had 30 multiple-choice questions, each with 4 possible answers, 120 correlations would have to be computed. Following is a simplified example involving six students and the Discrimination Index for one possible response to a hypothetical multiple-response question.

Calculation of the Point Biserial Correlation

Student	Exam Score	Marked Response "a"
1	75	NO
2	83	NO
3	97	YES
4	67	YES
5	22	NO
6	76	YES

Assume the following data relates to a multiple-choice question for which the correct response is "a". If it is a "good" question, there should be high positive correlation between whether a student answered this question correctly and their overall score on the exam (convergent validity).
The formula for the point biserial correlation coefficient r is:

$$r = \frac{X_{yes} - X_{no}}{S_x} (p)(q)$$

where X_{yes} is the mean exam score of those students choosing response "a" and X_{no} is the mean exam score for those that didn't.

S_x is the standard deviation of exam scores and p is the percentage of students choosing response "a", while q is the percentage of students that did not.

Substituting in the appropriate values,

$$r = \frac{80 - 60}{23.4} (.5)(.5)$$

$$= .43$$

Since values of r greater than .50 or .60 are seldom observed, this question demonstrates high convergent validity (high positive correlation) on the correct answer. For a complete analysis of the quality of this hypothetical multiple-choice question, however, the point biserial correlations should also be computed for each of the other possible responses. Those correlations will be highly negative if the question is high quality.

References

Airasian, P.W. and G.F. Madaus (1972), "Functional Types of Student Evaluations," *Measurement and Evaluation in Guidance* (January 1972), pp. 222-223.

Barcikowski, R.S. and H. Olsen (1975), "Test Item Arrangement and Adaptation Level," *The Journal of Psychology* (May 1975), pp. 87-93.

Davidson, S., C.P. Stickney and R.L. Weil (1980), *Intermediate Accounting: Concepts, Methods and Uses* (The Dryden Press, 1980) pp. viii-ix.

Ferguson, G.A. (1976), *Statistical Analysis in Psychology and Education*, 4th Edition (McGraw-Hill, 1976) pp. 415-418.

Frakes, A.H. and M.F. Foran (1978), "A Framework for Examining the Evaluative Function of Accounting Learning Activities," *The Accounting Review* (January 1978), pp. 148-154.

Helmstadter, G.C. (1964), *Principles of Psychological Measurement* (Appleton-Century-Crofts, 1964) pp. 162-164.

Howe, K.R. and B.A. Baldwin (1983), "The Effects of Evaluative Sequencing on Performance, Behavior and Attitudes," *The Accounting Review* (January 1983), pp. 135-142.

Krus, D. and R. Ney (1978), "Convergent and Discriminant Validity in Item Analysis," *Educational and Psychological Measurement* (Spring 1978), pp. 135-137.

Lemke, E. and W. Wiersma (1976), *Psychological Measurement* (Rand McNally, 1976), pp. 251-258.

Munz, D.C. and A.D. Smouse (1968), "Interaction Effects of Item Difficulty Sequence and Achievement-Anxiety Reaction on Academic Performance," *Journal of Educational Psychology* (October 1968), pp. 370-374.

Nunnally, J.C., Jr. (1970), *Introduction to Psychological Measurement*, (McGraw-Hill, 1970), pp. 209-212.

Womer, F.B. (1968), *Basic Concepts in Testing* (Houghton Mifflin Company, 1968), p. 76.

THE RELATIVE MERITS OF MULTIPLE TRUE-FALSE ACHIEVEMENT TESTS

David A. Frisbie
University of Iowa
Daryl C. Sweeney
University of Illinois at Urbana-Champaign

Of the several item formats typically used to test student achievement, the multiple choice (MC) type enjoys the greatest popularity for a wide variety of purposes. Research studies which compare the characteristics of MC with true-false, completion, and varieties of adapted MC forms have provided evidence that the MC type can yield efficient, valid, and reliable achievement measures. One seldom-used item format, the multiple true-false (MTF), has been subjected to little research but shows at least theoretical promise for achieving the same desirable ends as the MC form.

MTF items resemble MC items in their appearance. However, rather than selecting one best answer from several alternatives, examinees respond to each of the several alternatives as separate true-false statements. These separate statements have a common "lead" or stem just like an MC item. Content-parallel illustrations of both forms are shown in Figure 1. This use of the term, MTF, is consistent with Albanese, Kent and Whitney (1977), Kelley (1979), and Mendelson, Hardin and Canaday (1980), but differs from that of both Ebel (1978) and Whitely (1979). Ebel's format was very much like MC, except that it used a stem such as "Which of the following statements is true (false)?" Whitely's use of MTF is unusual, in that it referred to items which many have labeled complex multiple choice (CMC), response alternatives consisting of combinations of the typical MC alternatives.

The MTF format would appear to have several advantages over the MC format: a greater number of responses can be obtained in a given time period, the longer test is likely to be more reliable, a greater range of content can be examined because of the length, and a more valid measure should be obtained because of the increased reliability. In addition, students might indicate greater preference for MTF than MC because the additional test length gives more opportunities for them to show what they have learned.

Studies of MTF items reported in the literature have come from the medical and other health-related fields as measurement specialists have searched for an alternative to the CMC format. Gross (1978) supported the use of MTF items without a correction for guessing by showing that the maximum probable range of scores (difference between perfect and chance scores) for an MTF test would exceed that of an MC test which is comparable in terms of number of options. The expected advantage in terms of test

---

Reprinted by permission of <u>Journal of Educational Measurement</u>, Vol. 19, No. 1, (Spring 1982): 29-35.

reliability was documented by Albanese et al. (1977), Kelley (1979), and Mendelson et al.(1980). However, in each case comparisons were made by holding test content or test length constant. Because of differences in response rates between item formats (Frisbie, 1974; Frisbie & Ory, 1980), comparisons should be made by adjusting test lengths to equate testing time. The amount of time required for examinees to respond to items of the various formats was not reported by Albanese et al.(1977), Kelley (1979), or Mendelson, et al.(1980). The purpose of this study was therefore to compare MC and MTF content-parallel tests in terms of testing time required, reliability, concurrent validity, difficulty, and student preference.

METHOD

Subjects

Participants in this study were 574 students enrolled in Biology 110 during the Fall 1980 semester who took the final exam at the scheduled time. Based on achievement measures gathered throughout the semester, the instructor judged this Biology 110 class to be similar to those of recent years. Biology 110 is the first course in a two-course introductory sequence in which life science and pre-medicine majors enroll. Such students are highly capable academically and are highly motivated to succeed.

Figure 1. Sample multiple choice and multiple true-false items.

I. Multiple choice

   1. An ecologist losing weight by jogging and exercising is, in technical terms,

      a. decreasing maintenance metabolism.
      * b. decreasing net productivity.
      c. increasing biomass.
      d. decreasing energy lost to decomposition.
      e. increasing gross productivity.

II. Multiple True-False

   **An ecologist losing weight by jogging and exercising is, in technical terms,

      T 1. increasing maintenance metabolism.
      T 2. decreasing net productivity.
      F 3. increasing biomass.
      F 4. decreasing energy lost to decomposition.
      F 5. increasing gross productivity.

Instrumentation

The course instructor prepared 100 MC items which covered the entire range of course content. Each of these 5-choice MC items was converted to MTF form with only slight wording modifications to adapt to the new format. The substance of each converted item remained the same as its original counterpart in MC form; each MC item was associated with a quintet of MTF items by content.

Two test forms, A and B, were developed by randomly assigning each MC item to one form and its paired MTF cluster to the other form. This procedure resulted in two content-parallel test forms, each containing 50 MC and 250 MTF items. Items were content-ordered by item type subgroups within each form: 1-20, MC; 21-120, MTF; 121-140, MC; 141-290, MTF; 291-300, MC for Form A. The distribution of the number of true statements per MTF cluster is shown in Table 1 for each form. The only difference between forms on this dimension was the presence of three clusters in Form A in which all items were false and none such clusters in Form B. There was no attempt to control the number of true statements per cluster within or between test forms.

Two additional questions were appended to each form to solicit students' preference for the two item formats. Students were asked which format was easier and which they preferred. Response choices for the two questions were MC, MTF, and both the same.

Table 1
Distribution of the Number of True Statements
Per MC Cluster for Both Test Forms

Number of True Statements	Number of Clusters of MTF Form A	Form B
0	3	0
1	25	28
2	9	9
3	4	4
4	7	7
5	2	2
Total True Statements	93	96
Total False Statements	157	154

Procedures

Forms A and B were distributed in a non-systematic manner to students after they were seated in the testing room. Students had been told in advance that the test would consist of both MC and MTF items. Several sets of practice MTF, none of which appeared on the final exam, had been distributed to students throughout the semester to familiarize them with the MTF format. In addition, MTF items were used in two previous hourly exams.

After ten minutes of testing had elapsed, students were stopped and asked to circle the number of the test item they had last attempted. Testing then resumed without further interruption.

RESULTS

Testing Time

Students using Form A began with MC items and attempted 8.7 items on the average (median) during the first ten minutes, while students having Form B began with MTF items and attempted 29.9 items on the average (median) during the first ten minutes. The range of values for number of items attempted was 3-21 for MC and 14-65 for MTF. The ratio for these medians is 3.44 MTF items to one MC item. The frequency distributions for number of items attempted in the first ten minutes were examined to determine thestability of the ratio at several percentile points. At the 10th, 25th, 50th, 75th, and 90th percentiles, the corresponding ratios were: 3.51, 3.49, 3.44, 3.40, and 3.31. The ratios decrease slightly, as would be expected, as rate of response increases.

Reliability

Subtest coefficient alpha reliabilities for each form are presented in Table 2. The MTF clusters were scored 0-5 and cluster scores were used to estimate reliability because of the apparent within-cluster dependence between MTF items. As would be expected in view of test length differences, the MTF reliabilities exceeded the corresponding MC values by a meaningful amount. A more useful comparison of reliabilities for both practical and theoretical purposes requires an adjustment of the coefficient alphas for either testing time or test length. Because the rates of response are quite different for the two item types, the more meaningful adjustment would be for testing time.

The response time data showed that 3.5 MTF (25th percentile) items were attempted in the time required to try one MC item. In other words, 0.7 of an MTF cluster was attempted for each MC item. The MTF reliabilities shown in Table 2 were stepped down using the Spearman-Brown Prophecy Formula to make them comparable in testing time to the MC reliabilities. The adjusted MTF values were .749 and .786 for Forms A and B, respectively.

Validity

The two subtest correlation coefficients given in Table 2 can be used as concurrent validity evidence for the two item types. The simple correlations, .761 and .740, are similar to one another and are relatively high. Out of theoretical interest, the correlations were corrected for attenuation to determine the extent of the pure or infallible relationship between the variables. The unadjusted coefficient alpha values shown in Table 2 were used to correct for unreliability. The corrected values were 1.042 for Form A and .952 for Form B.

Difficulty

The difficulty levels of the subtests cannot be compared directly with mean scores because of the differences in both test lengths and mean chance scores for the two item types. To overcome these obstacles, the relative difficulty ratio (RDR) (Frisbie, 1981) was computed using the four subtest means. The RDR ratio compares a test mean to its ideal mean, the point midway between the expected chance score and the perfect score. The ratio can be used to calculate a linear transformation of the scores on one test scale to another test scale. In this case, the MC subtest means were transformed to the MTF score scale so that length differences (50 vs. 250 items) and mean chance differences (10 vs. 125) would not interfere with the assessment of test difficulty.

Values of the four subtest means, all on the MTF score scale, are depicted in Table 2. The results appear to be inconclusive in that the adjusted MC mean is higher in one pair (Form A) and lower in the other (Form B).

Table 2
Test Statistics For Item Type Subtests by Form

Statistics	Form A MC	Form A MTF	Form B MC	Form B MTF
n	279	279	295	295
$\bar{x}$	24.63	160.23	19.92	167.64
$\bar{x}'$	170.72		156.00	
s_x	5.44	16.93	5.90	17.49
k	50	250	50	250
α	.658	.810	.719	.840
r	.761		.740	

However, all subtests are relatively difficult by norm-referenced standards, and the Form B MC subtest is particularly difficult.

When asked which item type is easier, 47 percent of the 558 respondents indicated MTF and 22 percent indicated MC. About 31 percent of the students responded that the two were "about the same."

Student Preference

In response to the question, "Which do you prefer?" nearly half (47.8 percent) indicated MTF. About one-third (32.0 percent) preferred MC and 20 percent did not prefer one type over the other.

DISCUSSION

The results reported above provide evidence that MTF items compare favorably with MC items for measuring achievement. In fact, the data lend support to the theoretical expectation that MTF items may be superior to MC. The testing-time data showed that in a given period, students can attempt 3.5 times more MTF than MC items, assuming that the rate of response for the first ten minutes does not change differentially for the two item types in a longer testing period. In addition, the response-rate ratios indicated that the relationship is relatively stable in terms of fast- and slow-paced test takers. Certainly the additional test length available with MTF items permits greater sampling of the content in breadth and depth, and yields greater potential for a representative sampling of the content than with MC items.

The reliability data indicate that the increased test length achieved with MTF items is associated with increased reliability of scores even when MTF cluster scores are used. When the reliability estimates were adjusted to equate testing time, the advantage was still with the MTF items. Though the differences in adjusted reliability estimates may not be of practical significance, it is significant to note that reliability is not sacrificed by using MTF instead of MC.

The disattenuated correlation coefficients showed that the MC and MTF subtests in each form had high concurrent validity. The implication is that MTF and MC items measure the same thing, i.e., that the content of the subtests was similar and the test-taking tasks necessitated by the two item forms require the same or related skills. It is worth noting that students in this study had been exposed to the MTF format prior to the final exam through two hourly exams and several MTF self-tests. It seems logical that such prior exposure is necessary to avoid confusion on the students' parts during a graded examination.

That one format is more difficult than the other in a psychometric sense cannot be determined from the data in this study. All subtests were somewhat difficult by norm-referenced standards, but one MC subtest (Form B) in particular was more difficult than the others. The observed difficulty level of all subtests may have also reduced discrimination levels and in turn yielded lower reliability estimates than would be expected ideally.

It would be appropriate to revise these instruments to make them less difficult and replicate this study with another group. Under such circumstances one would expect all reliability estimates to increase and the gap between the MC and MTF estimates to narrow. Nonetheless, there is no reason to expect that the MC reliability estimates would exceed the MTF estimates.

It is significant that only 22 percent of the students perceived the MC items to be easier than the MTF. In addition, only a third of the students indicated a preference for MC over MTF. Although the strength of students' feelings was not assessed, these data support the further use of MTF items without expecting to affect negatively the psychological set of most students as they prepare for and take the exam. Students' responses were not necessarily a rejection of the MC format, but rather an endorsement of the MTF format.

This study then provides support for the use of MTF test items. The results suggest that on some dimensions MTF items may be superior to the popular MC format. It would be inappropriate to generalize far beyond the subjects and test content used in this study. But on logical grounds and in terms of the data reported here, additional research which would support or refute the claims made here seems to be justified.

References

Albanese, M. A., Kent, T. A., & Whitney, D. R. *A comparison of the difficulty, reliability, and validity of complex multiple choice, multiple response, and multiple true-false items.* Paper presented at the Annual Conference on Research in Medical Education, 1977.

Ebel, R. L. The ineffectiveness of multiple true-false test items. *Educational and Psychological Measurement,* 1978, 38, 37-44.

Frisbie, D. A. The effect of item format on reliability and validity: A study of multiple choice and true-false achievement tests. *Educational and Psychological Measurement,* 1974, 34, 885-892.

Frisbie, D. A. *A method for comparing test difficulties.* Paper presented at the Annual Meeting of the National Council on Measurement in Education, 1981.

Frisbie, D. A., & Ory, J. C. *Alternatives to the complex multiple choice item: An experimental comparison.* Research Report No. 370, Office of Instructional Resources, University of Illinois at Urbana-Champaign, 1980.

Gross, L. J. Considerations in scoring multiple true-false tests. *Health Professions Education Bulletin,* 1978, 7, 26-30.

Kelley, P. R. National Board of Medical Examiners, Personal communication, October 31, 1979.

Mendelson, M. A., Hardin, J. H., & Canaday, S. D. *The effect of format on the difficulty of multiple completion test items.* Paper presented at the Annual Meeting of the National Council on Measurement in Education, 1980.

Whitely, T. W. Some common flaws in multiple choice exam questions. *Nursing Outlook,* 1979, 27, 466-469.

MEASURING HIGHER LEVEL LEARNING OUTCOMES

Donna L. Street
James Madison University

Research indicates that the way students study is influenced by how they are tested [Frederiksen, 1984; Milton, Pollio, and Eison, 1986]. In recent years, the use of objective-type questions on classroom examinations has increased significantly. However, testing experts argue that objective-type questions cannot measure all of the higher level learning outcomes [Gronlund, 1985]. If higher level learning outcomes are not measured by examinations, students may not devote study time to acquiring these important skills.

The *Taxonomy of Educational Objectives* [Bloom, et al, 1956] provides a useful classification scheme for educational objectives. Educators may be concerned with learning objectives in the cognitive domain (knowledge outcomes and intellectual skills and abilities), the affective domain (attitudes, interests, appreciation, and modes of adjustment), and the psychological domain (motor skills).

This paper will focus on learning outcomes classified in the cognitive domain. In ascending order of complexity, Bloom's model includes the following cognitive skills: knowledge, comprehension, application, analysis, synthesis, and evaluation. In Table I each of these cognitive levels is defined and examples of each are provided.

Many college and university faculty members overestimate the level of learning outcomes measured by their examinations. For example, in a study conducted at the University of Kansas [Semb and Spencer, 1976] 17 faculty members representing various disciplines indicated that 31 percent of their test questions measured complex cognitive skills. Independent judges were then asked to categorize the test items used by these instructors.

According to the judges, only 8.5% required the use of complex skills; the remainder were of the recall or recognition variety. In their conclusion, Semb and Spencer stated, "many instructors are testing mainly over recall tasks. What is disturbing is that they do not even know it."

Educators need to become familiar with the advantages of measuring higher level learning outcomes and the techniques used to measure higher level skills and abilities. The purposes of this paper are (1) to review the education literature to determine the relationship between test format (true false, multiple choice, essay) and the types of knowledge, skills, and abilities which are measured and (2) to examine the test formats which can be used to measure higher level learning outcomes.

TABLE I
Major Categories in the Cognitive Domain*

Knowledge--the ability to remember previously learned material. All that is required is the recall of the appropriate information. Examples include the ability to define common terms and describe methods and procedures.

Comprehension--the ability to grasp the meaning of material. Examples include the ability to translate material from one form to another (words to numbers), interpret material (explain or summarize), and estimate future trends (predict consequences or effects).

Application--the ability to use learned material in new and concrete situations. Examples include ability to apply rules, methods, concepts, principles, law, and theories.

Analysis--the ability to break down material into its component parts so that its organizational structure may be understood. Examples include ability to identify the parts, analyze relationships between parts, and recognize the organizational principles involved. Learning outcomes at the analysis level require an understanding of both the content and the structural form of the material.

Synthesis--ability to put parts together to form a new whole. Examples include the ability to produce a unique communication (theme or speech), a plan of operations (research proposal), or a set of abstract relations (scheme for classifying information). Learning outcomes at this level stress creative behaviors which emphasize the formulation of _new_ patterns or structures.

Evaluation--the ability to judge the value of material (novel, research report) for a given purpose. The student's judgments are to be based on definite criteria which may be internal (organization) or external (relevance to the purpose). The student may be given the criteria or may be required to determine the criteria. These learning outcomes contain elements of all the other levels plus value judgments based on clearly defined criteria; therefore, they are considered to be the highest level of the cognitive hierarchy. Examples include the ability to: judge the consistency of written material and judge the adequacy with which conclusions are supported by data. In other words, the student has the ability to appraise, compare, conclude, contrast, criticize, discriminate, justify, interpret, relate, etc.

*From: Bloom [1956]

THE IMPORTANCE OF MEASURING HIGHER LEVEL LEARNING OUTCOMES

Several research studies [Vernon, 1962; Traub and Fisher, 1977; Ward, 1982] which examined the relationship between free response questions and multiple choice questions indicate that format does not influence what a test measures. However, these results may be biased since the studies were based on free response questions that were adaptations of multiple choice questions which tend not to measure higher level cognitive skills [Bowman and Peng, 1972; Levine, McGuire, and Nattress, 1970]. To overcome this limitation, other studies used multiple choice questions that were adaptations of free response questions designed to measure complex cognitive skills.

In one of these studies, Frederiksen and Ward [1978] developed a series of free response questions intended to simulate a type of problem frequently encountered by scientist. In each of the free response questions, the students were supplied with a description of a research study, the results of the study, and the findings of the study. Based on this information, the students were to supply possible explanations or hypotheses which supported the findings of the study and a list of competing hypotheses which should be considered. A series of multiple choice items were later constructed based on the free response questions. Scores were assigned to each set of tests to reflect quality, number, and unusualness of the hypotheses written or chosen. Correlations between the sets of scores indicate that the two test types do not measure the same knowledge, skills, and abilities.

Another study [Ward, Frederiksen, and Carlson, 1980] was conducted to determine specifically which knowledge, skills, and abilities were being measured by the two test types. Results of the study indicated that both test forms measured a knowledge factor and verbal and reasoning factors. But, the multiple choice form did not measure ideational fluency (skill in searching long term memory for relevant ideas) measures. On the other hand, the free response format did measure ideational fluency. These results indicate that format does influence what a test measures.

The studies discussed above focused only on the measurement of skills involved at the early stages of problem solving. Therefore, Frederiksen, Ward, Case, Carlson, and Samph [1981] conducted a study which focused on tests that measure the cognitive activities involved in seeking new information; using that information in evaluating, retaining, and discarding hypotheses; and deciding on a best solution. A problem solving test was designed to measure the clinical skills of medical students. To simulate real life, each problem was presented in incomplete form and the students were required to write hypotheses representing proposed solutions. Next, the students were asked to request additional information and write a new set of hypotheses. This cycle (write hypotheses, request additional information, rewrite hypotheses) was repeated six times; then the students were requested to write a solution. The test was administered to fourth year medical students in both the free response and multiple choice format.

Results indicate that for the free response test various methods of searching for hypotheses were used. These include: searching the problem statement for cues, making a broad search of long-term memory for ideas, and reconsidering previously rejected ideas based on new information. The extensional loadings indicate that ideational fluency and reasoning are primarily involved in these operations.

In contrast, the extension loadings for the multiple choice items were very low. The authors felt that the multiple choice format primarily measured the students' ability to make a narrow directed search of the memory store. They felt that reasoning and fluency were hardly involved at all. Once again, it appears that the multiple choice format did not measure the same skills and abilities that were measured by the free response format.

The studies cited above indicate that, when multiple choice tests are compared with their free response counterparts, format has little influence on the knowledge and abilities measured. Perhaps this is because the researchers tried to make the tests as similar as possible in all respects except format, even to the point of using identical item stems. As a result they ruled out any effects attributable to the influence of format on the context of the items.

However, if one begins with free response questions designed to measure complex cognitive skills, the results are different; the more complex cognitive skills are not measured by the multiple choice items. Unfortunately, the studies cited above all deal with a situation where students are required to use a hypothesize-and-test procedure. Others studies should be conducted to determine whether these results hold for other types of problems.

TEST FORMATS FOR MEASURING HIGHER MENTAL PROCESSES

Because of the importance of testing higher level learning outcomes and the research which indicates that objective type items may not measure many of these outcomes, educators need to ask themselves the following question: How do you measure understanding, reasoning, critical thinking, creative thinking and various problem solving abilities? This section will attempt to provide some insight for answering this important question.

Objective test items can be used to test some types of complex achievement [Gronlund, 1985]. For example, true-false items can be used to measure the ability to recognize cause-effect relationships, and multiple choice items can be used to measure some aspects of understanding and application. In addition to these popular methods, R. W. Tyler has developed other objective exercises which can be used to measure complex achievement. The most promising of these methods is the interpretive exercise. However, some of the other higher level learning outcomes cannot be measured using any of the objective formats. These outcomes are best measured using the essay.

True-False

The most common use of the true-false item is to measure simple learning outcomes such as the ability to identify the correctness of statements of fact, definitions of terms, and statements of principles. However, the true-false item can also be used to measure the ability to distinguish between fact and fiction and the ability to identify cause-and effect relationships [Gronlund, 1985].

When true-false items are used to measure the ability to identify cause-and-effect relationships, the item type usually contains two true statements and the student must decide whether the relationship between them is true or false. Examples of using true-false items to measure the ability to identify a cause-and-effect relationship follow:

Directions: In each of the following statements, both parts of the statement are true. You are to decide whether the second part explains why the first part is true. If it does, circle Yes. If it does not, circle No.

Yes No 1. For financial reporting purposes, a company should estimate and record interest on a seven-year note payable that has no stated interest rate

because

the accounting modifying convention of substance over form states when an apparent conflict exists between economic substance and the legal form of a business transaction, accountants tend to emphasize economic substance.

Yes No 2. Historical cost is generally used to measure such assets as inventories; property, plant, and equipment; and intangible assets

because

relevance is one of the primary qualitative characteristics of financial reporting.

Other examples of true-false items constructed to measure higher level learning outcomes can be found in Gronlund [1985] and Mehrens and Lehmann [1984].

Due to the severe limitations of true-false questions, Gronlund [1985] recommends that this question type should only be used in situations where there are only two possible alternatives, such as distinguishing fact from opinion, and distinguishing cause from effect. According to Gronlund, the limitations of true-false items include: 1) the reliability of each item is low, 2) the diagnostic value of a true-false exam is almost nil, 3) the validity of responses is questionable, 4) a limited number of learning outcomes can be measured with this item type, and 5) constructing unambiguous true-false items which measure significant learning skills requires much skill.

Others disagree with the Gronlund concerning the versatility of the true-false item. Ebel [1979] suggests that many of the limitations of the true-false format are not inherent in the item; instead, they are due to misuse and lack of skill in item construction. Jenkins and Deno [1971] argue that the true-false item can be written to measure comprehension, understanding, application, deduction, and problem solving.

Diekhoff [1984] states that true-false tests can be constructed which measure and promote structural understanding. He uses the true-false format to measure students' ability to determine whether or not pairs of concepts are related. Students indicated that the use of this form of true-false examination led them to think more about similarities between theories and principles presented in the course rather than simply trying to remember the theories singly.

Multiple Choice

One of the most popular testing formats is multiple choice. This popularity is primarily the result of the following: 1) the examiner can sample a larger portion of the content domain than could be sampled using nonobjective questions and 2) the items can be computer graded, thereby reducing scoring errors and grading time. In addition to measuring simple learning outcomes, multiple choice items can also be used to measure some more complex outcomes in knowledge, understanding, and application areas [Gronlund, 1985]. Knowledge outcomes based on vocabulary, facts, principles, and methods and procedures can be measured with multiple choice questions. Aspects of understanding such as the application and interpretation of facts, principles, and methods can also be measured using multiple choice. According to Gronlund, test formats other than multiple choice need to be used to measure the remaining higher level learning outcomes.
Illustrations of multiple choice items which measure higher level learning outcomes and suggestions for instructing them can be found in Gronlund [1985] and Mehrens and Lehmann [1984]. One of Gronlund's examples of a multiple choice item which measures a student's ability to identify a cause-and-effect relationship follows:

Investing money in common stock protects against loss of assets during inflation because common stock
- A. pays higher rates of interest during inflation.
- B. provides a steady but dependable income despite economic conditions.
- C. is protected by the Federal Reserve System.
- * D. increases in value as the value of a business increases

An example from the Board of Examiners of the American Institute of Certified Public Accountants (AICPA) [1987] which tests at the analysis level follows:

An auditor may conclude that depreciation charges are insufficient by noting
- a. Large amounts of fully depreciated assets.
- b. Continuous trade-ins of relatively new assets.
- * c. Excessive recurring losses on assets retired.
- d. Insured values greatly in excess of book values.

Research suggest that the difficulty involved in constructing multiple choice items that measure higher order cognitive skills tends to result in tests that measure factual knowledge rather than the higher level cognitive skills. For example, Bowman and Peng [1972] found that the majority of multiple choice questions on the GRE Advanced Psychology Test measure factual knowledge. Five psychologists were asked to judge whether memory, comprehension, analytic thinking, or evaluation was the primary ability required to answer each question. According to the judges, 70% of the items were memory items, 15% measured comprehension, 12% required analytic thinking, and only 3% involved evaluation. Even this professionally made test, which is widely used for admission to graduate schools, was found to be primarily a measure of factual knowledge.

In a similar study, Levine, McGuire, and Nattress [1970] asked trained judges to determine which cognitive processes were used by candidates in answering items on the Orthopedic In-Training Examination. This examination is used to measure competence in orthopedic medicine. Over half of the items were unanimously believed to measure only recall ability. Less than 25% of the items were believed, by at least one judge, to measure the ability to interpret data, apply a principle, or evaluate. Item writers were then asked to improve the test by increasing the number of questions which measured higher level cognitive skills. After the examination was revised, a majority of items were still judged to require only recall. The results of these studies illustrate the difficulty involved in constructing multiple choice questions which measure higher level learning outcomes.

Interpretive Exercise

An interpretative exercise consists of a series of objective questions which are answered based on a common set of data [Gronlund, 1985; Mehrens and Lehmann, 1984]. The questions usually are true-false or multiple choice; the data may be written material, tables, graphs, maps, or pictures. Using this format, a variety of complex learning outcomes can be measured. These include determining whether the student can identify relationships in data, recognize valid conclusions, appraise assumptions and inferences, and detect proper applications of data.

In the past, the interpretive exercise was most frequently used in commercially published reading comprehension and ability tests. Since it is rather difficult and time consuming to prepare, the interpretive exercise was rarely used in the classroom. However, these exercises are increasing in popularity due to their many advantages over the traditional items [Ebel, 1979; Wesman, 1971].

There are many different forms of the interpretive exercise. Illustrations of the various types of the interpretative exercise and suggestions for constructing these exercises can be found in Gronlund [1985] and in Mehrens and Lehmann [1984]. An example from Gronlund which requires students to recognize illustrations of a principle follows:

Directions: Read the principle and the statements following it. If a statement describes a condition that illustrates the principle, place a check (X) in the space to the left of the statement.

Principle: If the demand for a commodity or service is relatively constant, decrease in its supply will increase its market value.

( ) 1. The stock market has shown a general upward trend in the price of stocks since World War II.

(X) 2. Fresh fruits and vegetables cost more when not in season.

( ) 3. Medical costs are higher now than they were ten years ago.

Like the essay, the interpretive exercise makes it possible to measure more complex learning outcomes than can be measured with simple multiple choice and true-false items. The interpretive exercise also has advantages over the essay. With the interpretive exercise, students are not free to redefine the problem or to emphasize those thinking skills in which they are more proficient. They are forced to use only the mental process called for.

Therefore, specific problem solving skills can be tested and objective scoring procedures can be used.

The interpretive exercise has several limitations [Gronlund, 1985]. Constructing the exercises requires a great deal of time and greater skill than that needed to construct other types of objective questions. In contrast with the essay, the interpretative exercise cannot measure a student's global approach to problem solving; it does not measure a student's ability to integrate skills to solve a problem. Unlike the essay, the interpretive exercise is usually confined to learning outcomes at the recognition level. Only test questions such as the essay and free response problems can be used to measure the ability to define problems, to formulate hypotheses, to organize data, and to draw conclusions.

Numerical problem solving--objective format versus free response

The issue of whether multiple choice and other objective questions should be used to measure students' ability to solve numerical problems has been addressed in the education literature. According to Gronlund [1985], attempts are sometimes made to measure problem solving activities with objective type questions in areas such as mathematics and science, where the answer can be indicated by numbers or symbols. Unfortunately, these attempts commonly result in test questions that measure quite different learning outcomes than those measured by their free response counterparts. For example, the following multiple choice question may be written to determine whether students have learned to divide:

    86 / 2 =
       a. 41
       b. 42
  *   c. 43
       d. 44

However, this division problem can be solved by working backwards by multiplying 2 X 43 or even by multiplying 2 X 3. The problem obviously does not demand the problem-solving behavior it was written to measure.

In accounting, the issue of multiple choice versus free response problems has been much debated in recent years. Many classroom examinations include multiple choice problems and the Certified Public Accountant (CPA) examination includes many multiple choice problems. In their 1987 exposure draft, *Proposed Changes in the Uniform CPA Examination,* the AICPA Board of Examiners argues that objective items, if carefully constructed, can be used to measure higher level cognitive skills required by entry level public accountants. Following is an example of an objective item, which according to the Board, measures numerical problem solving skills at the analysis level.

Analysis: Hall Company's inventory at December 31, 1984 was $1,500,000 based on a physical count of goods priced at cost, and before any necessary year-end adjustment relating to the following:
---Included in the physical count were goods billed to a customer F.O.B. shipping point on December 31, 1984. These goods had a cost of $30,000 and were picked up by the carrier on January 10, 1985.
---Goods shipped F.O.B. shipping point on December 28, 1984, from a vendor to Hall were received on January 4, 1985. The invoice cost was $50,000.

What amount should Hall report as inventory on its December 31, 1984, balance sheet?
    a. $1,470,000   c. $1,520,000
    b. $1,480,000   * d. $1,550,000

    An alternative objective format suggested by the Board of Examiners presents the problem in free response format, but the responses are machine gradable. An example follows:
Analysis: Orr Company had the following bank reconciliation at March 31, 1986:

Balance per bank statement, 3/31/86	$46,500
Add: Deposit in transit	10,300
	56,800
Less: Outstanding checks	12,600
Balance per books, 3/31/86	$44,200

Data per bank statement for the month of April 1986 follow:
    Deposits $58,400
    Disbursements   49,700

All reconciliation items at March 31, 1986, cleared through the bank in April. Outstanding checks at April 30, 1986, totaled $7,500. What is the amount of cash disbursements per books in April?
```
0 0 0 0 , 0 0 0
1 0 0 0 , 0 0 0
2 0 0 0 , 0 0 0
3 0 0 0 , 0 0 0
4 0 0 0 , 0 0 0
5 0 0 0 , 0 0 0
6 0 0 0 , 0 0 0
7 0 0 0 , 0 0 0
8 0 0 0 , 0 0 0
9 0 0 0 , 0 0 0      (Answer $44,600)
```

When deciding between the free response question and the objective question, Gronlund offers the following guidelines. For simpler learning outcomes such as knowledge, changing to the objective format will not decrease the validity of the item and will increase objectivity of scoring. However, for the more complex learning outcomes, use of the objective format, instead of the short-answer, may result in a change in the learning outcomes measured. Gronlund recommends that "each learning outcome should be measured as directly as possible...."

Essay

Several instructional outcomes cannot be accurately measured using objective type items. Measuring outcomes such as the ability to recall, organize, and integrate ideas; the ability to express oneself in writing; and the ability to supply as opposed to simply identifying interpretations and applications of data requires less structuring of responses than that imposed by objective tests [Gronlund, 1985]. These outcomes are best measured by the essay examination.

Essay questions can be classified into two major types, restricted and extended response, based on the freedom of response provided by the questions [Gronlund, 1985; Mehrens and Lehmann, 1984]. Restricted response questions limit the form and content of the response. In the question, the student is told specifically the context that his/her answer is to take. Essay responses may also be restricted by basing the questions on specific problems. This can be accomplished by presenting introductory material like that used in interpretive exercises.

The restricted response question is used to measure learning outcomes requiring the interpretation and application of data in a specific area. When compared to the interpretive exercise, the advantage of the restricted essay is that the student is required to supply the answer instead of selecting the answer. In some instances, the interpretive exercise is preferable due to the ease and reliability of scoring. At other times, the restricted essay is preferable because of its direct relevance to the learning outcome (the student's ability to formulate valid conclusions).

A greater freedom of response than that associated with the restricted essay is needed when the objective is to measure learning outcomes which emphasize integration, organization, and originality. Extended response questions require students to select, organize, integrate, and evaluate ideas. However, this freedom of response makes the questions inappropriate for measuring specific learning outcomes and introduces scoring problems that restrict its use. It is at the levels of synthesis and evaluation of writing skills that the extended response essay makes the greatest contribution. Tests specialists argue that the extended response question does require complex behaviors that cannot be measured by objective questions. Unfortunately, the scoring of these questions is very unreliable; therefore, test specialists argue that extended response questions should not be used to measure achievement. Extended response questions should only be used as teaching devices [Mehrens and Lehmann, 1984].

There are several advantages associated with essay questions. Complex learning outcomes can be measured which cannot be measured using objective type questions. However, only well constructed essay questions can be used to measure these higher order learning outcomes. Writing good essay questions takes as much skill as writing good objective questions.[1]

In addition to being the only method of measuring certain complex learning outcomes, essay exams also have a desirable influence on students' study habits. When essay questions are part of classroom evaluation, research studies show that students tend to direct their attention toward the integration and application of larger units of subject matter [Coffman, 1971]. D'Ydewalle, Swerts, and DeCorte [1983] studied the effects of test expectation on study time and test performance and found that students anticipating essay examinations studied longer than those anticipating multiple choice examinations. Students anticipating an essay examination also performed better on both types of examinations than students anticipating the multiple choice format.

As mentioned previously, only essay questions can measure a student's overall approach to problem solving. Therefore, essay examinations play an important role in the education of professionals. For example, Milton [1979] examined the importance of essay examinations in the training of veterinarians. He concluded that multiple choice tests interfere with the development of clinical judgment. According to Milton, the thought processes involved in answering essay questions are similar to aspects of professional practice.

In addition to improving written communication skills, giving essay examinations and assigning essays as out of class projects should also help develop students' oral communication skills. Research tends to support the concept that written and oral communication are closely interrelated skills [Snipes, 1973; Groff, 1978; Jolly, 1980; Elbow, 1985].

The primary disadvantage of essay test is the high unreliability of scoring [Coffman, 1971]. Research studies lead to three conclusions: 1) when different raters are asked to judge the same essay they disagree in their judgments, 2)

---

[1] Guidelines for writing and grading essay questions can be found in several textbooks which address educational measurement and evaluation (i.e. Gronlund, 1985; Mehrens and Lehmann, 1984).

the same scorer will score answers differently on different occasions, and 3) the differences tend to increase as the essay question permits greater freedom of response. However, in most of these studies, the learning outcomes were not clearly defined [Gronlund, 1985]. Although uncontrollable variations will always influence the subjective scoring of essays, scoring reliability can be greatly improved by clearly defining the outcomes to be measured (factual content, organization of ideas, writing skill), properly framing the questions, carefully following scoring rules, and obtaining practice in scoring.[2]

Other disadvantages of essays include the time required to score the answers and the limited sampling they provide. Essays should only be used to evaluate those learning outcomes which cannot be measured using objective questions. This will allow the instructor to devote more time to the evaluation of each essay. Because of the limited sampling they provide, essays should not be used to test factual knowledge. However, this does not eliminate the problem since we would still like a larger sampling of complex learning outcomes. Therefore, essay tests that contain several questions requiring short answers are preferable to a test that asks only one question requiring a lengthy answer. Another way to use essays to evaluate a representative sample of complex learning outcomes is to assign essays throughout the semester/quarter. This will provide a larger sampling than would be obtained by using essays exclusively on examinations.

Because of their limitations, essays should only be used to measure those learning outcomes which cannot be measured using objective items. In these instances, the shortcomings of the essay are offset by the need for such measurement. The educational significance of measuring higher level outcomes justifies the expenditure of energy required to evaluate the answers.

IMPLICATIONS AND CONCLUSIONS

Many faculty members have not received training in preparing tests which measure higher level learning outcomes. These faculty are at a tremendous disadvantage when attempting to write test items which measure complex skills and abilities.

This article suggests a number of ways that test questions can be improved. For example, publisher-supplied questions that accompany many textbooks, which many faculty rely on, tend to measure lower-level learning objectives [Evans, Dodson, and Bailey, 1981; McMillan, 1979; Mentzer, 1982]. Textbook authors and publishing companies should include as part of their

---

[2] Valuable suggestions for scoring essay examinations can be found in several textbooks on measurement and evaluation (i.e. Mehrens and Lehmann, 1984).

ancillary materials test banks that include questions which measure higher level learning outcomes. Because of the difficulty involved in writing these types of test questions they, items should be written by individuals knowledgeable in both the specific subject area and in the area of test construction.

In order to encourage students to develop higher level cognitive skills, such as synthesis and evaluation, faculty should consider using a variety of measurement techniques. For example, an instructor can require students to take examinations which measure skills and abilities at the first four levels of Bloom's hierarchy, such as the ability to define common terms and the ability to apply rules, methods, concepts, principles, and theories. To measure and encourage development of higher level skills, alternative formats can be used.

The students can be required to prepare answers to cases and to make oral presentations of the results in class. Term papers and short essays can be assigned which require the student to appraise, compare, contrast, criticize, discriminate, justify, interpret, etc. Research shows that if educators do not evaluate higher level learning outcomes, many students will not develop these valuable skills and abilities.

In addition to classroom testing implications, there are implications for standardized examinations. Special emphasis needs to be placed on measuring more complex cognitive abilities in graduate school entrance examinations and professional examinations. As discussed previously, Bowman and Peng [1972] indicated that the GRE Advanced Psychology Test was primarily a measure of factual knowledge. Studies need to be conducted to determine if other graduate school entrance examinations, such as the Graduate Management Admission Test (GMAT), measure higher level learning outcomes or if they are also primarily measuring factual knowledge. Based on the results of these studies, the format and content of these examinations may need to be revised if the goal of these examinations is to measure higher level learning outcomes. In order to measure more complex cognitive abilities, some of these examinations may need to move away from the exclusive use of objective type items. Increased use of the interpretive exercise on graduate school entrance examinations may be another way to test higher level learning outcomes while maintaining the advantages of objective type items.

Research also needs to be conducted to determine the type of knowledge, skills, and abilities that is currently being measured by professional examinations. Future research projects should address the following types of questions: Do the examinations designed to test the entry level skills of accountants, lawyers, pharmacists, medical doctors, and other professionals measure the knowledge, skills, and abilities that are required by these professions? Or, do these tests need to be modified to test more complex skills and abilities? If the examinations need to be revised in order to measure more complex cognitive abilities, will this require changes in the format of the examinations? The results of these studies could have a significant impact on professional examinations. For example, the Board of Examiners of the AICPA is considering switching to an all multiple choice format for the examination which must be passed before receiving the CPA certificate. If future research studies yield results similar to those of Fredericksen and his colleagues, these results could be used to encourage the Board of Examiners to continue to include essay questions on the CPA examination.

More research needs to be conducted in the area of measuring higher level learning outcomes for all types of examinations. As mentioned previously, the research conducted by Fredericksen and his colleagues involved problems that required the students to use a hypothesize and test procedure; other studies need to be conducted which apply Fredericken's methodology to other problem areas.

Perhaps doctoral programs, regardless of the specialization area, should include a course in their curriculum on test construction, so their graduates will be better prepared for this important task. In addition, faculty members should be encouraged to participate in continuing education programs and seminars regarding testing and test construction.

References

Bloom, B. S., ed., at. *Taxonomy of Educational Objectives: Handbook I, Cognitive Domain,* New York: D. McKay, (1956).

Board of Examiners of the American Institute of Certified Public Accountants, *Exposure Draft: Proposed Changes in the Uniform CPA Examination,* American Institute of Certified Public Accountants, New York (March 16, 1987).

Bowman, C. M., & Peng, S. S. *A Preliminary Investigation Recent Advanced Psychology Tests in the GRE Program--An Application of a Cognitive Classification System,* Unpublished ETS Report, Princeton, NJ, (1972).

Coffman, W. E. "Essay Examinations," In *Educational Measurement,* ed. R. L. Thorndike. Washington, D.C.: American Council on Education, (1971).

Diekhoff, G. M. "True-False Tests That Measure and Promote Structural Understanding," *Teaching of Psychology,* 1984, 11, 99-100.

D'Ydewalle, G., Swerts, A., & DeCorte, E. "Study Time and Test Performance as a Function of Test Expectations," *Contemporary Educational Psychology,* January 1983, 8(1), 55-67.

Ebel, R. L. *Essentials of Educational Measurement,* 3rd ed. Englewood Cliffs, N.J.: Prentice-Hall, (1979).

Elbow, P. "The Shifting Relationships between Speech and Writing," *College Composition and Communication,* October 1985, 36(3), 283-303.

Evans, E., Dodson, P., and Bailey, D. "Assessment of Psychology Instructors' Perceptions and Use of Textbook Test-Item Manuals for Measuring Student Achievement," *Teaching of Psychology,* 1981, 8 (2), 88-90.

Frederiksen, N. "The Real Test Bias: Influences of Testing on Teaching and Learning," *American Psychologist,* 1984, 39, 193-202.

Frederiksen, N., & Ward, W. C. "Measures for the Study of Creativity in Scientific Problem Solving," *Applied Psychological Measurement,* 1978, 2, 1-24.

Frederiksen, N., Ward, W. C., Case, S. M., Carlson, S. B., & Samph, T. *Development of Methods for Selection and Evaluation in Undergraduate Medical Education.* (ETS RR 81-4). Princeton, NJ: Educational Testing Service, (1981).

Groff, P. "Children's Oral Language and Their Written Composition," *The Elementary School Journal.* January 1978, 78, 181-191.

Gronlund, N. E. *Measurement and Evaluation in Teaching.* New York: Macmillan Publishing Company, (1985).

Jenkins, J. R., & Deno, S. L. "Assessing Knowledge of Concepts and Principles," *Journal of Educational Measurement,* 8, 1971, 95-102.

Jolly, T. "Reading, Writing, Listening, Speaking," *Language Arts,* September 1980, 57(6), 664-668.

Levine, A. G., McGuire, C. H., & Nattress, L. W. "The Validity of Multiple-Choice Achievement Tests as Measures of Competence in Medicine," *American Educational Research Journal*, 1970, 7, 69-82.

McMillan, J. "Perceptions versus Potential of Multitple-Choice Tests," In Franz R., Hopkins, R. and Toma, A. (Eds.), Proceedings: Southern Marketing Association of 1979 Conference. Lafayette: University of South West Louisiana Press, (1979).

Mehrens, W. A., & Lehman, I. J. *Measurement and Evaluation in Education and Psychology*. New York: Holt, Rinehart and Winston, (1984).

Mentzer, T. "Response Biases in Multiple-Choice Tests," *Educational and Psychological Measurement*, 1982, 42, 437-443.

Milton, O. "Improving Achievement through Essay Exams," *Journal of Veterinary Medicine*, V6, N2, 108-112.

Milton, O., Pollio, H. R., & Eison, J. A. *Making Sense of College Grades*. San Francisco, California: Jossey-Bass Inc. (1986).

Semb, G., & Spencer, R. "Beyond the Level of Recall: An Analysis of Higher Order Educational Tasks," In L. Fraley and E. Vargas (eds.), Proceedings of the Third National Conference on Behavior and Technology in Higher Education. Atlanta: Georgia State University, (1976).

Snipes, W. C. "Oral Composing as an Approach to Writing," *College Composition and Communication,* May 1973, 24, 200-205.

Traub, R. E., & Fisher, C. W. "On the Equivalence of Constructed-Response and Multiple-Choice Tests," *Applied Psychological Measurement*, 1977, 3,355-369.

Vernon, P. E. "The Determinants of Reading Comprehension," *Educational and Psychological Measurement*, 1962, 22, 269-286.

Ward, W. C. "A Comparison of Free-Response and Multiple-Choice Forms of Verbal Aptitude Tests," *Applied Psychological Measurement*, 1982, 6, 1-12.

Ward, W. C., Frederiksen, N., & Carlson, S. "Construct Validity of Free-Response and Multiple-Choice Versions of a Test," *Journal of Educational Measurement*, 1980, 17, 11-29.

Wesman, A. G. "Writing the Test Item," In R. L. Thorndike (ed.), *Educational Measurement*. Washington, D.C.: American Council on Education (1971).

IMPROVING ESSAY TESTS

STRUCTURING THE ITEMS AND SCORING RESPONSES

Donald R. Coker, Rosemarie K. Kolstad, and Alonzo H. Sosa

Classroom examinations that require essay response are considerably more difficult for the teacher to construct and evaluate than are machine-scored or short-answer tests. Nevertheless, public pressure to upgrade the writing skills of students may necessitate more essay examinations to permit teachers to examine content learning and evaluate students' writing skills.

Advantages in Using Essay Questions

Essay items permit teachers to evaluate learning not measurable by objective tests (Gronlund 1985, p. 214). True-false, fill-in-the-blank, and other short-answer tests are limited to evaluating only the simplest levels of expected learning outcomes. And whereas the multiple-choice format can measure comprehension an problem solving, essay items can evaluate more complex skills (Wiersma and Jurs 1985, p. 166). Research studies by Benjamin Bloom have demonstrated "that over 95 percent of the items on teacher-made tests require nothing more than the recollection of facts" (Chance 1987, p. 46). The use of essay items discourages such rote testing by requiring students to demonstrate their critical thinking skills. Essay responses require students to compare, justify, contrast, compile, interpret, or formulate valid conclusions--all higher-order skills. Consequently, responses to essay questions give students the opportunity to display the broadest range of cognitive skills.

Preparation by students for an essay-type examination is more demanding than studying for short-answer or machine-scored tests. Undoubtedly this fact is related to the more complex learning skills needed to respond adequately to essay items. For example, responding adequately to an essay question is more difficult than displaying passive knowledge on a machine-scored item (Gronlund, p. 217-18). Students study more diligently for essay exams than for short-answer tests. The use of essay items permits the teacher to better differentiate students who have mastered the projected learning outcomes from those who have not.

Essay responses allow teachers to judge organizing skills, reasoning abilities, individual attitudes, and language capabilities of students. Excellent

---

Reprinted by permission of The Clearing House, Vol. 61 (1988): 253-255.

advise for the preparation of an essay examination is offered by Bloom (Chance 1987), who castigates American educators for their unfortunate tendency to assume that only those students genetically blessed can learn the higher cognitive skills. Bloom asserts that, on the contrary, problem-solving (in its broadest interpretation) can and should be taught, just as knowledge is taught. For example, students can be taught not only the financial versus agricultural biases of Alexander Hamilton and Thomas Jefferson, but also the impact of these contending viewpoints on the writing of the U.S. Constitution. An essay item on the subject could test higher cognitive skills and would apply to most, if not all, students. Enlarging on Bloom's philosophy, taking an essay test should be a repetition of classroom/homework activities. Essay questions, then, provide an opportunity for a more comprehensive evaluation than do other forms of written tests (Chance, p. 43-46).

Limitations of Essay Questions

A major limitation of essay tests is the difficulty of evaluating answers in a fair, equitable, and reliable way. Most experienced teachers are aware of the danger of becoming inconsistent in grading a stack of essays. Distractions during reading, the time of day (or night) the paper is read, exhaustion, preconceived expectations for certain students, and neatness of the writing all influence scoring. Two equally qualified readers using the same criteria will often disagree over how a paper should be scored (Gronlund, p. 218). Let us propose some methods to overcome these difficulties.

Improving Essay Items

1. *Clearly identify the responses and/or mental processes that are being assessed.* Many teachers favor essay examinations because they believe that essay questions are easy to construct (Gronlund, p. 218). Frequently, they write the questions on the chalkboard and attempt to develop the test items as they go along. However, constructing quality test questions designed to measure students' competencies accurately requires careful thought and effort. The test item must clearly focus the students' attention on the learning objective or mental processes that they are being asked to demonstrate, and this requires thoughtful consideration by the teacher prior to writing the essay question. In formulating test items, teachers should use specific terms such as organize, relate, discuss, or formulate to designate items appropriate to assessing desired responses (Storey 1970, p. 52).

2. *Use the essay format only when more objective formats will not suffice, that is, for complex objectives.* Simple learning outcomes can best be measured

through the use of objective-test formats such as multiple-choice or true-false (Storey, p. 219). In contrast, essay questions are used to measure the higher cognitive skills of analysis, synthesis, and evaluation (Hopkins and Antes 1979, p.91). At these levels, students are asked to demonstrate their mastery of skills such as relationships, organizing elements into wholes, comparing and contrasting, and making judgments and evaluations (Lien 1979, p.73).

3. *Carefully word each item so that the student clearly understands the range of responses you are seeking.* Often essay items do not sufficiently indicate the specific type of response the teacher expects from the student. Frequently, there is a critical difference between the answer the teacher expects a question to generate and the response produced by the individual being tested (Gronlund, p. 221). This miscommunication results when poor wording permits a too-broad translation of the question, making it possible for students to construct a wide range of equally correct answers. Since the teacher had intended a specific set of responses when formulating the question, however, the student often does not receive full credit for the answer, even though it is technically correct. A good essay question must find the middle path between being so narrow that a student's ability to respond is restricted and so broad that any reasonable response is correct. It is best to phrase the question to give hints concerning the structure of the answer expected" (Lien, p. 73). This not only gives the student direction in responding, but also provides a more reliable criterion for grading the accuracy of the response.

4. *Eliminate the practice of allowing students to select essay items to which they wish to respond.* Frequently, teachers present students with several essay items and instruct them to choose those they wish to answer. This practice is very popular among students for a number of reasons. First, it permits students to select the items they feel best qualified to answer. Usually this means selecting the less-demanding items. Only the best students may attempt the more challenging questions and, by doing so, risk receiving a lower grade. Second, students can often "outguess" the teacher, concentrating their study on the topics they expect to be among the test choices. If students are free to select items of their choice, it is obvious that individuals choosing different items will, in fact, be taking different tests. In this case assigning equitable grades may be impossible, or at best extremely difficult (Gronlund, p. 223-24).

5. *Do not make an essay test a speed contest.* In addition to producing the correct answer(s), an essay examination requires the student to organize and present appropriate responses in a logical and sequential manner. The style in which an answer is written is evaluated along with the subject content. Generally, the organization of an answer requires enough time to outline,

write, and read through the answer, plus additional time to edit and rewrite. The activities are time consuming. Teachers who want to evaluate a student's ability in these writing skills must allocate adequate time. Otherwise, the test becomes an exercise in quickness not quality.

Evaluating Essay Items

The chief difficulty in using essay items lies in the teacher's inability to evaluate the answers in an objective manner (Wiersma and Jurs, p. 175). But carelessness and bias in the grading of essay responses can be minimized when attention is given to specific points in the grading process.

1. *Score the essay items without knowing the identity of the examinees.* By shuffling the papers after grading each item, the teacher can enhance anonymity. This practice also randomizes problems caused by the increasing fatigue of the reader (Storey, p. 54). At best, have the students use a number system or write their names on the back of the final test page (Wiersma and Jurs, p. 177).

2. *Formulate a written answer to the item before you start grading.* A simple but effective way for a teacher to differentiate responses that are essential and acceptable from those that are not is to outline the major points expected in the student essay (Gronlund, p. 224). This technique permits the teacher to formulate a set of answers that can easily be used as a standard for uniformly evaluating the differing responses from all the students.

It should be emphasized that the outline must be written. Otherwise, there is a tendency on the part of the teacher to be influenced by answers from students and to deviate from the original model. Obviously, this is not fair, because answers read early would not be graded by the same standard as those read later. Frequently, an additional benefit occurs as a result of formulating a written answer in advance of grading: the preparation of an answer to an essay item often causes the teacher to rewrite the question in an improved format that makes the intent of the item clearer to the student. A prewritten response permits the teacher to evaluate uniformly clearly stated essay questions, and not practice the poor habit of developing standards for student performance as papers are being read.

3. *Determine how you are going to score the paper in advance of preparing the test items.* Essay items can be evaluated in several ways. The most common method is to compare the student's answer to the teacher's answer key, awarding points based on the completeness of the student's response. Awareness of how one is to score an item influences how the question is stated. Often a test consisting of several essay items will have certain items

that carry more point value than others. If this is the case, students should be given this information so that they can focus their attention and time on the items that offer them the greater potential for points. In addition, teachers must decide if spelling, penmanship, punctuation, grammar, or vocabulary are to be evaluated. If so, the students should know how the teacher intends to score these language components (Gronlund, p. 225).

4. *Grade all answers to the same item together.* The grade assigned to a paper may be influenced by the quality of the papers scored before and after it (Gronlund, p. 225). For example, an average paper is more likely to receive a lower score when it follows an exceptionally good paper, than if it follows one of very poor quality. In addition, papers that have strong answers to items appearing early in the paper, and weaker answers presented last, will fare better than papers having the poorer answers appearing first. Teachers can reduce these influences by grading all answers to the same item together. Although somewhat more time consuming, this organization increases the probability that the teacher's scoring procedure will be consistent.

5. *Rearrange the order of the papers in a random manner after each item is scored.* Changing the order reduces the possibility that a score is the result of location in relationship to other papers (Wiersma and Jurs, p. 177). This grading procedure requires little extra time and effort, but offers students the opportunity to have their papers scored more fairly. Teachers become more lenient as they make their way through a stack of papers (Wiersma and Jurs, p. 176). Teachers start the grading procedure with expectations that tend to diminish as they read students' answers.

Summary

Essay examinations require careful consideration if they are to be good measures of achievement. Construction and scoring require careful attention if consistency and fairness are to be maintained. Proper construction of essay items necessitates (1) clear identification of the desired responses, (2) proper selection of the formats, (3) careful wording of the individual items, (4) reducing unnecessary options, and (5) allowing sufficient time for completion. Evaluating essay questions requires (1) consciously maintaining the author's anonymity, (2) developing an answer key, (3) predetermining the method of awarding points, (4) scoring identical items together, and (5) scoring the papers in a random order.

References

Chance, P. 1987. Master of mastery. *Psychology Today*, April, p.46.

Gronlund, N. E. 1985. *Measurement and evaluation in testing.* New York: Macmillian.

Hopkins, C. D., and R. L. Antes. 1979. *Classroom testing: Construction.* Itasca, IL: F. E. Peacock.

Lien, A. J. 1970. *Measurement and evaluation of learning.* Dubuque, IA: William C. Brown Company.

Storey, A. G. 1970. *The measurement of classroom learning.* Chicago: Science Research Associates.

Wiersma, W., and S. G. Jurs. 1985. *Educational measurement and testing.* Boston: Allyn and Bacon.

SECTION III

Testing and Test Construction

IMPLICATIONS FOR ALTERING THE CONTEXT IN WHICH TEST ITEMS APPEAR: A HISTORICAL PERSPECTIVE ON AN IMMEDIATE CONCERN

Linda F. Leary and Neil J. Dorans
Educational Testing Service

ABSTRACT. Research into the effects of item arrangement has been motivated by the need to know the potential effects on item statistics of different item arrangement schemes. This review of the literature confirms that many of the salient and common features of the research can be identified as a function of the practical psychometric concerns of the time. The studies are separated into three periods. The earliest studies investigated the simple main effect of item order on test performance; the late 1960s reflected a change in emphasis to a design that included interactions between item order and factors of examinees' psychological and biological characteristics; current concern with test disclosure and development of individual adaptive testing instruments has shifted the emphasis to the effects of item order on the stability of item parameters. The literature has produced evidence of context effects, but has not demonstrated that the effects are so strong as to invalidate test theory or practice that is dependent on an assumption of item parameter invariance.

In any norm-referenced test, it is assumed that the test presents the same cognitive task to all examinees. This assumption is particularly important in the context of recent advances in psychometric theory. Some of the most promising applications of item response theory presume item parameter invariance. That is, the statistics associated with any test item, such as item discrimination and difficulty level, remain constant regardless of the ability of the examinee or the positions of the items in the test.

Impact of Legislation

Test disclosure legislation, as it currently exists, requires that test items that contribute to an examinee's score must be disclosed after the test has been administered. One consequence of this legislation is that methods of test equating that were dependent on reusing either previously administered intact tests or selected items from tests that were previously administered are no longer appropriate. As a result, methods for estimating equating parameters for new tests before they are administered for scoring are being developed. This practice is referred to as pre-equating. Often, pre-equating embeds individual items or sections of items that will not count toward the examinees' scores, and therefore, need not be disclosed, into a test that is being administered for scoring. Several methods, including Item Response Theory

---

Reprinted by permission of Review of Educational Research, Vol. 55, No. 3 (Fall 1985): 387-413.

(IRT) and Section Pre-equating (SPE) (Holland & Wightman, 1982), have used the unscored items to obtain equating parameters for a test that will later be administered for scoring. The unique contribution of SPE is that is does not require examinees to take two complete forms of the test. All sections of one form of the test are given to all examinees. The sum (or partial sum) of these sections comprises each examinee's score(s) for the test. The combination of the sections from which the score is derived is referred to as the operational test. The sections of the test to be pre-equated, referred to as the preoperational sections, are introduced into the operational test through the use of variable sections. Each test version contains only one or two sections of the new form. The content of the variable sections differs from one test book to another. That is, different versions of the test contain the same operational sections but different sections or combinations of sections from the preoperational test. Thus, each examinee takes the complete operational test but only one or two sections of the preoperational test. Missing data techniques (Holland & Thayer, 1983) are applied to estimate the parameters necessary to equate the preoperational test to the operational test.

The context in which the test items or sections of test items appear when they are pre-equated is different from the context in which they appear when the test is given for the purpose of score reporting regardless of the pre-equating method used. It must be assumed that the item parameters will not change when the test items or test sections are rearranged. The phrase "within-test context effects" refers to changes in performance on a particular type of test item which result from the context of questions that appear earlier in the same test (Stewart, 1981). The presence of within-test context effects violates the assumption of item parameter invariance.

Impact of Technology

Computerized adaptive testing (CAT) or tailored testing allows for the selection of each succeeding test item to be based on the performance of each examinee on the previously administered item. When adaptive testing is based on a measurement model, such as item response theory, the branching pattern need not be fixed. As a consequence, the same test items are administered to different examinees in different contexts and in different orders. Weiss (1982) has claimed three advantages to the implementation of this type of testing scheme: Adaptive testing can improve measurement quality and precision at all trait levels; it can improve measurement efficiency for test batteries using item pools designed for conventional test administration; and it can improve the accuracy and efficiency of testing for classification (e.g., mastery testing). When items are selected from an item pool, the item statistics associated with the item are assumed to be invariant. Again, if the order or the context in which the item appears affects any of the associated parameters, the assumption of invariance does not hold and the implementation of the adaptive testing mechanism becomes questionable.

Historical Perspective

Concern about the effects of item order and context on test performance is not new. Research in this area first appeared in the literature around 1950 (MacNicol, 1956; Mollenkopf, 1950). Many of the salient and common features of the research can be identified as a function of the practical psychometric concerns of the time, just as the renewed interest is a function of current psychometric concerns. Several important topics advanced rapidly in educational and psychological testing in the years following World War II. These topics included the advent of the computer and the development of statistics as a flourishing branch of mathematics, resulting in an increase in mathematical resources ranging from abstract theorems to more efficient and effective computational techniques. These events accelerated the development of psychometric theory.

The earliest literature on context effects, extending from 1950 to the late 1960s, was motivated by initial attempts to use new technology and resources to gain a better understanding of tests and their use. This research was concerned primarily with the simple main effect of item order on test performance. The late 1960s saw the introduction of concern about the effects of examinee psychological and biological characteristics on test performance. This concern was reflected in a change in emphasis in item order research from a test for main effects to a design that included interactions between item order and factors such as anxiety level, sex, and achievement level. The present concern regarding the moving of test items or sections to accomplish pre-equating or to develop adaptive tests has shifted the emphasis to the effects on item parameters that might result from changing item orders. To draw conclusions about the effects of item rearrangement on test performance for the purpose of answering the most recent questions, analysis of common characteristics of the research, across these three broad time periods, must be considered. This paper will provide a comparison of studies that have examined power tests with those that examined speed tests; a comparison of studies that have examined achievement tests with those that examined aptitude tests; and a comparison of studies that have used different item arrangement strategies.

Regardless of the specific questions posed or the time in which the study was conducted, research into the effects of item rearrangement has been motivated primarily by the need to know the potential effects on item statistics of different item arrangement schemes. Item rearrangement poses the following questions: If the items that compose a test are presented in one arrangement to one individual and the same items are then rearranged into a different sequence and administered to another individual, can one assume that the two individuals have taken the same test? This question can be answered by examining the invariance of item statistics and examinee performance.

Research Investigating Single Factor, Item Order Effects

One characteristic of the early studies of the effects of item rearrangement is that the investigators were looking for a simple main effect on the total score. These studies contrasted the sequencing options using either speeded or power test, achievement or aptitude tests, and standardized or teacher-made tests.

Random Rearrangement

The most common method of investigating context effects is to assign randomly the same set of items on two or more forms of a test. The various forms of the test could then be interspersed and administered. If the item context affects examinee performance, between-group differences should be statistically significant. One study that examined the effects of random assignment of items on a power test was conducted by Monk and Stallings (1970). Pairs of tests using random assignments of the same items had been given to students in Geography 101 (Elements of Geography) at the University of Illinois for several years. Data were available on 11 paris of these classroom tests for the period 1965-1968. They found that rearrangement produced significant differences in test performance in 2 of the 11 comparisons, and concluded that random arrangement of a power test does not markedly affect test scores, item difficulties, or test reliabilities. The authors, however, concluded by stating that the assumption of equivalence of scrambled test forms seems safe enough for the purposes of classroom testing where crowded classroom conditions exist, but added a caveat for large-scale testing programs. Presumably, this caveat is a result of concern for the individual students who may have been adversely affected by the order in which the test items appeared. Particularly in a large-scale testing program, this small proportion may represent a sizable number of individuals. In addition, the import of a few score points difference in a large-scale testing program (e.g., school admission, licensing, or certification testing) may have significant impact on the examinees affected.

Section Rearrangement

In addition to randomly scrambling items in a test, some investigations allowed for the rearrangement of sections of items in a test. By moving an entire section of test items, rather than moving individual items, investigators could isolate the effect of taking an item early of late in a test. That is, this type of design allowed the investigator to hold constant any effects on an item resulting from a change in context of the items immediately preceding it. The question under investigation was whether an item appeared to be easier or more difficult when it appeared earlier in a test than when it appeared later.

One of the earliest investigations into effects on item statistics resulting from rearranging sections of test items was conducted by Mollenkopf (1950). In his study, a verbal and a mathematics aptitude test were constructed and administered under power and highly speeded conditions. Each test contained three subsets of items. Extensive use was made of item analysis data in making the first and third sets parallel, with a grading of difficulty from easy to hard. The middle set in each test was reported to consist of items of medium difficulty. The p values ranged from about .35 to about .65, a fairly wide variation. Two forms of each test were prepared using the same items, with the set occurring first in one form appearing last in the other, and vice versa, that is x, y, z and z, y, x.

The verbal test consisted of 85 antonym items, with sets 1 and 3 having 30 items each and middle set having 25. The mathematics test contained 36 items, with 12 items in each of the three sets. The tests were administered to 382 11th and 12th grade students. Under power conditions, Mollenkopf found for the verbal forms that an item was easier (i.e., the p value of an item was higher) when the item appeared early than when it was presented late in the test. No similar position effect was noted on the mathematics forms. Under highly speeded conditions, Mollenkopf found that the item difficulty and item discrimination indices were significantly affected by position on both the verbal and mathematics forms; the item difficulty value was found to be higher when the item came late than when it came early. Also, the r biserial, which was used as a measure of item discrimination, was higher when that item appeared near the end of the test than when it came at the beginning. The Mollenkopf findings are consistent with item performance that would be anticipated from a highly speeded test. Typically, when a test is intended for administration under speeded conditions, all items are of equal difficulty and, in fact, are easy. When some of the items appearing at the beginning of the test were difficult, they probably required more time. When easy items appeared at the end of the test, they may well have appeared to be more difficult because many examinees who could have answered them under power conditions ran out of time. Similarly, the r biserial was higher for the item when it appeared near the end of the test under speed conditions because the less able examinees failed to reach the item, while the more able attempted that item and tended to respond correctly if the item was easy. Viewed in this way, the r biserials obtained in this study probably were not solely associated with the item, but were confounded between item and position.

In a similarly motivated study, the effect of repositioning sections of items on the difficulty level of an item in the Multistate Bar Examination was investigated by Klein (1981). In this study, 60 items from previously administered forms of the multiple-choice examination were selected and divided into two 30-item sets. Each set was considered to be three blocks of 10 items each. Two versions of each set were formed by reversing the positions of the first and third blocks. No information regarding item difficulties within or across blocks was presented. Differences between group means and standard deviations of the two versions of each set did not indicate a difference in total group performance as a result of rearrangement of item blocks.

Easy-to-Hard and Hard-to-Easy Sequencing Options

Most of the studies on the effects of item rearrangement on test performance contrasted three sequencing options: easy-to-hard, hard-to-easy, and random order. It has traditionally been recommended that test items in sections should be arranged in ascending order of difficulty (Conrad, 1951; Cronbach, 1984; Jordan, 1953; Remmers & Gage, 1943). One explanation for this recommendation has been that when an examination is administered under strict time constraints, some examinees could be at disadvantage as a result of spending time on hard items early in the test that they could more profitably have spent on easy items near the end. Another is that when an examinee is faced with difficult items early in a test, anxiety and discouragement could be fostered. It has been suggested that either lack of motivation or high levels of anxiety would affect performance on subsequent items, regardless of their difficulty.

Several studies investigated the effects of changing an easy-to-hard arrangement of item difficulties to either a random arrangement or a hard-to-easy arrangement under nearly pure power conditions. For example, in one study, one of three arrangements for a 50-item verbal analogies test was randomly administered to 1,500 high school students (MacNicol, 1956). *T* tests were performed to compare mean performances among all possible pairs of item arrangements. MacNicol found that the hard-to-easy arrangement was significantly more difficult than the easy-to-hard arrangement, while the random arrangement was not significantly different from the easy-to-hard arrangement. MacNicol's findings relative to the hard-to-easy arrangement may be a result of not having time to reach the easy items at the end of the tests used in her study. Although it was intended to be a power test, there was a 30-minute time limit on the test and there were differences in the number of examinees finishing each test.

In another study comparing the effects of different item difficulty sequencing, Sax and Cromack (1966) examined the effects on the test performance of college students when the Hemmon-Nelson Aptitude Test was administered using four types of experimental item orders: (a) an easy-to-hard arrangement; (b) a hard-to-easy arrangement; (c) an arrangement in which an easy item was interspersed on the average with every six items having a mean difficulty level of approximately .50; and (d) a random arrangement of items. They investigated the impact of theses orders under speeded and power conditions and found that under speeded conditions, the easy-to-hard arrangement yielded significantly higher scores than the other arrangements, while power conditions did not yield a significant effect. The effect found under speeded testing conditions is the same as the effect reported by Mollenkopf and the explanation offered for Mollenkopf's findings also apply here.

Studies that contrasted different item difficulty sequencing patterns were not only concerned with the effects on large-scale aptitude tests. For example, Brenner (1964) conducted four experiments to examine the effects of item difficulty order on test difficulty (average score), test reliability (K-R Formula 8), and discrimination (average point-biserial) for college students taking achievement tests in Educational Psychology. In two experiments, he compared an easy-to-hard arrangement to a hard-to-easy arrangement and found no significant effects on the three dependent variables. In another experiment, he examined a random arrangement in addition to the increasing difficulty and decreasing difficulty arrangements and found no significant effects on the dependent variables. In the fourth experiment, he found a significant effect on average point-biserial when half the class received a test in which the first 10 items were in a hard-to-easy arrangement and the remaining 30 items were randomly arranged, while the other half received a test in which the first 10 items were arranged in increasing difficulty and the remaining 30 items were randomly arranged. The number of subjects who participated in this experiment was not reported. It should be noted that Brenner viewed his tests as power tests with little or no time factor involved.

The practices of rearranging entire sections of test items to study possible effects on test performance, as was done by Mollenkopf and Klein, and of arranging individual test items according to patterns of item difficulty, as was done by MacNicol, Sax and Cromack, and Brenner, were incorporated into one study (Flaugher, Melton, & Myer, 1968),. The effects of item rearrangement on the verbal and quantitative scores of 5,000 high school students of the College Entrance Examination Board's Scholastic Aptitude Test (SAT) were examined.

Thirty-minute experimental verbal or quantitative sections were administered along with operational sections of the SAT under four possible item arrangements: (a) the standard arrangement, that is, easy-to-hard order within blocks of five items of similar item types; (b) reordering within blocks of five items, standard between blocks; (c) reordering between blocks of five items, standard within blocks; and (d) reordering between and within blocks. Flaugher et al. found that their verbal score was significantly affected by item rearrangement, while the quantitative score was not. This outcome occurred despite the fact that the quantitative test was more speeded than the verbal test. A possible explanation offered by the adheres was that in some of the verbal arrangements relatively easy items occurred last and were not reached by some students. They concluded that for those tests and under that degree of speededness, and a priori assumption of equivalence among different arrangements could be false. These results were consistent with those reported by both Mollenkopf and MacNicol.

Altering Context
A final sequencing option altered the items that preceded the item under investigation. This was accomplished by changing the content or the relative difficulty of the preceding items. For example, the effect of grouping items measuring the same subject matter together in separate subtests was compared with a spiral-omnibus arrangement (i.e., intermixing different types of items and placing them in ascending order of difficulty on a test of mental ability for college students) (Sax and Carr, 1962). Each student was tested using both item arrangements. To control for practice effects, half the group of 335 students took the subtest form first, and the other half took the mixed item type form first. Subjects in this study attempted significantly more items and obtained significantly higher scores when different types of items were intermixed and placed in ascending order of difficulty. The authors concluded that there was "evidence indicating the presence of a response set dependent upon test format."

The effect on the difficulty level of an item as a result of varying the difficulty level of the preceding item was investigated in two studies by Huck and Bowers (1972). In both studies, a balanced Latin square, in which the different test items served as the treatments, made up the experimental design. In the first study, a 60-item, multiple-choice final examination from an introductory undergraduate psychology course was administered in 10 forms. The forms, which differed only in item arrangements, were randomly assigned to 120 students. The test forms created a 10 X 60 matrix (i.e., 10 forms X 60 items) arranged so that the matrix actually consisted of six 10 X 10 adjacent balanced Latin squares. The statistical analysis of these data did not support the hypothesis of a sequence effect on the item difficulty level.

In the second study, 162 students from the same course were given scrambled versions of a 50-item mid-term examination. Only six forms of the test were produced to increase the number of examinees responding to each item. Again, a balanced Latin square design was used (which necessitated randomly eliminating two items from the test). As in the first study, the results did not support the hypothesis of a sequence effect.

Summary

The studies investigating the presence of a main effect of item order on test performance are grouped according to the sequencing design used and summarized in Table 1. Examination of the data in Table 1 suggests that speededness is the primary factor that mediates the effects of item arrangement on test performance. Among the studies with different difficulty arrangements for items in power tests, three obtained significant effects for verbal items. Flaugher et al. suggested that speed may have been a factor in their findings in that some easy items occurring at the end of the test were not reached by some students. Evidence of the same phenomenon was found in the MacNicol study, although she did not offer this as an explanation. The tests used in the Mollenkopf study were constructed for the purpose of the study, and they too may have required more time than was allocated during the power testing, resulting in easy items at the end of the test that were simply not reached.

Research Investigating Item Order Interaction Effects

Later studies attempted to uncover more complex relationships. In these studies, the researchers sought evidence of an interaction between various item sequences and individual examinee characteristics. Rationalization for the recommendation that items should be arranged in an order of increasing difficulty has been based on the belief that the anxiety aroused by the inability

TABLE I
Studies Investigating a Main Effect of Item Order on Test Performance

Item order	Investigator	Power/speed	Results[a]
Random item scrambling	Monk & Stallings (1970)	Power	ns
Random section scrambling	Mollenkopf (1950)	Power	Verbal: s
			Quant: ns
		Speed	Verbal: s
			Quant: s
	Klein (1981)	Power	ns
Easy-hard vs. hard-easy	MacNicol (1956)	Power	s
vs. random	Sax & Cromack (1966)	Power	ns
		Speed	s
	Brenner (1964)	Power	ns
Scrambling sections and	Flaugher et al. (1968)	Speed	Verbal: s
arranging difficulties			Quant: ns
of items within sections			
Context manipulation	Sax & Carr (1962)	Power	s
	Huck & Bowers (1972)	Power	ns

[a] ns = not significant, s = significant

to answer a difficult test item affects performance on succeeding items (McKeachie, Pollie, & Speisman, 1955). Interactions between item arrangement and variables such as test anxiety, achievement level, examinee knowledge of item arrangement, and sex were examined.

Item Order by Anxiety Interaction Effects

The majority of the studies were concerned with identifying the presence of an item order by anxiety interaction effect. The majority also used easy-to-hard, hard-to-easy, and random order item sequences in the investigations. The results of these studies are somewhat mixed. A series of three studies by one pair of investigators developed as a result of their attempts to explain and refine the relationships that they were observing (Munz & Smouse, 1963; Smouse & Munz, 1968, 1969).

The effects of item arrangement and test anxiety on achievement test scores were first investigated by Smouse and Munz (1968) through items on a 100-item multiple-choice final examination in psychology that were arranged in one of three sequences: easy-to-hard, hard-to-easy, or a random order. The examination was not speeded. One hundred thirteen undergraduates were randomly divided into two groups. In one group, anxiety-provoking information was introduced; in the other group, a normal test-taking atmosphere was maintained. An analysis of variance did not reveal significant differences in test scores among the three item difficulty orders or between the anxiety treatments. The interaction of these two variables also resulted in a nonsignificant F. This study did not support the hypothesis that item difficulty sequence affects scores on the type of power achievement test found in the classroom. However, the authors expressed concern that the high level of test anxiety found in both groups may have masked the effects of differential test performance for item difficulty sequences that affect test anxiety. This concern resulted in an expansion of the investigation to include the possibility that item difficulty arrangement affects test performance by interacting with test taking personality factors (Munz & Smouse, 1968). The authors used the same test and the same test item arrangements that they had used in the previous study. The Achievement Anxiety Test (AAT) was used to classify subjects into one of four achievement anxiety types (Alpert & Haber, 1960). Only the 40 subjects at the extreme ends of the scale were considered in this study. That is, the authors chose 20 students whose performance was most improved in anxiety situations and 20 students whose performance was most depressed under those conditions. An analysis of variance resulted in a statistically significant interaction between item sequence and achievement anxiety types.

Because the authors believed that the second study suggested that "criteria, differently sequenced, are measuring different things," a more complete analysis was conducted (Smouse & Munz, 1969). This study made use of the data obtained on all 181 subjects who participated in the second study. Scores on the AAT were used to predict final examination scores on the same three forms of the 100-item multiple-choice examination. The amount of variance in total score explained by response style varied systematically across the three forms. That is, more variance was accounted for by the AAT when items were sequenced randomly than when they were sequenced easy-to-hard, and the least amount was accounted for when they were sequenced hard-to-easy. The authors proffered these results as evidence of an effect of item sequencing on content validity in that sequencing produces noncontent-determined variance.

A study similar to the Smouse and Munz investigations was undertaken to determine the effects of the same variables on aptitude test performance (Berger, Munz, Smouse, & Angelino, 1969). Three forms of the Hemmon-Nelson Test of Mental Ability, Revised Edition, Grades 9-12, containing three different arrangements of items (easy-hard, hard-easy, and random) were produced. The forms were randomly administered to 330 high school seniors. A measure of anxiety reaction type was obtained as in the Munz and Smouse studies by using the AAT. An analysis of variance based on the aptitude data did not reveal any significant effects. The results of this study suggest that the test anxiety variable may not mediate the effect of item difficulty arrangement on aptitude scores in the same way it has been shown to do on achievement test scores. However, the authors caution that since one might expect to find greater variation in ability and motivation in a high school population, "it could be that this variability overshadowed any effects produced by an interaction between item sequence and achievement anxiety type" (p. 256). Some support for this conclusion was found in the studies by Munz and Smouse (1968) and Smouse and Munz (1969), both of which used a more homogeneous sample of college students and both of which found a significant order/anxiety interaction effect.

A later attempt to confirm the interaction effect found by Smouse and Munz was unsuccessful. Although the primary purpose of a study by Towle and Merrill (1975) was to investigate the interaction of item sequence and anxiety type, they also examined the effects of item sequence on test performance. Citing numerous studies by Munz and Smouse and their colleagues (Berger et al., 1969; Munz & Smouse, 1968; Smouse & Munz,1968), Towle and Merrill anticipated no item sequence effect on test performance but did anticipate an interaction between anxiety type and item sequence. Instead, they found a significant sequence effect: The mean score for an easy-to-hard arrangement was significantly higher than the mean score for a hard-to-easy sequence. In addition, neither the anxiety type main effect nor the anxiety type by item sequence interaction was significant. Although the anticipated result was confirmation, the Towle and Merrill findings conflicted with those of Munz and Smouse and their colleagues. One difference between these two studies was the item content. The Smouse and Munz studies used mathematics tests. The mathematics test might function more like an aptitude than an achievement test, suggesting that the Towle and Merrill study should have been consistent with the Berger et al. study, rather than with the Smouse and Munz studies.

Several later studies sought to establish evidence of an interaction between anxiety and item arrangement in achievement tests. However, none of them reported a significant interaction. For example, one such study examined the relationship between item arrangement and classroom test performance by examining two types of item arrangements (Marso, 1970). Arrangements based on item difficulty and on similarity of content were used in the first and second studies, respectively. Both studies were also concerned with the presence of an interaction effect between item arrangement and test anxiety. Undergraduate psychology students participated in both studies. The tests used for both studies consisted of multiple-choice items that were unspeeded. As a result of analysis of variance procedures, with test anxiety used as a classification factor, the author concluded that there was no anxiety by item arrangement interaction effect and that there was no effect due to arrangement of items for either item arrangement scheme.

Other Item-Order Interaction Effects

In a study by Plake (1980), differences in test scores were examined for different item orderings and student knowledge of item orderings. This study is related to those that investigated order by anxiety interaction effects in that the author posited that the impact of anxiety on test performance may be affected by knowledge of arrangement. A 96-item mid-term examination for nursing students was assembled into three orderings of items: easy-to-hard, spiral cyclical, and random. One half of the tests in each ordering included written directions explaining the arrangement of the items. She found no interaction effect between knowledge of arrangement and item order, and no significant order or knowledge of arrangements effects. One concern expressed by Plake was that it was possible that knowledge of test items might in fact increase test anxiety in highly anxious students taking items arranged easy-to-hard as the items increased in difficulty. This hypothesis could be tested by including test anxiety as a third effect in future studies. The effect was included in two subsequent studies conducted by Plake.

In a later study, Plake, Thompson, and Lowry (1981) investigated the effects of item arrangement, knowledge of arrangement, and test anxiety on number right scores and on elimination scores. A 48-item power mathematics achievement test was assembled and administered in three item-ordering forms: easy-hard, uniform, and random. Again, half the tests in each form contained information describing the ordering. Three anxiety measures were also administered to each subject. As a result of a multivariate analysis of variance, the authors concluded that none of the main effects and none of the interactions were significant. Since anxiety did not affect test performance, an additional analysis investigated the effects of item order and knowledge of ordering when the measures of anxiety were used as covariates. No significant effects for item order, knowledge of order, or the interaction of item order by knowledge were found.

In a follow-up study (Plake, Ansorge, Parker, & Lowry, 1982), the authors administered the same three arrangements of the test to a group of subjects whom they felt were highly motivated. This study investigated the effects of item arrangement, knowledge of arrangement, test anxiety, and sex on test performance. Significant sex by order effects were found: Males scored higher than females when item were ordered easy-to-difficult. The authors noted that this test was slightly speeded. They suggested that one cause of apparent difference in mathematics ability between males and females might be item arrangement under speeded conditions. However, this conclusion has not been supported by other researchers.

The sex by item interaction had been previously investigated by Hambleton and Traub (1974). They also used a mathematics achievement test, but it was administered to 106 11th grade students. Using a two-factor analysis of variance design, the authors examined differences in test performance between males and females. Neither the main effect due to sex nor the interaction between item order and sex was significant. They did demonstrate that the mean score on a mathematics test with items arranged in decreasing difficulty was significantly lower than the mean score on the same items arranged in increasing difficulty. The authors then investigated the effects of stress on test performance under different item arrangements. They did not find an anxiety by item order interaction effect. Hambleton suggested in his conclusion that it may not be possible to construct equivalent tests by any rearrangement of items. These authors did not address the possibility that their mathematics test, like that of Plake et al. (1982), might have been slightly speeded. Speed, rather than the variation in item arrangement, could have produced the difference in means. Such an explanation would be consistent with the other studies cited in this review.

Item Order by Achievement Level Interaction Effects

Several studies that have been cited for their concern with an item order by anxiety interaction effect were also interested in the interaction effects of other factors with item order. Examples are the Plake studies, which included factors of knowledge of item order and sex, and the study by Hambleton and Traub (1974), which also included a sex factor. Level of student achievement was considered to be a factor that might interact with the order in which test items are presented and affect test performance (Klosner & Gellman, 1973). They investigated the effects of item arrangement across two levels of student achievement. Fifty-four graduate students were classified as high or low achievers as a result of a median split on a mid-term examination. Three forms of a 75-item multiple-choice final examination in educational measurement, which differed only in item sequencing, were administered. Items were arranged either according to chronological presentation in the course, in increasing level of difficulty within subject matter topics, or in increasing level of difficulty regardless of topic. Although the interaction between item arrangement and achievement level, determined by means of a split plot analysis of variance, was fairly strong, the results were not significant ($p < .15$).

Summary

All of the studies presented in this section were concerned with the dependence of the effect of item arrangement on the level of some other variable. For example, does item arrangement have a different effect on performance for males and females? Or, does the effect of item arrangement depend on the anxiety level of the examinee? Table II summarizes those studies that investigated interaction effects.

The majority of the studies sought to confirm the presence of an order by anxiety interaction effect. The rationale for expecting to find such an effect has some intuitive appeal, but the research did not support this expectation. It can been seen from Table II that none of the studies found a significant item order by test anxiety interaction effect. All of these studies examined classroom test performance for high school of college students. The opinion expressed by Smouse and Munz that the anxiety level may have been so high among all of the students that an interaction effect could not be detected may also apply to these other studies. However, based on the evidence gathered to date, level of test anxiety has not been shown to relate to the effect of item arrangement on test performance.

A second group of studies refined the concept of test anxiety interacting with item order by defining performance anxiety types. This differentiation was based on the theory that some examinees' performance would improve in high anxiety situations, while for others, the effect would be just the opposite. Item order by performance anxiety type interaction effects were found in two studies by Smouse and Munz. However, attempts by Towle and Merrill and by Berger et al. to replicate their findings were unsuccessful. Berger suggested that his failure to replicate the findings of Smouse and Munz might have been the result of greater variability in ability and motivation in the sample he used.

Among the studies that examined factors other than anxiety, one significant interaction was reported. Plake et al. (1982) found a significant sex by order interaction term, but this finding has not been replicated.

Examining the Item Order Research Results from Different Perspectives

Tables I and II summarize some information gleaned from the studies that investigated single factor item order effects and item order interaction effects, respectively, to facilitate comparison of the similarities and differences across these studies. Some of the other areas in which these studies can be contrasted include whether the test(s) used in each study was (were) power, speeded, or both; whether the test(s) was (were) achievement or aptitude; the subject area(s) of the test(s) used; the age of the subjects; the factors that were investigated; the item sequence(s) that was (were) investigated; and the significance of lack of significance of the results. Consideration of some of the differences and similarities across all of these studies suggests that grouping some of these studies according to some common characteristics other than single factor versus item order interaction effects might lead to additional insights and conclusions regarding the effects of item arrangement on examinee performance.

TABLE II
Summary of Effects of Item Rearrangement on Test Performance
(Studies That Examined Interaction Effects)

Interaction	Investigator	Subject area	Item sequence[a]	Results[b]
Order/anxiety type	Smouse & Munz (1968)	Psych	E-H, H-E, R	ns
	Smouse & Munz (1969)	Psych	E-H, H-E, R	s(ord X anx)
	Berger et al. (1969)	V & M	E-H, H-E, R	ns
	Towle & Merrill (1975)	Math	E-H, H-E, R	s(ord)
Order/anxiety	Munz & Smouse (1968)	Psych	E-H, H-E, R	s(ord X anx)
	Marso (1) (1970)	Vocab	E-H, H-E, R	ns
	Marso (2) (1970)	Ed Psych	Order of the Instruction	ns
(also sex)	Hambleton & Traub (1974)	Math	E-H, H-E	s(ord)
(also knowledge of order)	Plake et al. (1981)	Math	E-H, SO, R	ns
(also knowledge of order & sex)	Plake et at. (1982)	Math	E-H, SO, R	s(sex X ord)
Order/knowledge of order	Plake (1980)	Psy nurs	E-H, SO, R	ns
Order/ach level	Klosner & Gellman (1973)	Ed meas	Cont areas	ns

[a] H = hard; E = easy; R = random; SO = spiral omnibus
[b] ns = not significant; s = significant

Power Versus Speed

One consideration is a comparison based on whether the tests administered were power or speed. This grouping is presented in Table III. The most consistent effect of item arrangement on test performance occurred under speeded conditions where an easy-to-hard arrangement of items repeatedly produced higher scores than a hard-to-easy arrangement. The avoidance of hard-to-easy arrangements of item difficulties under highly speeded conditions clearly is suggested by this literature. Confirmation of this conlusion is found in the work of Mollenkopf (1950), Sax and Cromack (1966), Flaugher et al. (1968), and Plake et al. (1982).

Conclusions about the effects of item rearrangement under power or near power conditions are not so easily deducted because in some cases item rearrangement had a significant effect on test performance, while in other cases no effect was observed. Most of the studies that were conducted under power or near power conditions reported no effect due to item arrangement. But there were exceptions. These included the studies by Mollenkopf (1950), MacNicol (1956), Monk and Stallings (1970), Towle and Merrill (1975), and Sax and Carr (1962). Even among the subset of studies that reported an effect under power conditions, results were not consistent within studies. Mollenkopf (1950) reported an effect on a verbal aptitude test but no effect on a mathematics aptitude test. For achievement tests in geography, Monk and Stallings (1970) reported significant effects in 2 out of 11 pairwise comparisons. The Monk and Stallings findings may partly be a consequence of sampling variation. All of the studies in which significant item order effects were found under power conditions were either aptitude tests or mathematics achievement tests. After considering the implications of this observation, the results of the studies being analyzed in this paper were grouped according to whether they were aptitude or achievement tests.

Aptitude Versus Achievement

Some of the distinctions that have been made between aptitude and achievement tests suggest that the effects of ordering items in differing arrangements of difficulty should be less for achievement tests than for aptitude tests. In particular, one distinction is that aptitude tests measure knowledge accumulated over a long time, while achievement tests tend to measure content specific information gained over a fairly short time. Related to this distinction, examinees are likely to have prepared (e.g., by studying or by obtaining some form of tutoring) for taking an achievement test because they are aware of the limits of the content. It is not unreasonable to assume that more study time was devoted to the more difficult content areas and less to the easy areas. One result might be that there is less distinction between relative difficulties of the items on the achievement test. One might also posit that because all of the information is in short-term memory at the time an

TABLE III
Summary of Effects of Item Rearrangement on Test Performance
(Grouped by Speed/Power)

Speed/power	Investigator	Item sequence[a]	Results[b]
Speeded	Mollenkopf (1950)	Section scrambling	Verbal: s Quant: s
	Sax & Cromack (1966)	E-H, H-E, vs. R	s
	Flaugher et al. (1968)	Scrambling sections and arranging difficulties of items within sections	Verbal: s Quant: ns
	Plake et al. (1982)	E-H, SO, vs. R	s (sex X ord)
Power	Mollenkopf (1950)	Section scrambling	Verbal: s Quant: ns
	MacNicol (1956)	E-H, H-E, vs. R	s
	Sax & Carr (1962)	Content areas	s
	Brenner (1964)	E-H, H-E, R	ns
	Sax & Cromack (1966)	E-H, H-E, R	ns
	Smouse & Munz (1968)	E-H, H-E, R	ns
	Munz & Smouse (1968)	E-H, H-E, R	s (ord X anx)
	Berger et al. (1969)	E-H, H-E, R	ns
	Smouse & Munz (1969)	E-H, H-E, R	s (ord X anx)
	Marso (1) (1970)	E-H, H-E, R	ns
	Marso (2) (1970)	Order of instruction	ns
	Monk & Stallings (1970)	Random item scrambling	ns
	Huck & Bowers (1972)	Context manipulation	ns
	Klosner & Gellman (1973)	Content areas	ns
	Hambleton & Traub (1974)	E-H, H-E	s (ord)
	Towle & Merrill (1975)	E-H, H-E, R	s (ord)
	Plake (1980)	E-H, SO, R	ns
	Klein (1981)	Section scrambling	ns
	Plake et al. (1981)	E-H, SO, R	ns

[a] H = Hard; E = Easy; R = Random; SO = Spiral Omnibus
[b] s = significant; ns = not significant

examinee takes an achievement test, examinees can respond correctly to those questions for which they have learned the content and cannot respond correctly to the others, regardless of where they appear on the test. When an examinee is taking an aptitude test, on the other hand, the method for performing the cognitive task required may be developed or recalled at the time the test is being administered. If this were true, it would seem that ordering the test items from easy to hard would increase an examinee's opportunity to answer the more difficult questions correctly. The studies presented in this paper are grouped according to the aptitude/achievement distinction and are summarized in Table IV. These data lend some support to the expectation that item order would be less important for achievement

TABLE IV
Summary of Effects of Item Rearrangement on Test Performance
(Grouped by Aptitude/Achievement)

Achievement/aptitude	Subject study area	Results[a]
Achievement		
Munz & Smouse (1968)	Psych.	s (ord X anx)
Smouse & Munz (1968)	Psych.	ns
Smouse & Munz (1969)	Psych.	s (ord X anx)
Marso (2) (1970)	Ed. psych.	ns
Monk & Stallings (1970)	Geography	ns
Marso (1) (1970)	Vocabulary	ns
Huck & Bowers (1972)	Psych.	ns
Klosner & Gellman (1973)	Ed. meas.	ns
Hambleton & Traub (1974)	Math	s (ord)
Towle & Merrill (1975)	Math	s (ord)
Plake (1980)	Psyc. nurs.	ns
Plake et al. (1981)	Math	ns
Klein (1981)	Law exam	ns
Plake et al. (1982)	Math	s (sex X ord)
Aptitude		
Mollenkopf (1950)	V & M	Verbal: s Quant: ns
MacNicol (1956)	Verb. anal.	s
Sax & Carr (1962)	V & M	s
Brenner (1964)	Ed. psych.	ns
Sax & Cromack (1966)	V & M	ns
Flaugher et al. (1968)	V & M	Verbal: s Quant: ns
Berger et al. (1969)	V & M	ns

[a] s = significant; ns = not significant.

tests than for tests of aptitude. Significant item order effects were found in only 2 of the 14 studies that used achievement test data. Both of the studies in which item order results were found were mathematics achievement tests (Hambleton & Traub, 1974; Towle & Merrill, 1975). It should be noted that other studies found no significant item order effect on mathematics tests. These included the work by Mollenkopf (1950), Sax and Cromack (1966), Flaugher et al. (1968), Plake (1980), and Plake et al. (1981, 1982). The item arrangement schemes used in these studies differed, as did the ages and the homogeneity of the ability levels of the subjects. Examinees in the Flaugher et al. study took the SAT to gain admission to college; examinees in the Mollenkopf study took an examination constructed by the experimenter; in the Plake study, a set of math items was taken from the ACT College Mathematics Placement Program and administered to undergraduates in an educational psychology class. An additional explanation for the apparent differences among the results of these studies may be that mathematics tests incorporate both aptitude and achievement characteristics. The way in which rearranging items on any particular mathematics test influences examinee performance may depend on the mix between aptitude and achievement characteristics present in the items.

Verbal aptitude tests provided more consistent findings. Mollenkopf (1950), Flaugher et al. (1968), MacNicol (1956), and Sax and Carr (1962), all reported significant effects on verbal scores in their studies. Some recent research investigating section placement effects suggests that one explanation for the findings might be the presence of practice and fatigue for different item types. For example, Mollenkopf observed that when the easy-to-hard order within sections of the test was held constant, verbal items were more difficult when they appeared later than when they appeared earlier in the test. Flaugher et al. also found an effect on verbal test performance when blocksof items were moved. The research investigating section placement effects will be expanded on in a later section of this review.

TABLE V
Summary of Effects of Item Rearrangement on Test Performance
(Grouped by Age of Subjects)

Age of subjects	Investigator	Results[a]
High school	MacNicol (1956)	s
	Flaugher et al. (1968)	Verbal: s, Quant: ns
	Hambleton & Traub (1974)	s (ord)
	Mollenkopf (1950)	Verbal: s, Quant: ns
	Berger et al. (1969)	ns
College	Sax & Carr (1962)	s
	Brenner (1964)	ns
	Sax & Cromack (1966)	ns
	Munz & Smouse (1968)	s (ord X anx)
	Smouse & Munz (1968)	ns
	Smouse & Munz (1969)	s (ord X anx)
	Marso (2) (1970)	ns
	Monk & Stallings (1970)	ns
	Marso (1) (1970)	ns
	Huck & Bowers (1972)	ns
	Towle & Merrill (1975)	s (ord)
	Plake (1980)	ns
	Plake et al. (1981)	ns
	Plake et al. (1982)	s (sex X ord)
Graduate school	Klosner & Gellman (1973)	ns
	Klein (1981)	ns

[a] s = significant; ns = not significant.

TABLE VI
Summary of Effects of Item Rearrangement on Test Performance
(Grouped by Item Arrangement Scheme)

Item arrangement	Investigator	Power/ speed	Results
Random items	Monk & Stallings (1970)	Power	ns
Random sections	Mollenkopf (1950)	Power	Verbal: s
			Quant: ns
		Speed	Verbal: s
			Quant: s
	Klein (1981)	Power	ns
Easy-hard vs.	MacNicol (1956)	Power	s
hard-easy vs.	Brenner (1964)	Power	ns
random	Sax & Cromack (1966)	Power	ns
		Speed	s
	Munz & Smouse (1968)	Power	s (ord X anx)
	Smouse & Munz (1968)	Power	ns
	Smouse & Munz (1969)	Power	s (ord X anx)
	Berger et al. (1969)	Power	ns
	Marso (1) (1970)	Power	ns
	Hambleton & Traub (1974)	Power	s (ord)
	Towle & Merrill (1975)	Power	s (ord)
	Plake (1980)	Power	ns
	Plake et al. (1981)	Power	ns
	Plake et al. (1982)	Speed	s (sex X ord)
Scrambling sections and arranging difficulties of items within sections	Flaugher et al. (1968)	Speed	Verbal: s
			Quant: ns
Content areas	Sax & Carr (1962)	Power	s
	Marso (2) (1970)	Power	ns
	Klosner & Gellman (1973)	Power	ns
Context manipulation	Huck & Bowers (1972)	Power	ns

Age of Test Takers

The presence of context effects does not seem to be a function of the age of the test taking population. Table V groups the studies by the age of the subjects who participated. Significant order effects and order by students characteristic interaction effects were found among both high school and college test takers. None of the studies examined the effect of item rearrangement on the test performance of elementary school or younger examinees.

Item Rearrangement Strategy

In Table VI, the studies are grouped according to the item rearrangement strategy that was used. As shown in Table VI, most of the studies examined the effects on performance of three basic item sequences:

easy-to-hard, hard-to-easy, and random. A variety of other item rearrangement strategies are possible, but little research on these strategies has appeared in the literature. The Mollenkopf (1950), Sax and Carr (1962), Flaugher et al. (1968), Marso (1970), Huck and Bowers (1972), Klosner and Gellman (1973), and Klein (1981) studies are exceptions. Mollenkopf switched the first and third sections, each of which followed an easy-to-hard arrangement. Klein also switched the first and third sections, but no information pertaining to the arrangement of items within sections was provided in the study. Flaugher et al. were confined to the format used by the SAT (described earlier in this review). Huck and Bowers produced 10 random sets of item difficulty arrangements in Latin square designs. Sax and Carr, Marso, and Kosner and Gellman compared items grouped by content area to items intermixed across content areas.

As Table V reveals, results considered by item arrangement scheme tend to be inconsistent. Approximately half of the studies that paired hard-to-easy with easy-to-hard arrangements found significant effects. As mentioned when discussing Table II, speed of response seems to be the most important moderator in these studies.

Summary
In sum, the research on the effects of item rearrangement on test performance has shown experimentation with a wide range of item arrangement schemes, test types, testing conditions, subject areas, and examinee samples. The most definitive result is that hard-to-easy arrangements of items yield lower scores on speeded tests than do easy-to-hard arrangements. The research also suggests that aptitude tests might be more subject to variation in examinee performance than are achievement tests.

Research Investigating Section Placement Effects

Recent investigations into the effects of repositioning intact test sections were motivated by the impact of test disclosure legislation on data collection designs for the equating of new test forms. Most of this research has evolved in conjunction with development of new equating methods that require flexibility of section arrangement. Section pre-equating (SPE) and item response theory (IRT) pre-equating methods, which involve embedding sections of test items of similar item type or by content, have
introduced two related concerns regarding the effects of context on test performance.

The first is an assumption that the item parameters and/or the estimated section difficulty based on examinee performance during pre-equating will be the same when the section is administered operationally, that is, when it counts toward the examinee's score. Evidence of context effect would negate this assumption. The second concern is that the introduction of pre-equating sections into intact tests introduces the concept of practice as an additional factor influencing test performance. That is, each pre-equating section will be parallel to some section from the operational test. To the extent that practice on any item type enhances an examinee's performance on subsequent sections containing similar item types, examinees could be differentially advantaged by the content of the pre-equating sections that appear on the test form that they receive as well as the positions in which they appear. In that sense, having the opportunity to practice an item type alters the context in which later sections of the same item type appear for various students. If practice is a factor that influences test performance, arranging the items so that a preoperational action precedes the parallel operational section would result in different test performance, different item parameters, and different equating parameters than would be obtained if the items were rearranged so that the preoperational section came after the operational section of the same type. Several studies have investigated the effects of intact section rearrangement on test performance in various national testing programs.

Faggen and McPeek (1981) examined the effects of within-test practice for four verbal reasoning item types. Data were obtained from samples of examinees participating in two different administrations of a graduate level testing program. Lord's C statistic (Lord, 1950), which is based on the assumption that the size of the practice effect is constant throughout the score range and is proportional to the standard deviation of the section score, was used to evaluate the size of the practice effect. Transformations of Lord's C were also computed to provide additional indices for comparison. The size of the practice effects found in this study varied across item types. One type showed no appreciable practice effect; the effects for the other items ranged from 9.2 to 2.1 scaled score points on a scale with a standard error of approximately 2.2. However, the authors warned that the impact of practice effects of this size on equating is unknown and that the size of a practice effect that would necessitate psychometric action has not yet been determined.

Within-test practice effects have also been examined in the Graduate Management Admissions Test (GMAT) from the same perspective as the Faggen and McPeek study (Wightman, 1981). Three item types were examined using data obtained from samples participating in two separate test administrations. Again, the results varied across item types. One item type showed statistically significant positive practice effects, one showed negative practice effects, and the last showed small positive effects. However, the author noted that the "practical size of the effects on scaled scores was minimal relative to the errors of measurement" (p. 13).

In a subsequent study, Wightman and Leary (1983) investigated practice effects in section pre-equating. The process of section pre-equating in which sections that were practiced were considered separately from sections that had no opportunity for practice was compared with pre-equating in which the effects of practice were ignored. Empirical data were used to demonstrate that ignoring the effects of practice in equating resulted in parameter estimates that yielded lower scaled scores than when only unpracticed data were selected. The data also suggested that the magnitude of the differences might be related to the proportion of practiced and unpracticed data in the operational and preoperational sections of the tests. The authors concluded that the method of taking practice into account seems to be the fairest treatment for examinees, all of whom do not necessarily receive the same benefits from the opportunity for practice. The results of this study offer confirmation to the concern that rearranging the order in which test items are administered (i.e., items are practiced or unpracticed) affects examinee performance on those items and, consequently, affects statistics associated with the items.

Within-test context effects of several item types on the Graduate Record Examination (GRE) General Test were investigated in three separate studies (Swinton, Wild, and Wallmark, 1982). In Study 1, the practice effect was estimated after three types of analytical questions were repositioned on three different editions of the test. The data were analyzed using analysis of covariance, with group and form as main effects. The second study was undertaken to evaluate possible restructurings of the analytical measures. Two versions of an experimental test were used. The results were analyzed using repeated measures analysis of covariance with group and form as main effects. Study 3 was conducted to investigate the practice effect for verbal and quantitative items as well as to replicate the earlier findings on analytical item types. The study used two editions of the GRE General Test. The results were analyzed using analysis of covariance as they were in Study 2. The result of these analyses showed that there were large practice effects for some item types. It is noted parenthetically that as a result of this and other supporting studies, those item types showing such susceptibility to context practice effects were eliminated from the GRE General Test.

The recent studies into the effects of section placement that were conducted for national testing programs, as a result of their need to consider and/or implement alternative equating data collection designs, produced results that suggest within-test context effects may be item-type dependent. Faggen and McPeek (1981), Swinton et al. (1982), Wightman (1981), and Wightman and Leary (1983) all found at least one item type that exhibited sensitivity to material the preceded it in the testing sequence. These results suggest that systematic, careful research studies should be conducted to assess how invariant across intended uses particular item types are before they are used in different ways.

Research Investigating Item Parameter Invariance

The assumption of item parameter invariance that is associated with the item response theory model is central to both IRT pre-equating and to the development of computer adaptive testing. Only a few studies that test this assumption have been reported.

Item Parameter Invariance

Whitely and Dawis (1976), for example, conducted one of the first studies explicitly designed to assess parameter invariance associated with models of item response theory. They investigated the "context stability" assumption of IRT models by studying context effects on classical item difficulties (percent pass) and Rasch item easiness for a verbal analogies test. A set of 15 core items was placed in seven different tests along with seven sets of 45 unique items to produce seven 60-item tests that were administered under essentially unspeeded conditions to seven random samples of examinees, ranging from an N of 210 to an N of 241. One-way analyses of variance were conducted on item difficulties for the core items across tests/samples. Nine of the 15 core items had statistically significant differences in classical item difficulties and showed similar patterns in Rasch item easiness. Although the practical importance of the difference magnitudes obtained in the study was not addressed by the authors, the cumulative effect of the changes in item difficulties would make a difference in obtained total score for some examinees. It is not clear what that difference would be relative to the standard error of measurement already associated with the instrument, but it is clear that an additional source of error has been introduced.

A later study was concerned with the extent and importance of context effects on item parameters for two latent trait models, the three-parameter logistic and the Rasch models (Yen, 1980). The purposes of the study were to gauge the extent of context effects on latent trait model item parameters, explore their causes, and evaluate their importance. The study compared "different context" parameter estimate variation with "same context" parameter estimate variation, which provided baselines for sampling variability in item parameter estimates. Based on pretest item parameter estimates, Yen separated four-choice reading comprehension and five-choice mathematics concepts and applications items into three classes: one set of anchor items with a range of difficulties and relatively good model fit; two sets of context-altering items that had relatively poor fit and, in some cases, extreme difficulties or low discriminations; and two sets of items with relatively good model fit, good discrimination, and nonextreme difficulties that would be the items of major interest. Using these classes of items, 14 test booklets (7 reading and 7 math) were created. In each booklet, items from different sets were presented in different orders. The reading and math booklets were administered to students in grades 4 and 6, respectively. Liberal item limits were allowed. All students were tested twice. First, each student took one of six booklets; 2 weeks later, the students took the remaining booklet. Sample sizes ranged from 183 to 460. Item calibrations were run on various combinations of test booklets with sample sizes ranging from 224 to 1,352. Correlations, chi-square tests of differences, and mean absolute differences between item characteristic curve values and test characteristic values were used to compare item parameter estimates. Changes in item arrangements decreased the stability of item difficulty for both models. In addition, chi squares for test of parameter differences usually were much larger for the different context condition than they were for the same context condition. And context effects were apparent in the item characteristic curves.

Yen concluded that context effects were evident in the study, particularly for discrimination parameter estimates. The data did not support the hypothesis that inclusion of the context-inducing items would reduce the strength of relationships between item parameter estimates. The results indicated that number of items calibrated might affect the stability of item discrimination parameter estimates. Some support was found for an item location hypothesis. In particular, Yen found that items in reading passages generally were more difficult when they appeared at the end of a test than when they appeared at the beginning.

Item Arrangement Effect on Score Equating

The influence of context effects on item statistics generated from IRT resulted in several studies that looked anew at IRT score equating. The main purpose of one study was to assess within-test context effects on IRT true score equating (Kingston & Dorans, 1984). Item statistics estimated from a three-parameter IRT model were used to investigate the effects of item position on student behavior using the same data set as the one in the Swinton et al. (1982) study. The authors examined whether performance on certain item types was affected by exposure to the same item types earlier in the test.

The five types of analyses for the different item positions were based on (a) item difficulty, (b) item discrimination, (c) pseudoguessing parameters, (d) differences between equatings resulting from the administration of items located in different positions, and (e) regression of the difference between item difficulties on item position. The analysis of item difficulty showed a large improvement in performance on two types of items (analysis of explanations and logical diagrams) found in the GRE analytical section and a moderate decrease in performance on reading comprehension items. Analyses of the other item characteristics failed to produce consistent results.

The difference between equatings reflected the differences between item difficulties.

Finally, the analysis of the regression of the differences between item difficulty on item position showed a rather consistent relationship for the analysis of explanations and logical diagrams items on both forms of the test. Additional research on these two item types (Powers, 1983; Powers & Swinton, 1982; Swinton & Powers, 1983) demonstrated that performance on each item type is improved from formal coaching and from less formal test familiarization materials. This research suggests that the results found by Swinton et al. and by Kingston and Dorans are at least partially a consequence of the complexity and novelty of the item types. Kingston and Dorans concluded that any equating method that includes item types that exhibit within-in test context effects should provide for administrations of the items in the same position in the old and new forms.

Eignor and Cook (1983) investigated the feasibility of using IRT in the pre-equating of aptitude tests. The purpose of the study was to determine if the SAT verbal test can be pre-equated using pretest item parameters generated from IRT. The authors employed a complex item parameter estimation and linking design. Item responses for 143,499 examinees were involved in the calibrations. Although the primary purpose of the study was to evaluate the feasibility of IRT pre-equating based on precalibrated items, the authors became interested in item position effects when their pre-equating results did not replicate across test forms. Upon examining the data, they found that some items on the reading passage tended to exhibit a lack of item parameter invariance with respect to location. In particular, some items that appeared at the ends of pretest sections were easier when final form location was not at the end of a section. This effect was observed on both final forms used in the study. This result was consistent with the effect reported by Yen (1980).

Summary

All four studies that investigated item parameter invariance found some context effects. In particular, the Yen (1980), Kingston and Dorans (1984), and Eignor and Cook (1983) studies found that reading passage items generally were more difficult when they appeared at the end of a test or section than when they appeared near the beginning. Wightman (1981) also found a negative practice effect when two reading comprehension sections appeared in the same test. That is, mean section score for the reading comprehension items was lower when it was the second reading comprehension section to appear on the test than when it was the first. This phenomenon raises several questions about the construct being measured by reading comprehension items. Is the item measuring complex processing that is fatiguing to examinees? Is it the complexity of the item that makes if difficult? Might there be a change in cognitive processing between reading passages and responding to comprehension questions that is slower or more difficult for some examinees than for others? Does the change in processing become slower as it is repeated more times or as readers become fatigued? Regardless of the explanation, the consistent effect of position on item difficulty for reading comprehension item suggests that item arrangement cannot be ignored or dismissed for this item type.

Conclusions

Concern about within-test context effects has spanned 30 years, beginning with the work of Mollenkopf (1950) and others in the 1950s and 1960s who studied the simple main effects of item order on test performance, through the studies of interactions between item arrangement and examinee characteristics that occurred in the 1960s and 1970s and are continuing today by Plake and her associates, to the recent studies that have accompanied the development of item response theory and section pre-equating. Research concerned with the development and implementation of methods of pre-equating and with computerized adaptive testing or tailored testing is being actively pursued. The use of pre-equated tests or test items, whether for traditional test administration or for use with computerized adaptive testing, will necessitate a shift in emphasis from the test to the item. The test score, which is based on an aggregate of items, will be replaced by ability estimates that are based both on individual examinees' responses to individual items and on a model relating item performance to ability (e.g., the item response function or item characteristic curve of IRT). Current models of item performance that are used in adaptive testing presume that item performance is not sensitive to the context effects discussed in this review. To the extent that item performance is, in fact, sensitive to context, the models underlying adaptive testing are inappropriate and resultant ability estimates may be biased.

This review of the literature of item rearrangement and section placement has produced examples of position effects on test performance and item statistics. Evidence of effects has been demonstrated
throughout the 30 plus years of research. Although results have not been entirely consistent, some conclusions appear to be justified. Hard-to-easy arrangements yield lower scores than easy-to-hard arrangements under speeded conditions. This result virtually has no implication for computerized adaptive testing if time is irrelevant. Item arrangement does, of course, affect pre-equating research and practice if time limits affect performance for some of all examinees, and items appear in different relative positions when they are pre-equated than when they are given operationally.

A second conclusion supported by the literature is that random rearrangement of items or sections of items of the same type under power conditions does not seem to affect examinee performance. These data are important in instances in which scrambled forms of the same test might be desirable as a hedge against copying when tests must be administered under crowded or other undesirable testing conditions. The data are also important in that they suggest that item parameter invariance can be anticipated if pretesting or pre-equating items are randomly interspersed into an intact power test of homogeneous item types.

The effect of item order on test performance for easy-to-hard or hard-to-easy sequencing designs is less well anticipated. Some studies found evidence of an effect, and others did not. One difference among the studies investigating item order effect appears to be definition of the terms "hard" and "easy." Items defined as difficult in the Sax and Cromack study were much more difficult than those defined under the same terminology in the Marso study. Mollenkopf defined items with p values ranging from .35 to .65 as "medium difficulty." It appears that items used in these three studies would have been categorized differently by the different investigators. Beyond the statistical criterion to define item difficulty (e.g., a predetermined minimum or maximum p value), there is a more complex question about the definition of equal difficulty. Item difficulty is confounded with item complexity. That is, an item may be difficult because it is complex or because it is obscure. Both the complex and the obscure item may result in a low p value, but they may well not be equally susceptible to item order effect. The obscure item will remain obscure no matter where it is presented. The complex item may be more easily answered after some easier items have been successfully completed; for example, direction might be better understood or anxiety might be reduced. On the other hand, a complex item may be more difficult later in the test after fatigue has set in. Issues of optimal and least desirable item location, as well as differential susceptibility of statistically equivalent items are in need of further study. Understanding what makes an item difficult and developing a method for uniform classification of item difficulty are necessary parts of this research.

A third conclusion suggested by this review is that aptitude test items seem to be more sensitive to item arrangement than achievement test items. Related to this third conclusion is that some item types are particularly sensitive to context effects. Several studies demonstrated that items in reading passages tend to be more difficult when they appear at the end of a section than when they appear near the beginning. In addition, in their respective studies, Faggen and McPeek, Wightman, and Kingston and Dorans each identified one or more item type on which examinee performance was affected by within-test practice. Familiarity with the item type and time available to answer the item are plausible explanations for these consistent effects. The items identified in each of these studies were all verbal item types. Coupled with the sensitivity of reading passages to item arrangement, it seems likely that the finding of significant item order effects in so many of the verbal aptitude tests may well be a consequence of the practice and fatigue effects to which verbal item types seem to be subject.

In sum, the research literature has found evidence of context effects. Current testing models and techniques make stronger assumptions about item performance than traditional testing practice has needed to make in the past. The evidence does not suggest that the effect of test item or test section rearrangement is so detrimental as to invalidate test theory or practice that is dependent on the assumption of item parameter invariance. The effects, if known, can be taken into account. One such example is the separation of practiced from unpracticed parameter estimates in section pre-equating, allowing for the calculation of equating parameters based only on unpracticed data. A second example is the elimination of item types that are subject to context effects as was done with the GRE items as a consequence of the Swinton et al. (1982) and the Kingston and Dorans (1984) studies. Researchers or practitioners should, of course, avoid using item parameters based on data collected under speeded conditions when testing in an unspeeded adaptive mode. Likewise, parameter estimates for the novel item types that are bound to accompany the administration of items by computer should be collected under widely varying conditions and studied for context effects.

Perhaps the most important immediate direction for additional research on this topic is to define more clearly the significance of the context effects that have been identified. For example, what is the impact of item position effect on equating? What magnitude of variation in IRT generated item parameter estimates affects the estimation of an examinee's true score? Is item position effect confounded with mode of test administration (i.e., paper and pencil versus computer)? Are there identifiable subgroups of examinees who are more affected by variation in item position? As test theory practice increasingly implement variation in item arrangement, the answers to these question become increasingly important.

References

Alpert, R., & Haber, P. N. (1960). Anxiety in academic achievement situations. *Journal of Abnormal and Social Psychology, 61,* 207-215.

Berger, V. F., Munz, D. C., Smouse, A. D. & Angelino, H. (1969). The effects of item difficulty sequencing and anxiety reaction type on aptitude test performance. *Journal of Psychology, 72,* 253-258.

Brenner, M. H. (1964). Test difficulty, reliability, and discriminations as functions of item difficulty order. *Journal of Applied Psychology, 48,* 98-100.

Conrad, H. S. (1951). The experimental tryout of test materials. In E. F. Lindquist (Ed.), *Educational Measurement.* Washington DC: American Council on Education.

Cronbach, L. J. (1984). *Essentials of psychological testing.* New York: Harper and Row.

Eignor, D. R., & Cook, L. L. (1983). *An investigation of the feasibility of using item response theory in the preequating of aptitude tests.* Paper presented at the annual meeting of the American Educational Research Association, Montreal.

Faggen, J., & McPeek, M. (1981). *Practice effects for four different item types.* Paper presented at the annual meeting of the National Council on Measurement in Education, Los Angeles.

Flauger, R. L., Melton, R. S., & Myer, C. T. (1968). Item rearrangement under typical test conditions. *Educational and Psychological Measurement, 28,* 813-824.

Hambleton, R. K., & Traub, R. E. (1974). The effects of item order on test performance and stress. *Journal of Experimental Education, 43,* 40-46.

Holland, P. W., & Thayer, D. T. (1983, April). Section pre-equating in the presence of practice effects. In P. W. Holland (Chair), *Section pre-equating: A new equating technique for the era of national test disclosure.* Symposium conducted at the annual meeting of the American Educational Research Association, Montreal.

Holland, P. W., & Wightman L. E. (1982). Section pre-equating: A preliminary investigation, In P. W. Holland and D. B. Rubin (Eds.), *Test equating.* New York: Academic Press.

Huck, S. W., & Bowers, N. D. (1972). Item difficulty level and sequence effects in multiple choice achievement tests. *Journal of Educational Measurement, 9,* 105-111.

Jordan, A. M. (1953). *Measurement in education.* New York: McGraw-Hill.

Kingston, N. M., & Dorans, N. J. (1984). Item location effects and their implications for IRT equating and adaptive testing. *Applied Psychological Measurement, 8,* 147-154.

Klein, S. P. (1981). *The effect of time limits, item sequence and question format on the California bar examination*. A report prepared for the Committee of Bar Examiners of the State of California and the National Conference of Bar Examiners.

Klosner, N. C., & Gellman, E. K. (1973). The effect of item arrangement on classroom test performance: Implications for content validity. *Educational and Psychological Measurement, 33,* 413-418.

Lord, F. M. (1950). *Notes on comparable scales for test scores* (ETS RB50-48). Princeton, NJ: Educational Testing Service.

MacNicol, K. (1956). *Effects of varying order of item difficulty in an unspeeded verbal test.* Unpublished manuscript, Educational Testing Service, Princeton, NJ.

Marso, R. N. (1970). Test item arrangement, testing time, and performance. *Journal of Educational Measurement, 7,* 113-118.

McKeachie, W. J., Pollie, D., & Speisman, J. (1955). Relieving anxiety in classroom examinations. *Journal of Abnormal and Social Psychology, 50,* 93-98.

Mollenkopf, W. G. (1950). An experimental study of the effects on item analysis data of changing item placement and test-time limit. *Psychometrika, 15,* 291-315.

Monk, J. J., & Stallings, W. M. (1970). Effect of item order on test scores. *Journal of Educational Research, 63,* 463-465.

Munz, D. C., & Smouse, A. D. (1968). Interaction effects of item-difficulty sequence and achievement-anxiety reaction on academic performance. *Journal of Education Psychology, 59,* 370-374.

Plake, B. S. (1980). Item arrangement and knowledge of arrangement on test scores. *Journal of Experimental Education, 49,* 56-58.

Plake, B. S., Ansorge, C. J., Parker, C. S., & Lowry, S. R. (1982). Effects of item arrangement, knowledge of arrangement, test anxiety, and sex on test performance. *Journal of Educational Measurement, 19,* 49-58.

Plake, B. S., Thompson, P. A., & Lowry, S. (1981). Effect of item arrangement, knowledge of arrangement and test anxiety on two scoring methods. *Journal of Experimental Education, 41,* 214-219.

Powers, D. E. (1983). *Effects of coaching on GRE Aptitude Test scores* (GREB Research Report 81-3R; also ETS RR-8387). Princeton, NJ: Educational Testing Service.

Powers, D. E., & Swinton, S. S. (1982). *The effects of self-study of test familiarization materials for the analytical section of the GRE Aptitude Test* (GREB Research Report 79-9). Princeton, NJ: Educational Testing Service.

Remmers, H. H., & Gage, N. L. (1943). *Educational measurement and evaluation.* New York Harper.

Sax, G., & Carr, A. (1962). An investigation of response sets on altered parallel forms. *Educational and Psychological Measurement, 22,* 371-376.

Sax, G., & Cromack, T. R. (1966). The effects of various forms of item arrangements on test performance. *Journal of Educational Measurement, 3,* 309-311.

Smouse, A. D., & Munz, D. C. (1968). The effects of anxiety and item difficulty sequence on achievement testing scores. *Journal of Psychology, 68,* 181-184.

Smouse, A. D., & Munz, D. C. (1969). Item difficulty sequencing and response style: A follow-up analysis. *Educational and Psychological Measurement, 29,* 469-472.

Stewart, E. E. (1981). *Methodological Issues related to the study of context effects in multisection tests.* Paper presented at the annual meeting of the National Council on Measurement in Education, Los Angeles.

Swinton, S. S., & Powers, D. E. (1983). A study of the effects of special preparation on GRE analytical scores and item types. *Journal of Educational Psychology, 75,* 104-115.

Swinton, S. S., Wild, C. W., & Wallmark, M. (1982). *Investigation of practice effects on item types in the Graduate Record Examination Aptitude Test* (GRE Report No. 80-1). Princeton, NJ: Educational Testing Service.

Towle, N. J., & Merrill, P. F. (1975). Effects of anxiety types and item difficulty sequencing on mathematics test performance. *Journal of Educational Measurement, 12,* 241-249.

Weiss, D. J. (1982). Improving measurement quality and efficiency with adaptive testing. *Applied Psychological Measurement, 6,* 473-492.

Whitely, S. E., & Dawis, R. V. (1976). The influence of test context on item difficulty. *Educational and Psychological Measurement, 36,* 329-337.

Wightman, L. E. (1981). *GMAT within-test practice effects studies.* Paper presented at the annual meeting of the National Council on Measurement in Education, Los Angeles.

Wightman, L. E., & Leary, L. F. (1983). *Dealing with practice effects in section pre-equating.* Paper presented at the annual meeting of the American Educational Research Association, Montreal.

Yen, W. M. (1980). The extent, causes and importance of context effects on item parameters for two latent trait models. *Journal of Educational Measurement, 17,* 297-311.

COLLEGE STUDENT PERFORMANCE UNDER REPEATED TESTING AND CUMULATIVE TESTING CONDITIONS: REPORT ON FIVE STUDIES

Rosalie A. Rohm
University of Montevallo

Frank J. Sparzo
Carson M. Bennett
Ball State University

ABSTRACT This study was designed to shed light on three questions: (a) Are repeated single-unit tests given every-other-week as effective in improving end-of-course achievement as non-repeated cumulative tests given ever-other-week? (b) What is the effect on achievement of coupling the frequency of this testing? (c) Are weekly repeated cumulative tests more effective than either weekly non-repeated cumulative or weekly repeated single-unit tests? After assigning subjects randomly to experimental conditions, analysis of covariance (ANCOVA) procedures were applied to the final examination scores of undergraduate preservice teachers enrolled in an introductory course in behavior analysis. Repeated testing led to better performance than cumulative testing under every-other-week but not weekly conditions. However, repeated cumulative tests promoted better achievement than either non-repeated cumulative or repeated single-unit tests under weekly testing conditions.

A recent report on higher education calls for greater concern for the effects of testing on student performance (National Institute of Education; 1984). Because testing procedures are easily controlled by teachers and can have profound influences on the learning process (Popham, Cruse, Rankin, Sandifer, & Williams, 1985), determining the most beneficial procedures of testing may well improve the effectiveness of teaching.

An account of the most desirable testing procedures may some day emerge. However, serious gaps in knowledge now exist. One such gap is related to the relative effect of repeated single-unit and non-repeated cumulative testing procedures on improved academic performance.

Repeated single-unit testing formats typically incorporate only content that is currently under study and provide two or more opportunities to reach a prespecified level of achievement on comparable tests before the student is administered a subsequent unit test (Crouse, 1974; Deboer, 1980, Fitchem & Adler, 1977, Glucksman, 1973; Martin & Srikameswaran, 1974; Stauffer, 1973). Cumulative tests typically incorporate content from the current unit as well as from former units of study. Although cumulative exams have been found in education for many years as terminal measures of achievement (e.g.,

---

Reprinted by permission of the Journal of Educational Research, Vol. 80 No. 2 (Nov/Dec 1986): 99-104.

Turney, 1931), few investigations have evaluated the effects of cumulative testing on student performance during instruction (Grosser, Packwood, & Walters, 1979).

Opportunity to retake tests have been found to increase student study time (Barkmeier, Duncan, & Johnson, 1978), course grades (Barrall & Axelrod, 1978), and final exam performance (Cantanzano & Wilson, 1976). Retesting to mastery is a central feature of personalized systems of instruction (PSI) and other mastery-oriented approaches to teaching (Johnson & Ruskin, 1977; Kulik, Kulik, & Cohen, 1979). With few exceptions (e.g., Hertzburg, Heilman, & Levenberger, 1932; Noll, 1939; Olsen, Weber, & Dorner, 1968; Selakovich, 1962), most studies have concluded that frequent testing leads to increased academic achievement (Dustin, 1971; Fitch, Drucker, & Norton, 1951; Gaynor & Milham, 1976; Keys, 1934; Kulp, 1933; Marso, 1970; Schunert, 1951; Standlee & Popham, 1961; Turney, 1931, 1931). The single study investigating the effects of cumulative testing during instruction found an increase in final examination performance (Gosser et al., 1979).

If retesting improves academic performance, the logistical demands and additional teacher and student time involved in such testing may be justified. But if non-repeated cumulative testing procedures during instruction are as effective as retesting patterns, the greater demands of retesting would be neither necessary nor justified. While weekly rather than monthly testing and cumulative rather than single-unit tests have been shown to promote end-of-course achievement, there are apparently not reported studies that focus on the relationship between test frequency and repeated and cumulative testing procedures.

This article reports the results of five studies that were designed to shed light on three questions: (1) Are repeated single-unit tests given every-other-week as effective in improving final exam performance as non-repeated cumulative tests given every-other-week? (2) What is the effect on final exam performance of doubling the frequency of testing? that is, are weekly repeated single-unit tests as effective in improving final exam performance as weekly non-repeated cumulative tests? (3) Are weekly repeated cumulative tests more effective in improving student performance than either weekly non-repeated cumulative or weekly repeated single-unit tests?

Study 1

This study investigated the effect of every-other-week single unit and every-other-week cumulative testing on final exam performance. Subjects (n =32) were undergraduate preservice teachers enrolled in two introductory classes in behavior analysis at a moderately sized midwestern university during a winter quarter.

Students in each class were assigned randomly to one of two experimental conditions: An every-other-week repeated single-unit or an every-other-week cumulative testing condition. Thus both testing conditions were administered in both classes. The instructor/examiners were given random teaching assignments in each class to minimize possible teacher effects. Topics were assigned randomly to each instructor/examiner who presented the topic to both classes. The result was that each instructor/examiner taught each class half the time. Students in both classes were assigned the same course materials and requirements and followed the same schedule of events. Syllabi were also the same except for the description of the students testing condition.

On the first day of class students were informed of the research study and told of their random assignment to their respective testing condition. They were assured that final grades would be adjusted if a systematic difference between experimental groups was found in total points earned on the four unit tests and the final exam. No students declined to participate. Students in the retest group were administered a total of four unit tests and up to two retests per unit if they failed to reach the criterion for an "A" grade of 88% (or 35 items correct). Retests were taken outside of class prior to the next scheduled unit test. If a student did not attain an 88% on either of the retests, his recorded score for the unit was the average of his two highest scores for that unit. (It was assumed that this provision would maintain motivation across all three retest administration.) The remaining half of the students were administered one cumulative test per unit which was constructed as follows: Half the items were based on content from previous units; half were based on content from the unit currently under study. The four unit tests (single-unit and cumulative) and the unit retests were forty items in length and consisted of true-false and completion items. The same types of items in approximately the same proportion were used in the construction of the one-hundred item comprehensive final. This final was the dependent measure for the first four studies in this series. Items for the unit tests and retests were drawn randomly from an item pool. New items were developed for the final in proportion to the topical emphasis in the course. Items were included on tests only when at least two of the authors agreed on their technical adequacy or their modification. All tests except retests were administered at the same time to students in the classroom.

Results

An analysis of covariance (ANCOVA) procedure was applied to the 400-point final examination scores from the two experimental groups. Grade point averages (GPA) were used as a covariate. The retesting group mean ($M = 299$) was significantly different from the cumulative group mean ($M = 278$),

$F(1,29) = 8.7, p < .006$. Effect size was 1.05 standard deviation units after adjustment for GPA.

Study 2

Study 2 was a replication of Study 1. Subjects ($n = 22$) were undergraduate preservice teachers enrolled in the introductory class in behavior analysis the spring quarter following Study 1.

Course content, the schedule of events, teaching methods, and testing procedures were essentially the same as those used in Study 1. As in Study 1, students were assigned randomly to the two testing formats.

Results

The results from Study 2 were similar to those reported for Study 1. The retesting group mean ($M = 308$) was significantly different from the cumulative group mean ($M = 272$), $F(1,19) = 10.28, p < .005$. Effect size was 1.37 standard deviation units after adjustment for GPA. Pooling the data from Study 1 and Study 2 yielded an overall effect size of 1.17.

Discussion

The results of the first two studies in this series indicate that repeated single-unit testing is more effective in enhancing end-of-course achievement than cumulative testing when tests are administered every-other-week. Given this schedule of testing, the additional time and effort involved in implementing repeated testing procedures may be justified.

Study 3

Study 3 was an extension of Study 1. Tests were administered every week rather than every-other-week. Subjects ($n = 25$) were undergraduate preservice teachers enrolled in the introductory class in behavior analysis during the subsequent fall quarter.

Materials and procedures were the same as those used in the former studies. The syllabi were also the same except for the sections describing the testing procedures--repeated single-unit and non-repeated cumulative tests were administered weekly. Students were again assigned randomly to experimental conditions. Almost all of the items of the eight 20-item tests (single-unit and cumulative) were drawn from the previous 40-item every-other-week tests. The tests were shortened to hold the number of items constant while increasing test frequency. Thus, aside from test frequency, students in Study 3 (and Study 4) were exposed to essentially the same course content, procedures, and test items as in Study 1 and Study 2. Students in the repeated testing condition took eight unit tests and, if necessary, one or two retests per unit to meet criterion. Students under the cumulative testing condition also took eight tests. After the initial test, half the items on each cumulative test (10) were drawn from previous content and half (10) covered content currently under study. The dependent variable was the same final exam used in Study 1 and Study 2 (except that each item was scored 1 point rather than 4 points).

Results

Data were analyzed as before. In contrast to the results from the two preceding studies, no significant difference on the 100-points final exam was found between the repeat ($M = 63.7$) and cumulative testing groups ($M = 63.4$), $F(1,22) = .002, p > .05$.

Study 4

Study 4 was a replication of Study 3. Subjects ($n = 23$) were undergraduate preservice teachers enrolled in an introductory course in behavior analysis in the subsequent winter quarter.

Course content, procedures, and the schedule of events remained essentially the same as in Study 3. Random assignment to experimental conditions was once again conducted.

Results

The results paralleled those from Study 3. No significant difference was found between the repeated ($M = 63.25$) and the cumulative testing groups ($M = 61.55$), $F(1,20) = .222, p > .05$.

Discussion

This series of four studies answers, albeit tentatively, two of the questions with which we began: Under testing conditions of every-other-week, a repeated single-unit testing procedure will probably lead to better end-of-course performance than cumulative testing procedures. However, when weekly tests are given, cumulative testing may serve as well without the greater logistical demands associated with repeated testing.

Study 5

This study was designed to (a) investigate the relationship between weekly repeated cumulative testing on the one hand, and weekly non-repeated cumulative and weekly repeated single-unit testing on the other hand, and (b) to determine whether the results of Study 3 and Study 4 would hold in a different context. Course content and test item differed from that reported in the four previous studies.

The subjects ($n = 28$) were undergraduate preservice teachers enrolled in a human growth and development class during the spring quarter following Study 4.

The first author was the instructor for the course. As in the previous studies, a within-class control condition was implemented. All unit tests--cumulative tests and retests and single-unit tests and retests--were 20 items in length. In contrast to the four earlier studies, all items for the unit tests and the 60-item comprehensive final were four-alternative multiple-choice items. The test items were constructed by the instructor. One or two retests were administered to students who did not achieve an 88% criterion score on the repeated cumulative and single-unit tests. Retests were taken out of class prior to the next scheduled unit test.

Results

Data were analyzed by means of an ANCOVA procedure; GPA was the covariate. As in Study 3 and Study 4, there was no significant difference between weekly non-repeated cumulative testing and weekly repeated single-unit testing on the comprehensive final. However, the difference between the final mean score of the repeated cumulative testing group ($M = 45.12$) and the composite of the means for the cumulative and single-unit testing groups ($M = 39.20$) was significant, $F(2,24) = 7.15, p < .004$. The effect size was 1.42 standard deviation units after adjustment for GPA.

Discussion

Study 5 parallels the results of Study 3 and Study 4. That is, there was no statistically significant difference between weekly cumulative and repeated single-unit testing procedures on an end-of-course measure of achievement. However, under a weekly testing condition, there was a statistically significant difference when the tests were repeated and cumulative.

Table 1 summarizes the statistical analyses for all five studies.

Table 1. Results of Testing Procedures

Comparison	Overall F	Probability level	Effect size
Study 1 Biweekly repeated single-unit to non-repeated cumulative	8.705	p < .006	1.05
Study 2 Replication of Study 1	10.282	p < .005	1.37
Study 1 and Study 2 pooled	18.517	p < .001	1.17
Study 3 Weekly repeated single unit to non-repeated cumulative	.002	p > .05	
Study 4 Replication of Study 3	.222	p > .05	
Study 5 Weekly repeated single-unit and non-repeated cumulative to repeated cumulative	7.15	p < .004	1.42

Table 2. Proportion of Test Items By Topic on Final and Across Testing Conditions

	Behavioral assessment	Reinforcement	Stimulus control	Aversive control	Applications
Study 1 and Study 2					
final test	22	30	18	10	20
repeated testing	25	23	13	9	30
cumulative testing	43	22	7	6	22
Study 3 and Study 4					
final test	22	30	18	10	20
repeated testing	24	22	12	12	30
cumulative testing	40	22	9	9	20

Note. All numbers are percentages.

Two questions are pertinent to the interpretation of the data from Table 1:

What is the relative distribution of test items by topic on the final and across testing conditions? Because one plausible explanation for the effect of cumulative testing is that topics covered in each successive test were also topics which received greatest emphasis on the final examination, this is essentially a content validity question. Table 3 presents the percent of items in the five major topic areas on the final and across testing conditions for the first four studies. Inspection of the table reveals that the distribution of test items is approximately proportional. The possible exception to this conclusion can be found for the cumulative tests in the column labeled behavioral

Table 3. Mean Final Exam Scores for Cumulative, Low-Item, and High-Item Groups

Group	n	M	F level	Probability
Cumulative	24	66.92	7.392	$p < .002$
Low-item	8	82.00		
High-item	15	59.60		

assessment (43% and 40%). Undoubtedly these percentages are due to the fact that behavioral assessment was the first topic covered in the course. A similar analysis conducted for Study 5 also yielded a proportional distribution across major topic areas.

Might the results of these studies be due simply to the number of test items taken? That is, did the students who performed better on the final do so because they took more test items? In response to this question, data from students in Study 2 and Study 3 were pooled ($n = 47$). Treating GPA as a covariance, a one-way ANCOVA was applied to the final exam scores (percentage of items correct) of three groups of subjects: the cumulative testing group (all students took 160 items), a low-item repeat testing group who responded to 160-280 items, and a high-item repeat testing group who responded to 320-480 items. Table 3 presents the results of this analysis. It shows that the number of items taken is inversely related to final examination performance. Students in the repeat testing condition who responded to fewer items throughout the quarter did better on the final than those who responded to a greater number of items.

Within the limitations of course characteristics, sample size, test structure, etc., the following conclusions are warranted:

1. Under every-other-week testing conditions, non-repeated cumulative testing does not promote end-of-course achievement as well as repeated single-unit testing.
2. Repeated single-unit testing loses this advantage under weekly testing conditions.
3. Repeated cumulative testing promotes better end-of-course achievement than either non-repeated cumulative of repeated single-unit testing under conditions of weekly testing.

If a teacher administers tests every-other-week, repeated single-unit rather than non-repeated cumulative tests should be administered. If the teacher uses weekly tests, repeated cumulative tests are recommended.

Although these studies were planned for different purposes, taken together they imply a 2 X 2 X 2 design with fully-crossed independent variables as follows: (a) repeated testing opportunity or not, (b) cumulative testing or not, and (c) weekly or every-other-week testing. Future investigations might well employ such a design. Because the condition of repeated cumulative testing on an every-other-week schedule was not investigated, no conclusion can be made as to preference for that approach over repeated single-unit testing on an every-other-week schedule.

Finally, this research suggests the need for a variety of additional studies. For example, it is noteworthy that the testing procedures in these studies differed from most mastery models of teaching in that there was no requirement for continuous testing to mastery. Would such a requirement change the results of these investigations? Would repeated cumulative testing retain an advantage under every-other-week and monthly testing conditions? Which, if any, of the findings would hold across other subject matter areas? How might item type (Ulman & Sparzo, 1978) and the cognitive level of items interact with the testing formats examined in this article? How effective is a more traditional single-unit testing procedure compared with repeated single-unit, repeated cumulative, and non-repeated cumulative testing? Are the effect sized reported here large enough to have practical as well as statistical value?

These are important questions to answer. They serve to remind us of the serious gaps that exist in our knowledge of how different kinds and amounts of testing affect student performance.

References

Barkmeier, D. R., Duncan, P. K., & Johnson, J. M. (1978). Effects of opportunity for retest on study behavior and academic performance. *Journal of Personalized Instruction, 3,* 89-92.

Barrall, M. E., & Axelrod, S. (1978). The effects of learning partners and retests on pretest-posttest scores, final course grades, and student attitudes. *Research in Higher Education, 8,* 177-187.

Catanzano, R., & Wilson, M. S. (1977). The effect of retesting contingencies of achievement, anxiety, and attitude in seventh grade science. *Science Education, 61,* 173-180.

Crouse, J. H. (1974). Acquisition of college course material under conditions of repeated testing. *Journal of Educational Psychology, 66,* 367-372.

DeBoer, G. E. (1980). Can repeated testing of en route objectives improve end-of-course achievement in high school chemistry? *Science Education, 64,* 141-147.

Dustin, D. S. (1971). Some effects of exam frequency. *The Psychological Record, 21,* 409-414.

Fitch, M. L., Drucker, A. J., & Norton, J. A. (1951). Frequent testing as a motivating factor in large lecture classes. *Journal of Educational Psychology, 42,* 1-20.

Fitchen, C., & Adler, L. (1977) Examination retest procedures: Effects on performance, test anxiety, and attitudes. *Improving College and University Teaching, 25,* 247-250.

Gaynor, J., & Milliham, J. (1976). Student performance and evaluation under variant teaching and testing methods in a large college course. *Journal of Educational Psychology, 68,* 312-317.

Glucksman, M. D. (1973). The use of retesting as a teaching device in an elementary algebra course. *School Science and Mathematics, 73,* 725-729.

Gosser, J., Packwood, G., & Walters, W. (1979, July). The effect of repeated testing on long term retention and generalization in a general psychology course. Paper presented at the meeting of the AERA North Central Region Special Interest Group for Community-Junior College Research, Ann Arbor, MI.

Hertsberg, O. E., Heilman, J. D., & Leuenberger, H. W. (1932). The value of objective tests as teaching devices in educational psychology classes. *Journal of Educational Psychology, 23,* 371-379.

Johnson, K. R., & Ruskin, R. S. (1977). Comparing behavioral and conventional instruction. In *Behavioral Instruction: An Evaluative Review.* Washington, DC: APA.

Keys, N. (1930). The influence on learning and retention of weekly as opposed to monthly tests. *Journal of Educational Psychology, 25,* 427-436.

Kulik, J. A., Kulik, C. L., Hertzier, E. C. (1977). Modular college teaching with and without required remediation. *Journal of Personalized Instruction, 2,* 70-75.

Kulp, D. H. (1933). Weekly tests for graduate students? *School and Society, 38,* 157-159.

Marso, R. N. (1970). Classroom testing procedures, test anxiety, and achievement. *Journal of Experimental Education, 38,* 54-58.

Martin, R. R., & Srikameswaran, K. (1974). Correlation between frequent testing and student performance. *Journal of Chemical Education, 51,* 485-586.

National Institute of Education (1984). *Involvement in Learning: Realizing the Potential of American Higher Education,* Washington, D. C.: U. S. Department of Education.

Noll, V. H. (1939). The effect of written tests upon achievement in college classes: An experiment and a summary of evidence. *Journal of Educational Research, 32,* 345-358.

Olsen, R. E., Weber, L. J., & Donner, J. L. (1968). Quizzes as teaching aids. *Journal of Medical Education, 43,* 941-942.

Popham, W. J., Cruse, K. L., Rankin, S. C., Sandifer, P. D., & Williams, P. L. (1985). Measurement-driven instruction: It's on the road. *Phi Delta Kappan, 66,* 628-634.

Schunert, J. (1951). The association of mathematical achievement with certain factors resident in the teacher, in the teaching, in the pupil, and in the school. *Journal of Experimental Education, 10,* 221-238.

Selakovich, D. (1962). An experiment attempting to determine the effectiveness of frequent testing as an aid to learning in beginning college courses in American government. *Journal of Educational Research, 55,* 178-180.

Standlee, L. S., & Popham, W. J. (1960). Quizzes' contribution to learning. *Journal of Educational Psychology, 51,* 322-325.

Stauffer, A. J. (1973). The validity of a test for improving learning and measuring achievement when administered repeatedly. *Educational and Psychological Measurement, 33,* 951-954.

Turney, A. H. (1931). The effect of frequent short objective tests upon the achievement of college students in educational psychology. *School and Society, 33,* 760-762.

Ullman, J. D., and Sparzo, F. J. (1978). Differential effects of two types of unit quiz modes on final exam performance. *Journal of Personalized Instruction, 3,* 187-191.

EDUCATION RESEARCH

Jack E. Kiger, Editor

ON THE BENEFITS OF CUMULATIVE EXAMS: AN EXPERIMENTAL STUDY

Thomas P. Edmonds

> ABSTRACT: This study analyzes the effect of two review strategies on performance, effort, and attitude measures. The two review strategies are compared with a control strategy that does not include a review treatment. The review treatments are administered through two separate testing procedures. One procedure includes individualized review questions on each succeeding examination. The other includes randomized review questions on succeeding exams. The results indicate that reviews are a cost-effective means of improving student performance. The random review treatment proved to be the more efficient strategy. Further, the data implied that students were unable to assess properly the benefits of reviews. This finding suggests that instructors should take the initiative to employ strategies that force students to review on a regular basis.

Pawliczek [1978] found that an individualized review treatment improved student performance as measured by the final examination scores of introductory accounting students. The review treatment was administered via individualized cumulative exams; that is, succeeding interim tests for each student included new material plus material that the student had missed on previous exams. Pawliczek's findings were consistent with other studies that had indicated that student performance could be improved by reviews of course material. Indeed, Clayton [1973] found reviews administered through two types of testing strategies (i.e., testing only and testing with explanations) increased learning for grammar school, junior high school, and college students who were studying mathematical concepts. Employing a different strategy, Ross and Di Vesa [1976] reported that an oral review of prose material had a positive influence on retention.

While these studies have shown that reviews in general and cumulative examinations in particular lead to improved student performance, they have not addressed the cost/benefit issues that are crucial to the widespread use of review strategies. For example, while accounting educators are interested in improved performance, they may be deterred from using Pawliczek's review strategy because of the substantial professional and clerical effort required to prepare and score individualized examinations. In addition to professional and clerical effort, the impact of review strategies on the students' effort

---

Reprinted by permission of the American Accounting Association from The Accounting Review, Vol. LIX, No. 4 (October 1984): 660-668.

should be evaluated. Review strategies that cause students to prolong the study of particular course material may drain the base of study time that could otherwise be applied more efficiently to different subject matter.

Improved student performance, like any other benefit attribute, must be balanced against the effort required. Accordingly, accounting instructors need to know whether review strategies cause students, teachers, and support staff to work harder (i.e., expend more effort) or to work more efficiently. Likewise, it is important to know whether different review strategies affect performance and efforts measures differently. The purpose of this study is to provide some insight into these cost/benefit considerations. Specifically, the study analyzes the impact of two examination review strategies on certain performance, effort, and attitude measures. These two review strategies are compared with a control strategy that does not include a review treatment.

FORMATION OF HYPOTHESES

The research findings cited earlier lead to an *a priori* expectation that experimental subjects who receive review treatments will outperform control subjects who do not receive review treatments. However, no expectations exist regarding the potential for different review strategies to affect performance measures differently. If cost differentials exist for alternative review strategies, then the use of strategies that require greater costs can only be justified by the provision of commensurate benefits (e.g., higher performance). The following null hypothesis was established to test for differences in the measurement of performance.

H_1: No significant differences exist in the performance measures of subjects who receive different review treatments.

Different review strategies may cause instructors, clerical staff, and students to expend more or less effort to attain a certain level of performance. For example, improved performance may result from the fact that experimental groups spend more total time on a topic than do control groups. This effect is called the total-time hypothesis. It has been used as a factor that competes with the treatment effect in explaining performance differentials in studies involving a variety of educational research experiments [e.g., Faw and Waller, 1976]. While the total-time hypothesis undoubtedly explains some variation in performance in some studies, researchers have also shown that when time is held constant, performance differentials can be attained through the employment of different teaching strategies [Nungester and Duchastel, 1982]. These related studies imply that performance could be affected by differentials in review treatments or differences in the amount of effort expended. Accordingly, the evaluation of time spent and other effort measures is essential to a cost/benefit analysis of different review strategies. A second null hypothesis was used to test for significant differences between efforts measures.

H_2: No significant differences exist in the effort expended for groups that receive different review treatments.

The Pawliczek [1978, p. 987] study raised an interesting question regarding the potential of a Hawthorne effect that may result from an individualized review treatment. Specifically, the study noted that the superior performance of a group which received an individualized review treatment may have been attributable to the fact that the students were receiving the individual attention of the instructor, rather than the repetition benefits associated with the review treatment. If such a motivational impact is present, is could have significant cost/benefit implications. Indeed, other teaching strategies may provide a more cost-effective means of obtaining motivational benefits than the administration of review treatments. The following null hypothesis was established to assess the potential impact of different review treatments on student attitudes.

H_3: No significant differences exist in the attitudes of students that review different review treatments.

TEST OF HYPOTHESES

A classroom laboratory experiment was conducted with subjects consisting of three groups of graduate-level introductory accounting students. Group A acted as the control group. Groups B and C were used as experimental groups. Classes were scheduled from 5:30 to 6:50 on Monday and Wednesday evenings for students assigned to Group A. Groups B and C met from 5:30 to 6:50 and from 7:00 to 8:20, respectively, on Tuesday and Thursday evenings. The control and experimental groups were intentionally assigned to meet on different days of the week to minimize the students' awareness that they were receiving differential treatments.

The review treatments used in this study were administered via differentiated testing procedures. Each group received five interim examinations and a final examination. After the first exam, successive interim tests for the control group covered only material that had been introduced since the last examination. In contrast, Groups B and C received cumulative examinations. Students in Group B received and individualized review treatment; that is, each student received a different examination that contained review questions on material that he or she had missed on a previous exam. Students in Group C received a random review treatment;

that is, all students received the same examination including review questions on material that the class as a whole had missed on previous exams.

The review questions (individual and random) tested the subject areas that had been missed on previous exams but were not exact replicas of the questions that were used in those examinations. Multiple-choice questions were used exclusively for all examinations. All grading was conducted on an objective basis. No partial credit was assigned for any reason. The interim examinations were administered to each group at is regularly scheduled classroom meeting time. However, all three groups took the same, examination, at the same time and in the same physical setting.

Sample Size

Initially, the sample of subjects contained 111 students. Twenty-one of these students were removed from the sample because they failed to complete the course. Another nine students were removed from the sample via random selection in order to obtain balanced data sets. As a result, the final sample consisted of 81 students, who were subdivided into three groups of 27 subjects each.

Variables

The control and two experimental review treatments constituted the independent variables that were employed in the study. The dependent variables were measures of performance, effort, and attitude.

Performance

Performance was measured by the group mean scores for the final examination. The final exam was comprehensive. To avoid biasing the performance measure of any particular group, the exam consisted of modifications of multiple-choice question drawn randomly from a test bank that had been developed for the course over a two-year period prior to the experiment. Since all three groups received the same final, at the same time, in the same location, the amount of available study time for each group was equalized and the potential for the exchange of exam information between the groups was eliminated.

Effort

Two distinct categories of effort measures were examined in the study. The first dealt with the professional and clerical effort that was required to prepare and score the exams. The second centered on the students' effort that was devoted to studying for the exams.

There was no significant difference in the amount of professional and clerical effort required to prepare the exams for the control versus the random group. Each group required the preparation of one examination that contained 25 multiple-choice questions. Every individual within each group received the same examination. The exams were machine graded and a computer printout identified the most frequently missed questions. Accordingly, the administration of a random review treatment did not increase the effort required to prepare and score examinations.

The administration of the individualized review treatment did result in the incurrence of significantly higher levels of professional and clerical effort. Since the review treatment was individualized, it was necessary to analyze each student's exam to determine which questions the student had missed. Modified forms of the missed questions had to be prepared for inclusion on the subsequent examinations. In addition to the questions covering new material, the interim exams required the preparation of 15 to 20 modified exam questions. While the questions covering new material were standardized, the inclusion of the individualized review questions required that a portion of each exam be individually typed. Thus the clerical effort was significantly increased. Further, since the exams were not standardized, machine grading was precluded. Even the distribution of the exam to the students required more effort because each student had to be matched with his or her particular examination. In this study, the individualization of the review treatment more than doubled the amount of professional and clerical effort that was required to prepare and score the interim examinations.

Two variables measured student effort: the average number of hours of study time per week and the average number of hours of study time devoted to the final examination. Higher averages for the time-spent variables represent higher costs to students in the form of a greater depletion of the base of available study time. These variable were measured by self-reporting. A recent study by Ganster, Hennessey and Luthans [1983] found that self-reported effort measure may be affected by a social desirability (SD) influence.[1] However, this study did not attempt to discover how many hours students spend studying, but whether one group reported more or less study hours than another group. Unless SD affected one of the groups differently than the others, it is unlikely that it would affect the comparisons used in the study. Hence, it is not likely that the effort measures used in this study are affected by a self-reporting bias.

---

[1]Social desirability is defined as a tendency for an individual to present him or herself in a way that makes the person look positive with regard to culturally derived norms and standards.

The study examined four attitude measures. Students were asked to register their level of agreement with four statements on a seven-point Likert scale, with one representing complete agreement and seven representing complete disagreement: 1) The instructor exhibited exceptional concern for the students in the class; 2) The instructor's attention to me as an individual motivated me to improve my performance in the course; 3) I should have spent more time reviewing the course material during the semester rather than waiting until the end of the semester to start my review; and 4) I crammed for the final examination. The attitude measures, like the effort measures, are subject to the social desirability effects inherent in self-reported data. The arguments stated in the discussion on effort measures would hold equally for the attitude measures. Accordingly, it is not likely that the research conclusions regarding the attitude measures are affected by a self-reporting bias.

An intercorrelation matrix (see Table 1) indicates that the seven dependent variables are relatively independent of each other. Only two of the correlation coefficients were significant at the .10 level of significance.

CONTROL FEATURES

The following steps were taken to assure the comparability of the three groups. Classes for all three groups were conducted in evening sessions. This eliminated any bias which may have resulted from differences in day versus night students. All three groups met in similar physical settings with the same instructor, thereby reducing the potential for bias resulting from differences in physical surroundings or teaching styles.

TABLE 1
DEPENDENT VARIABLE INTERCORRELATION MATRIX

	1	2	3	4	5	6
Performance Measure:						
1. Final Exam Score						
Effort Measures:						
2. Average Hours Per Week	.01					
3. Average Hours on Final	.04	.18				
Attitude Measures:						
4. Instructor Concern	-.03	.13	.04			
5. Individual Attention	-.05	.03	.37*	.12		
6. Review During Semester	.33*	.17	-.06	.03	-.10	
7. Cramming	.16	.07	.08	.19	.11	.02

*Significant at $\alpha < .1$.

Other variables beyond the organizational control of the researcher were subjected to statistical control procedures. Three categories of variables that contained potentially contaminating influences were analyzed in the study. These categories were: 1) the ability of the students to perform; 2) the level of the instructor's performance; and 3) certain demographic variables.

Two measurements of students' ability were analyzed. These were the students' scores on the AICPA Orientation Test, Form D, and their grades on the first classroom examination. The orientation test was used as a measure of the students' aptitude, while the first exam score was intended to measure examination performance. Performance on the first classroom examinationwas not contaminated by the review treatments, because there were no previous exams available for review prior to the administration of the first examination.

The instructor's performance was measured by the students' responses to a summary question that was included on the university's teacher evaluation form. The subjects were asked to rate the instructor's effectiveness by using a five-point Likert scale, with one representing unsatisfactory and five indicating excellent performance. The question used read as follows: *"Disregarding your personal opinion of him as an individual,* what is your overall rating of this instructor's teaching effectiveness?"

The demographic data were collected during the first week of class. The subjects were asked to provide information regarding five variables. These variables were age, sex, number of hours employed per week, number of previous semester hours of college-level accounting, and number of hours of course work enrolled in during the current semester.

The eight control variables were tested to determine whether they were distributed equally among the three groups. Each of the variables was analyzed by using a one-way analysis of variance (ANOVA) test, with the control and experimental treatments acting as the independent variables. These and other tests employed in this study were conducted by using the

TABLE 2
ANALYSIS OF CONTROL VARIABLES

Variables	Control	Individual	Random	Total	Significance level
AICPA Test	64.1	66.4	69.5	66.7	.06*
Test I	82.8	75.8	75.0	77.9	.03*
No. Hrs. Acct.	1.3	2.0	2.2	1.8	.55
No. Hrs. Work	28.8	28.8	30.8	29.5	.88
No. Hrs. Class	5.2	5.4	5.8	5.5	.64
Sex (% M)	56%	72%	76%	68%	.29
Age	26.6	27.6	26.4	26.9	.51
Inst. Performance	4.5	4.6	4.6	4.6	.76

*Significant at $\alpha < .1$.

TABLE 3
ANALYSIS OF DEPENDENT VARIABLES

	Performance	Efforts		Attitude			
	Final	Week Hours	Final Hours	Instructor Concern	Individual Attention	Review During Semester	Cramming
Adjusted Mean Scores:							
Control	74.18	4.81	11.63	3.51	1.71	4.32	2.01
Individual	78.63	5.21	8.30	3.29	2.45	3.33	2.97
Random	79.64	4.89	8.56	2.96	2.44	3.24	3.33
Levels of Significance for F test:							
Main Effect	.06	.86	.07	.35	.05	.07	.01
Covariates:							
AICPA Test	.05	.85	.59	.58	.71	.43	.38
Test 1	.02	.10	.06	.79	.38	.65	.36
Levels of Significance for t test:							
Control vs. Individual	.08	.60	.05	.57	.04	.10	.02
Control vs. Random	.03	.91	.06	.15	.03	.07	.00
Individual vs. Random	.69	.68	.88	.41	.99	.88	.36

programs contained in the Statistical Analysis System [Ray, 1982]. Table 2 shows the mean values of the control variable measurements and the level of significance of the F-statistic for each ANOVA test.

Two of the tests produced F-statistics with associated levels of significance which fell below ten percent. Accordingly, the results indicated that the AICPA Orientation test scores (.06) and the first classroom examination grades (.03) were distributed unequally among the three groups. The null hypotheses regarding no differences among the groups in the other control variables could not be rejected.

RESULTS

Analysis of covariance models were used to test the three hypotheses. Each of the seven dependent variables was tested with the control and review treatments acting as the independent variables. The scores on the AICPA

Orientation Test and the grades on the first classroom examination were introduced as covariates in each of the seven tests. Repeated *t*-tests were used to identify differences between the individual means.

Table 3 provides a summary of the results of the analysis of covariance tests and the repeated *t*-tests. The table includes the significance levels for the main effect *F*-test and the two covariates and the significance levels for the *t*-tests between the individual means.

At an alpha level of less than or equal to ten percent, both of the covariates had a significant effect (AICPA Test .05 and Test I .02) on the final exam scores of the subjects. The only other significant effect of the covariates centered on the relationship between the Test I covariate and the two time-spent measures (weekly hours .10 and final exam hours .06).

The data support the *a priori* expectations of Hypothesis 1 that reviews improved student performance. The main effect *F*-statistic for the performance variable final exam scores was significant (.06). Further, the *t*-test revealed that the differences between the control and both review treatments (individual .08 and random .03) were significant. In both cases the review groups had significantly higher mean scores (individual 78.63 and random 79.64) than the control group (74.18). The difference between the mean scores of the two review treatments was not significant (.69).

The only effort measurement with a main-effect significant *F* (.07) was the number of hours devoted to studying for the final exam. The individual *t*-tests for this variable indicate that the control group was significantly different from the individual group (.05) and the random group (.06). There was no significant difference between the individual group and the random group (.88). The mean measurement of 11.63 hours for the control group was significantly higher than the 8.30 hours for the individual group or the 8.56 hours for the random group. While this finding would suggest a rejection of Hypothesis II, the other effort measure supports the hypothesis with results showing no significant differences in the average number of weekly study hours of the three groups.

Three of the attitude measure suggested a rejection of Hypothesis III, the null hypothesis concerning attitudes. The two measures regarding instructor concern had conflicting results. No significant difference (.35) was found with regard to the mean scores of the general level of instructor's concern. However, there were significantly different (.05) mean ratings regarding the students' perception of the effect of the instructor's individualized treatment on their performance. The *t*-test revealed that the control group had a significantly different perception ranking from both the individual (.04) and the random (.03) groups. The mean difference between the individual and the random treatment groups was not significant (.99). This result is surprising because the control group ranked its perception of individualized attention higher (1.71) than the group that received the individualized review treatment (2.45).

Significant differences existed for both of the attitude measures regarding the subjects' perceptions of the value of reviews. Recall that the subjects were asked to register their level of agreement with certain statements on a seven-point Likert scale with one representing complete agreement, seven representing complete disagreement, and four representing the neutral point. The control group disagreed (4.32) with the statement that it should have reviewed more during the semester, while both the individual (3.33) and the random (3.24) groups agreed with the statement. The t-test indicates that the spread for this variable was significantly different between the control group and both review treatments (individual .10 and random .07). The difference between the two review treatment groups was not significant (.88). All three groups agreed with the statement that they crammed for the final exam. However, the control group's level of agreement was significantly higher than the individual group (.02) or the random group (.00). Once again there were no significant difference between the rankings of the two review treatment groups (.36).

CONCLUSION

The purpose of this study was to provide insight into cost/benefit considerations associated with certain test review strategies. The results supported the *a priori* expectation that student would be improved by the review treatments. More importantly, the study found no significant differences in student performance when the review treatment was randomized instead of individualized. These findings, when coupled with the results of the efforts and attitude measures that were examined in the study, have significant implications for accounting educators.

The review treatments increased student performance and held constant or reduced the student cost measures. Hence, the study indicates that from the students' perspective, the review treatments are a cost-effective learning strategy. Further, the findings suggest that the random review treatment is the more efficient strategy. Note that the performance measure was not affected by the more expensive individualization procedure. Finally, the attitude measure indicated that the subjects were not able to perceive the benefits of a continual review strategy unless they had experienced a test review treatment. These findings suggest that instructors should develop and employ a strategy that forces students to review throughout the duration of a course.

This study provides evidence that a testing policy that includes randomized review questions is a cost-effective means of improving student performance. In a broader sense, it suggests that future research should be more sensitive to the cost/benefit trade-offs that are essential to the acceptance of any new discovery. The benefit of improved performance must ultimately be restricted by the cost necessary to attain its accomplishment.

REFERENCES

Clayton, McLouis, *The Differential Effects of Three Types of Structured Reviews on the Learning and Retention of Mathematics,* Unpublished Ph.D. dissertation (North Carolina State University of Raleigh, 1973).

Faw, H.W. and T.G. Waller, "Mathemagenic Behaviors and Efficiency in Learning from Prose," *Review of Educational Research* (February 1976), pp. 691-720.

Ganster, D.C., H.W. Hennessey and F. Luthans, "Social Desirability Response Effects: Three Alternative Models," *Academy of Management Journal* (June 1983), pp. 321-331.

Nungester, R.J. and P.C. Duchastel, "Testing Versus Review: Effects on Retention," *Journal of Educational Psychology* (February 1982), pp. 18-22.

Pawliczek, R.B., "Modifications of Examinations: A Focus on Individual Weaknesses," *The Accounting Review* (October 1978), pp. 985-988.

Ray, A.A., ed, *SAS User's Guide: Statistics* (SAS Institute, 1982).

Ross, S.M. and F.J. Di Vesa, "Oral Summary as a Review Strategy for Enhancing Recall of Textual Material," *Journal of Educational Psychology* (December 1976), pp. 689-695.

SECTION IV

Test Anxiety

CORRELATE, CAUSES, EFFECTS AND TREATMENT OF TEST ANXIETY

Ray Hembree
Adrian College

> Results of 562 studies were integrated by meta-analysis to show the nature, effects, and treatment of academic test anxiety. Effect sizes were computed through the method invented by Glass (Glass, McGaw, & Smith, 1981). Correlations and effect-size groups were tested for consistency and significance with inferential statistics by Hedges and Olkin (1985). Test anxiety (TA) causes poor performance. It relates inversely to students' self-esteem and directly to their fears of negative evaluation, defensiveness, and other forms of anxiety. Conditions (causes) giving rise to differential TA levels include ability, gender, and school grade level. A variety of treatments are effective in reducing test anxiety. Contrary to prior perceptions, improved test performance and grade point average (GPA) consistently accompany TA reduction.

Last year (1987) the test anxiety construct observed its 35th birthday. Offspring of the omnibus phenomenon *anxiety*, the construct has matured within a huge cocoon of attention, tempting hundreds of researchers to explore its nature, reveal its effects, and develop a treatment. This attention has "intensified" over the years (Sarason, 1980, p. 3). The construct may seem remarkable less for its age than for its enduring fascination.

Its study began at Yale University. Based on their responses to a Test Anxiety Questionnaire (Sarason & Mandler, 1952), groups of students were categorized as high- or low-test-anxious. On subsequent intelligence tests, the low-anxious students outperformed their high-anxious peers in both the scores and their variability (Mandler & Sarason, 1952; Sarason, Mandler, & Craighill, 1952). As learning continued through successive trials of Block Design and Digit Symbol subtests, however, performance differences tended to disappear.

Mandler and Sarason (1952) interpreted the difference in performance on the basis of learned psychological drives. Two kinds were said to be evoked by the test situation. First are *task-directed drives*. These stimulate behaviors to reduce the drive by completing the task. Second are learned *anxiety drives*. These stimulate two opposite and incompatible behaviors: (a) task-relevant efforts to finish the task and thereby to reduce the anxiety and (b) self-directed, task-irrelevant responses, manifested by "feelings of inadequacy, helplessness, heightened somatic reaction, anticipations of punishment or loss of status and esteem, and implicit attempts to leave the testing situation" (Mandler & Sarason, p. 166). Persons with strong anxiety drives are prompted to enact the task-irrelevant behaviors that impair performance. Low-test-anxious persons, less burdened by self-centered tendencies, can attend more easily to task-directed behaviors that enhance achievement.

Reprinted by permission of the Review of Educational Research, Vol. 58, No. 1 (Spring 1988): 47-77.

Theorists after Mandler and Sarason built on their behavioral interpretation:
1. Proposing a bidimensional theory, Alpert and Haber (1960) labeled the drives that lead to task-directed and task-irrelevant behaviors as *facilitating* and *debilitating* anxieties, respectively. Mandler and Sarason (1952) had believed these constructs to be highly correlated; they devised their Test Anxiety Questionnaire (TAQ) with only a debilitating scale and inferred the presence of one anxiety from an absence of the other. Alpert and Haber suggested that the constructs may be independent, such that "persons may possess a large amount of both anxieties, or of one but not the other, or of none of either" (p. 213). They provided a self-report instrument, the Anxiety Achievement Test, equipped with facilitating (AAT+) and debilitating (AAT-) subscales.
2. From factor analyses of the TAQ, Liebert and Morris (1967) proposed that debilitating test anxiety (hereafter called "test anxiety" or "TA") is itself bidimensional, consisting of the components *worry* and *emotionality*. Worry is "any cognitive expression of concern about one's own performance" (p. 975). Emotionality refers to autonomic reactions to the test situation, for example, perspiration and accelerated heartbeat. Liebert and Morris composed two scales to measure these components. Their experiments suggested that worry interferes with performance, but emotionality and performance are not related except for persons low on the worry component (Morris & Liebert, 1969).
3. The work of Liebert and Morris shifted TA theory toward a cognitive orientation. Wine (1971) proposed an attentional theory to explain how Ta harms performance: Test-anxious persons divide their attention between task-relevant activities and preoccupations with worry, self-criticism, and somatic concerns. With less attention available for task-directed efforts, their performance is depressed.
4. Spielberger (1972) has distinguished between two aspects of anxiety. *A-State* is "a transitory emotional state" (p. 39) of tension and nervous reaction, whereas *A-Trait* is a chronic anxiety proneness characterized by A-State reactions in a wide range of stimulus situations. According to trait-state theory, TA is a form of trait anxiety (Spielberger, Anton, & Bedell, 1976). High-anxious persons respond to testing with elevations in A-State (or emotionality). Worry is then triggered by the A-State manifestations. These latter reactions also activate random error tendencies. Hence, emotionality and worry both contribute to depressed performance.
5. These theories all conceptualize an *interference* model of test anxiety, wherein TA disturbs the recall of prior learning and thus degrades performance. This model has been challenged by continuing reports

(e.g., Tyron, 1980) that treatment can effectively reduce test anxiety but better performance usually fails to accompany TA reduction. An alternative *deficits* model of TA has been proposed, wherein "the lower test scores obtained by test-anxious students are attributable to inadequate study habits, or to deficient test-taking skills" (Tobias, 1985, p. 185). In this model, TA does not cause poor performance; the reverse is true. Awareness of poor past performance causes test anxiety.

The conflicts within this discussion suggest that TA, despite its age, is a construct in search of identity. Is it a cognitive construct, or is it behavioral? Are AAT+ and AAT- independent dimensions or simple reflections? The TA/performance relationship is a fundamental concern, yet its causal direction has remained at issue. How could 35 years of research have failed to deliver more insight into the construct? Do potentials for insight exist, scattered and thus hidden in the massive body of evidence?

It seems to be time to unwrap the cocoon and discover what we know.

Problem Statement

The study's central purpose was descriptive and generic: to integrate the findings of the research on test anxiety, regarding its nature, effects, and treatment. Methods of meta-analysis were selected for this synthesis, to describe relationships and effects with scale-invariant metrics. Focus was supplied by the pursuit of a second objective: the use of results to reduce or resolve theoretical issues surrounding the construct.

Related Reviews

Early TA research was led by S. Sarason at Yale University and I. Sarason at the University of Washington. S. Sarason and his colleagues studied test anxiety in children. Their work (surveyed by Hill, 1972) found TA to appear at about second grade and then to increase grade by grade, with consistently higher levels for girls than for boys. Across the elementary years, the construct seemed increasingly related to poor performance, marks in school, and grade repetition. The strongest inverse relationships were found in stressful as opposed to gamelike test conditions. High-test-anxious (HTA) children functioned poorly when expected to achieve, but low-anxious children did well in this environment. Similar findings were reported at the college by I. Sarason (as reviewed by Spielberger, Anton, & Bedell, 1976). Under ego-involving instructions, HTA students declined in performance. "Under neutral or reassuring conditions high and low anxious subjects do not differ in their performance levels" (Sarason, 1961, p. 205).

Research of test anxiety burgeoned during the late 1960s, largely through a desire to treat its symptoms Tobias, (1979). Early interventions were behavioral in nature, stressing relaxation training and desensitization through counterconditioning or extinction. Allen (1972) summarized the findings of 12 studies. All the treatments appeared to reduce self-reported TA; five treatment groups improved their performance compared with untreated controls. By the 1980s, TA had become such a "target for therapy" that the range of treatments encompassed the "overall evolution" of anxiety reduction (Denney, 1980, p. 209). Allen, Elias, and Zlotlow (1980) reviewed 49 treatment studies of college students. Most treatments produced significant TA reductions; however, only 18% of the treated groups showed significant performance improvement. Tyron's (1980) review of 85 studies supported these findings. She suggested that desensitization and other behavioral techniques attend to the emotional rather than the cognitive (worry) aspect of test anxiety, so improved performance through these methods should not be expected. Cognitive modification or study counseling combined with desensitization seemed more likely to reduce TA and raise performance.

None of these reviews employed an exhaustive collection of studies. All focused on selected aspects rather than a comprehensive view of test anxiety. There seemed to be a consensus that a relationship between the construct and performance has been established. However, a causal direction has not been defined. The reviewers also agreed that most interventions are effective in TA reduction, but without assurance of performance improvement. No review used quantitative methods beyond vote-counting, so sizes of treatment effects could not be compared.

Research Questions

The present study was designed to provide a statistical synthesis of the research on test anxiety. Regarding its nature, effects, and treatment, four tasks were defined to identify (a) variables that correlate with test anxiety, (b) variables that exhibit differential levels of test anxiety, (c) variables affected by test anxiety, and (d) variables affected by *treating* test anxiety. Within each task, a question regarding each variable was developed, for example:

1. What is the correlation between TA and self-esteem?
2. What is the difference between females and males in TA level?
3. What is the effect of TA on performance?
4. What is the effect of treatment on TA level?

All these questions were treated by inferential statistics. Implicit in each question were inquiries into relationships between the *outcomes* of studies and *properties* the changed across the studies, such as school grade level, kinds of tests, and lengths of treatment.

These previous questions addressed the study's first purpose. The following questions relate to the issues discussed in the opening section.

1. Is the nature of test anxiety cognitive or behavioral?
2. What kinship exists between AAT+ and AAT-?
3. In the relationship between TA and test performance, what is the direction of causality?
4. Which model of test anxiety, interference or deficits, does the evidence support?

Method
Collecting the Studies

The identification of studies to be used in the meta-analysis began with computer searches of the data bases for *Psychological Abstracts, Dissertation Abstracts International,* and the Educational Resources Information Center (ERIC). This initial list of references was extended by two bibliographies in ERIC documentation (Ribordy & Billingham, 1980; Wildemuth, 1977). Additional studies were found by manually searching the data bases, soliciting studies directly from authors, and tracking citations from study to study. All candidate reports were screened against the following criteria for acceptance:

1. The research concerned *academic* test anxiety, using English-speaking subjects in mainstream education.
2. The report provided product-moment correlation coefficients and their sample sizes or, in the case of experiments, sufficient data for effect-size calculations.
3. Test anxiety was measured by a validated instrument specific to the construct.
4. TA treatments used at least two groups, including a control.
5. Each experimental group contained at least 10 subjects (for rigor in the meta-analytic tests of homogeneity). This requirement was extended to permit sample sizes of nine or eight subjects, so long as these smaller samples affected just a small fraction of any effect-size group to be analyzed.

The screening delivered a body of 562 studies: 369 journal articles (which included summaries of 67 doctoral dissertations and 18 master's theses), 22 ERIC documents, 4 monographs, 16 reports in research anthologies, 2 master's theses, 148 doctoral dissertations, and 1 unpublished report. A bibliography is present in ERIC documentation (Hembree, 1987). (Specific study titles that relate to the data analysis are available from the author.)

Distribution of these studies in each decade from the 1950s to date is as follows:

	1950-1959	1960-1969	1970-1979	1980-1986
Number of studies	30	150	271	111

An additional 149 studies could not meet the screening criteria--109 with insufficient data, 25 with sample sizes smaller than eight, 13 without control groups, and 2 with unvalidated instruments.

Overview of the Data

Some studies dealt with more than one grade, so the total exceeds 562. The studies produced 944.

Shown below is the number of studies involved with each grade level K through 12 and postsecondary.

Grade Level	Number of Studies
1	9
2	21
3	31
4	63
5	73
6	73
7	35
8	30
9	23
10	24
11	27
12	26
Undergraduate	360
Graduate	12

correlations and 1,558 effect sizes, with 351 effects related to causes, 465 to effects of test anxiety, and 742 to effects of treating test anxiety. Treatments ranged in length from 1 to 12 hours, with a median value of 6. Research design ratings from 1.4 to 2.7, with a median value of 2.0.

Correlational Findings

The first task of the study set out to identify possible correlates of test anxiety and to answer the question, What is the extent of each correlation?

Tables 1-6 present the findings. The data regarding each correlate are summarized by (a) providing the number of correlations along with the total number n of students involved, values of outliers (if any), smallest and largest values of r (excluding outliers), and the grades involved, (b) providing the group mean as *the correlation* that, in the presence of homogeneity, describes the relationship, and (c) indicating whether or not the mean was significantly different from zero.

TABLE 1 Mean correlations of test anxiety and performance

Correlate of TA	Number of studies	n	Outliers	End values	Grade levels	Mean *p < .01
IQ by grades						
1, 2	5	992	None	-0.20/0.05	1,2	-0.10*
3-P	61	8,438	None	-0.52/-0.08	3-P	-.023*
Aptitude/achievement by grades						
2	2	346	None	-0.07/-0.04	2	-0.06
4-P	44	6,390	None	-0.55/-0.03	4-6,8-12,P	-0.29*
Aptitude/achievement by subject						
Reading & English						
Grade 2	5	1,231	None	-0.19/-0.03	2	-0.15*
Grades 3-P	46	10,761	None	-0.65/0.06	3-P	-0.24*
Mathematics						
Grade 2	2	346	None	-0.07/-0.02	2	-0.05
Grades 4-P	46	6,534	None	-0.44/0	4-P	-0.22*
Natural sciences	10	1,831	-0.61	-0.39/-0.02	5-8,P	-0.21*
Social sciences	9	1,637	None	-0.53/-0.16	5,6,P	-0.25*
Foreign language	4	1,110	None	-0.14/-0.02	P	-0.12*
Mechanical knowledge	7	1,695	None	-0.27/-0.03	10,P	-0.12*
Psychology	22	2,017	-0.65	-0.53/-0.05	P	-0.23*
Electives	4	1,114	None	-0.14/-0.01	P	-0.07
Other performance						
Problem solving	7	1,225	None	-0.39/-0.12	5,6,P	-0.20*
Memory task	4	172	None	-0.44/-0.16	P	-0.28*
Course grade	14	1,664	None	-0.38/0.12	6,9,12,P	-0.15*
GPA						
High school	8	1,164	None	-0.26/-0.01	9-12	-0.12*
College						
TAQ	9	1,499	None	-0.37/-0.01	P	-0.12*
AAT-	9	1,423	None	-0.39/-0.25	P	-0.29*
Worry component						
Aptitude/achievement	13	1,112	None	-0.41/-0.25	9-12,P	-0.31*
Course grade	3	272	None	-0.34/-0.08	12,P	-0.26*
Emotionality						
Aptitude/achievement	13	1,112	None	-0.28/-0.01	9-12,P	-0.15*
Course grade	3	272	None	-0.33/-0.01	12,P	-0.19*

Performance correlates. Table 1 presents the mean correlations between performance measures and test anxiety. These measures include IQ, aptitude, and achievement tests, problem-solving and memory tasks, course grades, and cumulative GPA.

Sixty-six correlations had examined the relationship between IQ and TA. For grades 1 and 2 combined, the mean was -0.10 of marginal significance. Grades 3-P (postsecondary) showed consistent correlation at a level of -0.23. These findings suggest that higher TA associates with lower intelligence. However, it needs to be reclassed that IQ scores are gathered by testing; these IQ measures were possibly confounded by test anxiety.

Correlations between TA and scores of aptitude and achievement measures were consistent for the two styles of tests, and so their values were combined. THe mean results were nonsignificant for grade 2 and significant for grades 4-P. These measures were studies further with respect to subject matter. All relationships were inverse. The largest correlations regarded reading and English, mathematics, natural and social sciences, and psychology. No relationship was found between TA and performance in elective courses.

Results of problem-solving tasks (e.g., solution of anagrams) and tasks involving the immediate recall of memorized materials showed negative relationships with TA at levels consistent with the correlations for test performance. Measures of course grades and GPA were also related inversely to test anxiety. Different levels were observed for college GPA as measured by the Test Anxiety Questionnaire (TAQ) and the debilitating subscale of the Anxiety Achievement Test (AAT-).

In addition to the correlates of debilitating test anxiety, Table 1 shows performance correlates of its worry and emotionality components. Their relationships with test scores and course grades were inverse and significant, more strongly for worry than emotionality.

Personal/personality correlates. Table 2 presents relationships between TA and measures of student characteristics, including performance-related attitudes and skills, thinking styles, self-concept variables, socioeconomic status (SES), defensiveness (a tendency to deny one's anxiety), and psychological attitudes and needs.

A group of 31 correlations had examined the relationship between need for achievement and test anxiety. The group was heterogeneous; a relationship was found between grade level and the correlations. In the elementary grades, the relationship was inverse, suggesting that high-test-anxious (HTA) students had lower needs to achieve. The relationship shifted in sign for high school students and became nonsignificant for college students. No relationship was found between TA and students' levels of aspiration. HTA students displayed strong fears of negative evaluation and negative feelings toward tests. Their study skills appeared attenuated. An outcome regarding fear of failure could not be determined; these correlations stayed heterogeneous.

No significant relationships were found between TA and creative (divergent) thinking or level of curiosity. A strong inverse relationship appeared between self-esteem and test anxiety. HTA students were inclined to an external locus of control and were prone to feel unprotected. A small relationship existed between SES and test anxiety. Ta and defensiveness were strongly related, with boys a little less inclined than girls to admit their

TABLE 2 Mean correlations of test anxiety and personal/personality variables

Correlate of TA	Number of studies	n	Outliers	End values	Grade levels	Mean[a] *p < .01
Performance-related						
Need for achievement						
Elementary grades	5	629	-0.60	-0.27/-0.09	4-8	-0.16*
High school	7	1,154	None	0.10/0.44	10-12	0.26*
College	19	1,744	None	-0.43/0.23	P	0.03
Level of aspiration	8	431	-0.62	-0.18/0.15	4,8,P	-0.05
Fear of negative eval	4	229	None	0.35/0.65	5,6,P	0.54*
Fear of failure	7	222	None	-0.38/0.66	P	(0.07)
Feelings about tests						
Positive	6	950	None	-0.36/-0.07	3,5,6,P	-0.18*
Negative	5	878	None	0.20/0.48	5,6,P	0.33*
Study skills	4	399	None	-0.40/-0.22	9-12,P	-0.27*
Thinking styles						
Divergent thinking	6	525	None	-0.34/0.12	6,9-12,P	-0.07
Curiosity	3	206	None	-0.11/-0.03	9-12,P	-0.07
Self-concept						
Self-esteem	36	8,839	-0.08	-0.71/-0.29	4-12	-0.42*
Locus of control	16	2,222	None	-0.16/0.36	5,9-12,P	0.22*
Lack of protection	6	829	None	0.30/0.47	10,12,P	0.37*
Socioeconomic status	8	826	None	-0.20/0.10	4-7,10,11	-0.13*
Defensiveness						
Girls	17	1,748	None	-0.73/-0.32	1,3-6,8	-0.49*
Boys	16	1,557	None	-0.65/-0.28	1,3-6,8	-0.41*
Personality						
Needs						
Dominance	10	1,531	None	-0.28/-0.10	6,9,12,P	-0.19*
Nuturance	3	361	None	-0.11/0.16	6,9,12,P	0.04
Exhibition	3	361	None	-0.28/0.17	6,9,12,P	-0.07
Teacher dependency	5	557	None	-0.25/-0.02	4,7,10,12,P	-0.16*
Blame assignment						
On others	4	199	None	0.23/0.36	5,6,P	0.28*
On self	4	199	None	-0.21/0.58	5,6,P	(0.16)
Sociability						
Grades 1-12	10	1,046	None	-0.11/0.26	4-7,9	0.06
Undergraduate	6	627	None	-0.35/-0.19	P	-0.26*

[a]Entries in parentheses are mean effects for heterogeneous data.

TABLE 3 Profile of 627 test-anxious college students (based on subscales of the California Psychological Inventory)

Correlate of TA	End values	Mean
Sense of well-being	-0.53/-0.22	-0.33*
Self-acceptance	-0.30/-0.10	-0.19*
Self-control	-0.41/-0.19	-0.24*
Responsibility	-0.32/-0.18	-0.22*
Capacity for status	-0.35/-0.21	-0.26*
Tolerance	-0.52/-0.30	-0.39*
Flexibility	-0.15/-0.02	-0.08
Intellectual efficiency	-0.51/-0.29	-0.38*

Note. No outliers were found.
*p < .01.

anxiety. HTA students seemed less dependent on teacher behavior than LTA students. They tended to blame others for failure. Their needs for dominance and TA were inversely related; needs for nuturance and exhibition did not correlate significantly with the TA construct. In early grades, the HTA students seemed as sociable as less anxious students. This tendency declined, however, until HTA students in college seemed significantly less sociable than their LTA peers. As shown in Table 3, test-anxious college students possesseda lower sense of well-being, less self-acceptance, less self-control, less acceptance of responsibility, lower capacity for status, less tolerance, and lower intellectual efficiency that LTA students.

Teacher-related correlates. Table 4 presents relationships between TA and variables regarding teachers. The first mean correlation relates teacher ratings of test anxiety with the students' self-reports. Later evidence will show that TA levels tend to be low among children in the early grades, so teachers

TABLE 4 Mean correlations of test anxiety and teacher variables

Correlate of TA	Number of studies	n	End values	Grade levels	Mean[a] *p < .01
Ratings of student TA					
Lower grades	4	1,148	0.09/0.31	2,3	0.14*
Intermediate grades	6	1,951	0.18/0.34	4-6	0.29*
Teacher manifest anxiety	10	234	0.47/0.75	3	0.64*
Perception of teacher					
Negative/unfriendly	10	1,073	0.04/0.32	4-7,9	0.16*
Positive/supportive	10	1,073	-0.17/0.20	4-7,9	-0.03

Note. No outliers were found.

were better able to judge TA at intermediate grades, where the levels where higher. The extent of teachers' anxiety (as measured by the Taylor Manifest Anxiety Scale) correlated strongly with students' TA. Perceptions of the teacher as negative and unfriendly were moderately related to the construct, but perceptions of the teachers as positive and friendly showed not significant relationship to test anxiety.

Correlations among anxieties. Table 5 presents the results of relating TA and other anxieties. The construct related directly and strongly to general anxiety proneness, more in grades 1-12 than in college. Similar large correlations were found between TA, A-State (transitory) anxiety, and A-Trait (chronic) anxiety. TA was significantly related to its worry and emotionality components, and the components themselves were strongly related in both the state and trait senses. Results from the debilitating (AAT-) and facilitating (AAT+) subscales of the Anxiety Achievement Test correlated at a significant level of -0.49.

Correlations of AAT+. Table 6 identifies correlates of AAT+, a construct much less studied than its debilitating counterpart. Higher levels of AAT+ related to better IQ, aptitude, and achievement tests scores and to higher GPA. No relationships were found between AAT+ and need for achievement or locus of control. AAT+ and general anxiety were inversely related at a modest level.

TABLE 5 Mean correlations of test anxiety and other anxiety measures

Correlate of TA	Number of studies	n	Outliers	End values	Grade levels	Mean *p < .01
General anxiety						
Grades 1-12	57	7,271	None	0.23/0.78	1-12	0.56*
College	20	3,586	1.07	0.31/0.64	P	0.48*
A-Trait	10	961	0.27	0.42/0.75	P	0.53*
A-State	8	790	None	0.29/0.59	4,P	0.45*
Worry	8	708	None	0.32/0.67	P	0.57*
Emotionality	8	544	None	0.35/0.72	P	0.54*
Worry vs. emotionality (state)	13	1,206	None	0.55/0.76	12,P	0.67*
Worry vs. emotionality (trait)	7	1,237	None	0.70/0.80	9-12,P	0.78*
AAT- vs. AAT+	20	2,322	None	-0.77/-0.30	9-12,P	-0.49*

TABLE 6 Mean correlations regarding facilitating test anxiety

Correlate of AAT+	Number of studies	n	Outliers	End values	Grade levels	Mean $p < .01$
Test performance						
IQ	3	315	None	0.28/0.47	P	0.30*
Aptitude/ achievement	23	2,624	0.09	0.12/0.56	9-12,P	0.29*
GPA	9	1,664	None	0.17/0.58	P	0.32*
Need for achievement	3	327	None	0.03/0.26	P	0.14
Locus of control	5	879	0.82	-0.01/0.15	10-12,P	0.05
General anxiety	4	993	None	-0.40/-0.17	P	-0.26*

Findings Related to Causes

The second task of the study set out to identify causes and sources of test anxiety (variables that exhibit differential levels of the construct) and to answer the question, What is the difference in TA level between two elements of a cause? By Equation 1, each difference was converted to an effect size (e.g., to compare the TA levels of females and males). The effect-size group accrued for each cause was analyzed through the procedures given before.

Tables 7 and 8 present the findings, where a positive mean effect assigns a higher TA level to the first component of a comparison. A negative mean accuses the second component of higher TA.

Causes of debilitating test anxiety. Table 7 presents the mean effects for causes and sources of debilitating test anxiety, including ability level, sex, school grade level, ethnicity, birth order, and the school environment.

Ability level. A group of 10 effects compared the TA levels for students of high, average, and low abilities or aptitudes. The subset comparing high and average abilities displayed a significant mean effect of -0.49. For low and average abilities, the subset showed a mean effect of 0.52. Hence, TA was greater for average students than those with high ability and, with nearly the same proportion, greater for low than for average-ability students.

Sex. Females consistently showed higher levels of test anxiety than males. A small sex difference appeared in the early school years, increased to a peak in grades 5-10, and declined through upper high school and college. In studies where the TA scores of highly defensive students were removed, the female-to-male comparisons still displayed a significant mean of 0.40. Thus, the TA gender difference seemed to be a true effect.

Adjacent grades. A group of 78 effects examined TA differences between adjacent grades from 2 through 12. After increasing in the early grades, TA appeared to stabilize near grade 5, remain essentially constant through high school, and show a small decline in college. It should be noted that the

TABLE 7 Mean effects for causes of test anxiety

Causes and comparisons	Number of studies	n	Outliers	End values	Grade levels	Mean[a] *p < .01
Ability level						
High vs. average	7	625	None	-0.59/-0.17	7-9,P	-0.49*
Low vs. average	3	339	None	0.34/0.62	9,P	0.52*
Sex (female vs. male)						
Grades 1,2	5	7,758	None	0.40/0.34	1,2	0.14*
Grades 3,4	26	2,643	None	-0.58/0.85	3,4	0.28*
Grades 5-10	73	13,244	None	0.17/1.10	5-10	0.43*
Grades 11,12,P	39	10,615	None	-0.02/1.07	11,12,P	0.27*
Low-defensives	11	2,119	None	-0.02/0.57	1-4,7-12	0.40*
Adjacent grades						
2-3, 3-4	8	949	None	-0.64/0.10	2-4	-0.24*
4-5	5	1,397	None	-0.40/0.26	4,5	-0.11
5-6 through 11-12	65	15,192	-0.61	-0.41/0.66	5-12	0.08*
Ethnicity						
Black vs. white						
Grades 2-4	4	7,539	None	0.38/0.60	2-4	0.52*
Grades 5-8	8	1,446	None	-0.25/0.62	5-8	0.21*
Grades 9-12	4	2,570	None	-0.51/0.16	9-12	0.02
Hispanic vs. white	5	2,894	None	0.05/0.68	4-12	0.36*
Birth order						
Only child vs. first	4	280	None	-0.31/0.06	10-12,P	-0.11
Later-born vs. first	9	687	None	-0.14/0.80	10-12,P	0.22*
Instrument-related						
Prior measure vs. none	8	304	None	-0.92/0.48	3,6	0.03
TA-GA vs. GA-TA[b]	8	160	None	-0.97/0.20	3-6	-0.17
Stranger vs. teacher	4	320	None	-0.37/0.06	6	-0.17
School environment						
New vs. old building	16	2,410	None	-0.49/0.40	6,7,9,10	-0.01
Sex grouping						
Boys vs. coed	4	154	None	-0.92/0.24	7,8	-0.26
Girls vs. coed	4	154	None	-0.82/0.91	7,8	(0.02)
At-risk vs. passing	3	209	None	0.33/0.60	7,P	0.51*
Test conditions						
Low vs. high stress	8	442	None	-1.00/-0.08	P	-0.27*
Hard test vs. easy	3	590	None	0.31/0.68	4,6,9,P	0.35*
IBI[c] feedback of answers vs. none	4	239	None	-0.93/-0.21	3,P	-0.64*
Item arrangements vs. easy-to-hard	6	334	None	-0.22/0.84	P	0.25
Matching vs. MC	3	393	None	0.47/0.80	11,12	-0.58*

[a] Entries in parentheses are mean effects for heterogeneous data.
[b] GA = general anxiety. [c] IBI = item-by-item

tendency toward lower TA scores in college may reflect attrition more than developmental trends.

Ethnicity. In the early grades, black students displayed significantly higher TA levels than white students. This difference declined to marginal significance in grades 5-8, and by high school the levels for black and white students were essentially equivalent. A significant effect of 0.36 was observed for TA differences between Hispanic and white students across grade levels.

Birth order. Comparisons of TA levels for only children versus firstborns showed a nonsignificant effect. However, the mean effect comparing later-borns and firstborns was significant at 0.22, so later-borns were somewhat more prone to higher TA.

Instrument-related effects. Eight items compared the *present* TA levels of students who had received the TASC 1 year previously with students receiving TA measurement for the first time. No significant difference was observed. On occasion, TA and general anxiety (GA) have been measured one after the other, potentially creating confounded results because of a position (order-of-administration) effect. Eight items compared the test anxiety measured before general anxiety (TA-GA) with TA levels measured afterward (GA-TA). The mean position effect was not significant. No TA differences were found when a stranger instead of the teacher administered the instrument.

School environment. TA levels were compared when students were housed (because of promotion or transfer) in a new instead of a familiar building and when students attended classes that were segregated by sex instead of being coeducational. Neither condition appeared to affect test anxiety. Comparisons of students by status, whether at risk or passing, showed a significant effect of 0.51, so at-risk students possessed higher levels of test anxiety. Two conditions of testing seemed related to high TA levels: ego-involving high-stress versus non-evaluative low-stress conditions and test perceived as difficult rather than easy. Conditions that related to low TA levels included (a) item-by-item (IBI) feedback of correct answers during the test and (b) a matching test format as compared with multiple choice. Test item arrangement with respect to difficulty (e.g., easy to hard) showed no significant effects on TA levels.

Causes of worry, emotionality, and AAT+. Table 8 gives mean effects for causes of worry, emotionality, and facilitating test anxiety. Sex differences continued to appear, with females scoring higher than males on both TA components. Males scored higher than females on AAT+. The presence of music during tests exerted no apparent effect on either worry or emotionality.

TABLE 8 Mean effects for causes of worry, emotionality, and AAT+.

Causes and comparisons	Number of studies	n	End values	Grade levels	Mean *p < .01
Worry component					
Sex (female vs. male)	6	2,225	-0.21/0.41	3-8, P	0.24*
Presence of music					
Sedative vs. none	3	84	-0.19/0.26	P	0.05
Lively vs. none	3	84	-0.06/0.78	P	0.44
Emotionality					
Sex (female vs. male)	6	2,222	-0.20/0.60	3-8, P	0.34*
Presence of music					
Sedative vs. none	3	84	-0.13/0.24	P	0.05
Lively vs. none	3	84	0.12/0.65	P	0.42
Facilitating (AAT+)					
Sex (female vs. male)	13	3,185	-0.45/0.14	9-12, P	-0.21*

Note. No outliers were found.

Findings on Effects of Test Anxiety

The study's third task set out to identify variables possibly affected by TA and to calculate the extent of those effects. Each effect was measured by Equation 1, where the resulting statistic compared the scores of a variable determined at two TA levels, for example, performance scores for HTA versus LTA students. Where scores of a middle-test-anxious (MTA) group were also provided, comparisons were drawn between MTA and LTA subjects. Typically, the high- and low-test-anxious groups were formed as upper and lower thirds or fourths of the TA distribution. All groups were determined before obtaining scores on any measure, so the data were collected ex post facto. Comparisons thus represented *implicit* effects. No cause could be ascribed to test anxiety.

Effects between TA levels. Table 9 presents mean effects of test anxiety with regard to test performance and performance-related variables. Entries that bear no special notation are HTA-versus-LTA comparisons. Effects involving MTA students are cited accordingly.

Performance data. Seventy-three comparisons were made between the scores of HTA and LTA students on IQ, aptitude, and achievement tests. The group was homogeneous with a significant mean of -0.48. (An effect size represents the number of pooled standard deviations between the scores of the two groups being compared. For example, with an s of 12 for average scores on a 100-point scale, the effect size of -0.48 depicts an advantage of about 6 points for LTA over HTA students.) No sex differences in performance were observed. Sixteen effects for MTA versus LTA students

TABLE 9 Mean effects of test anxiety between TA levels

Related variable	Number of studies	n	Outliers	End values	Grade levels	Mean[a] p < .01
Test performance						
IQ/aptitude/ achievement	73	6,316	-1.85	-1.19/0.11	1-12, P	-0.48*
(MTA)[b]	16	1,709	None	-0.58/-0.04	4-6,8,9,11,P	-0.34*
GPA	4	226	None	-0.61/-0.30	P	-0.46*
GPA (MTA)	4	303	None	-0.65/0.41	P	-0.27
Problem solving	14	780	None	-1.01/-0.19	2-9, P	-0.45*
Free recall	13	1,021	-1.98	-0.74/-0.05	2,4,10-12,P	-0.40*
Time to do test	13	924	None	-0.26/0.88	4,6,9,P	0.30*
Performance by ability						
High ability	10	466	None	-0.69/-0.02	2,3,5,6,10	-0.19
Low ability	10	456	None	-0.78/0.07	2,3,5,6,10	-0.32*
Performance by test difficulty						
Perceived as hard	13	874	None	-1.51/-0.10	4,6,10,P	-0.45*
Perceived as easy	12	849	-1.34	-0.75/0.64	4,6,10,P	-0.07
Performance-related						
Encoding difficulty	3	264	None	0.64/1.54	2,4,6,P	0.74*
Cognitive interference	11	872	None	0.24/1.42	2,4-6,P	0.88*
Study hrs/week	3	216	None	0.41/0.68	P	0.53*
Success expectation	7	491	None	-0.64/-0.42	P	-0.53*
Good study habits	3	220	None	-2.10/-0.05	P	(-0.90)
A-State during test	11	873	None	0.50/1.52	P	0.81*
Attitudes						
Positive	6	672	None	-1.16/0	3,5,6,P	-0.57*
Positive (MTA)	3	538	None	-0.36/-0.16	5,6,P	-0.26*
Negative	8	760	2.24	0.52/2.03	3,5,6,P	0.93*
Negative (MTA)	3	538	None	0.51/0.74	5,6,P	0.63*

[a] Entries in parentheses are mean effects for heterogeneous data.
[b] MTA = middle-test-anxious

showed a significant mean of -0.34, so the MTA students scored between their HTA and LTA associates. Similar results among the TA levels were observed for GPA comparisons. In problem solving and in tests of free (uncued) recall of memorized material, the LTA students consistently scored higher. The mean time spent in working tests was significantly longer for HTA students.

The foregoing test performance effect of -0.48 was derived for students of all abilities, so this effect may be said to apply for "average" students. Two groups each of 10 effects compared the performance of HTA and LTA students separated into high- and low-ability subsets. For high-ability students, the mean effect was nonsignificant at -0.19; however, all 10 effects were negative in sign, so the students were not immune to test anxiety. Low-ability students displayed a significant mean effect of -0.32. Thus, among the ability levels, the performance of average students seemed to be the most depressed with respect to test anxiety. Performance was also seen to vary with the students' perception of test difficulty. Where tests were believed to be difficult, LTA students possessed the advantage, but where tests were thought to be easy, there was not significant difference between the scores of HTA and LTA students.

Performance-related variables. HTA subjects experienced more encoding difficulty and more cognitive interference than LTA students. The high-test-anxious students spent more time in study, but their expectation of success remained lower, and their state anxiety during tests was higher than that of LTA students. Effects comparing the effectiveness of study habits stayed heterogeneous.

Attitudes. HTA students were significantly less positive and more negative toward themselves and toward evaluation than MTA and LTA students.

Effects within TA levels. In a number of experiments, TA and performance had been examined with another condition present that could moderate performance. For these experiments, effects were determined *within* the TA levels, using variations of the moderator to establish the comparison. Table 10 gives the findings.

Test instructions. Effects were computed within TA levels for IQ/aptitude/achievement scores derived under ego-involving conditions versus neutral or low-stress test instructions. HTA students did not seem affected by test instructions in elementary and high schools, but the HTA students in college scored best *without* ego-involvement. No effect of instructions was found for MTA students. LTA subjects at all grade levels appeared to fare better *with* ego-involvement; however, the effects in elementary school stayed heterogeneous.

Incentives. Subjects at all TA levels found a small but significant benefit from the presence of performance incentives, for example, praise, reproof, or external reward. Effects of these incentives did not differ from each other or with respect to TA level.

Feedback of results. The effects of providing item-by-item feedback of correct answers during tests or of feeding back correct results during programmed instruction were not significant.

Item difficulty sequence. The effects of arranging test items with respect to difficulty (hard-to-easy or randomly as opposed to easy-to-hard) were not significant for HTA students. For LTA students, the effect was significant and negative; their scores were higher with the easy-to-hard arrangement.

Frequency of testing. HTA students appeared better served by frequent testing, but the mean effect (0.36) was not significant. Adjusting the frequency of tests did not affect the LTA subjects.

TABLE 10 Mean effects of moderating variables on performance within TA levels

Comparisons	Number of studies	n	Outliers	End values	Grade levels	Mean[a] p < .01
Test instructions, high vs. low stress						
HTA[b]						
Precollege	16	1,120	-1.43	-0.77/0.33	4-6,8,10-12	-0.05
College	17	640	None	-1.04/0.52	P	-0.26*
MTA	5	440	None	-0.22/0.18	5,6,P	-0.04
LTA						
Elementary	12	980	None	-0.54/1.11	4-6,8	(0.32)
After elementary	22	974	None	-0.35/1.11	10-12,P	0.29
Incentives vs. none						
HTA	21	866	None	-0.11/0.92	2,4-7,P	0.26*
MTA	7	246	None	-0.08/0.78	5,6,P	0.24
LTA	21	855	None	-0.49/1.27	2,4-7,P	0.21*
IBI[c] feedback of answers vs. none						
HTA	10	489	None	-0.18/1.04	5,6,P	0.13
LTA	10	515	None	-0.73/0.90	5,6,P	-0.10
Item arrangements vs. easy-to-hard						
HTA	11	534	None	-0.32/0.84	4-6,P	0.16
LTA	11	549	None	-0.94/0.92	4-6,P	-0.23*
Test frequency more vs. less						
HTA	3	112	None	0.27/0.49	P	0.36
LTA	3	98	None	-0.08/0.14	P	0.06
Memory support vs. none						
HTA	3	148	None	0.80/1.54	5,6	0.90*
LTA	3	148	None	-0.07/0.59	5,6	0.42
Distraction, high vs. normal						
HTA	3	79	None	-2.08/-0.52	6	-0.87*
LTA	3	106	None	-0.70/-0.29	6	-0.48
Music vs. none						
HTA	3	229	None	0.84/1.14	10-12,P	0.97*
LTA	3	231	None	-0.50/-0.10	10-12,P	-0.39*
Observers vs. none						
Motor task						
HTA	14	280	None	-2.80/-0.85	2-5	-1.84*
LTA	14	280	None	1.25/2.18	2-5	1.46*
Classroom test						
HTA	5	114	None	-0.66/0.18	4,P	-0.30
LTA	5	114	None	-0.32/0.22	4,P	0.01

[a] Entries in parentheses are mean effects for heterogeneous data.
[b] HTA, MTA, LTA = high-, middle-, low-test anxious.
[c] IBI = item-by-item

Memory support. In three experiments, cues were provided (or not provided) to trigger recall of information helpful in solving a problem. Memory support appeared to benefit performance, especially for the HTA subjects.

Presence of distractions. Test scores were gathered under high versus normal levels of auditory and visual activity. HTA subjects seemed significantly more distractible than LTA students; their performance was accordingly depressed.

Presence of music. The scores of HTA subjects were significantly enhanced by the presence of unobtrusive classical music during the test. In contrast, the scores of LTA students were depressed in the presence of music.

Presence of observers. Parents, teachers, peers, adult strangers, or known adults looked on while elementary school boys performed a repetitive motor task (marble-dropping). Severely degraded results were obtained by HTA boys, but observers enhanced the performance of LTA boys. (No similar experiments had been performed with female students.) Effects of being observed during IQ and achievement tests were not significant for either gender within TA levels.

Findings From Test Anxiety Treatments

The final task of the study set out to determine effects of treating test anxiety. One hundred thirty-seven studies were examined--28 with placebotreatments, 55 with waiting-list control groups (promised treatment at a laterdate), 69 with minimal-contact controls, and 15 with both a placebo and a second control group. According to Equation 1, effect sizes were computed to compare the posttreatment scores of treated versus untreated HTA subjects. These data were partitioned on two dimensions: posttreatment measures (e.g., TA level or test performance) and type of treatment. *Behavioral* treatments attended to the emotionality component of test anxiety. *Cognitive* treatments attended to worry, and *cognitive-behavioral* treatments attended to worry but also provided elements to reduce emotionality. *Study skills* included study training by itself or training combined with other forms of treatment. *Testwiseness training* furthered academic test-taking skills. Placebo treatments were *pseudotherapy*, whose outcomes were compared with untreated controls. The group of effects for each posttreatment measure and treatment style was analyzed through the procedures given before. Tables 11-14 give the findings. A positive mean effect implies the treated group scored higher, whereas a negative mean shows favor to the control group.

Effects on test anxiety. Table 11 displays the mean effects of treatment on TA, worry, emotionality, and facilitating test anxiety.

TA. Behavioral treatments included systematic desensitization (or SD, the most common treatment), relaxation training, modeling, covert positive

TABLE 11   Mean effects of treatment on test anxiety level

Result by treatment	Number of studies	n	Outliers	End values	Grade levels	Mean *p < .01
Behavioral treatment						
Systematic desensitization						
Precollege	13	870	None	-1.39/0.07	5-12	-0.54*
College						
Taped individual	8	227	None	-1.56/-0.15	P	-0.59*
Other styles	58	1,623	None	-2.47/-0.22	P	-1.08*
Relaxation training	32	953	None	-1.89/-0.18	7-12,P	-0.68*
Other behavioral	14	384	-2.73	-1.94/-0.48	P	-1.10*
Cognitive treatment						
Group counseling	6	165	None	-0.91/-0.09	7,8,P	-0.34
Cognitive-behavioral						
Precollege	5	486	None	-0.64/-0.21	2,3,5,8-12	-0.53*
College	43	1,311	None	-1.63/-0.42	P	-0.87*
Study skills (SS)						
Study skills training	6	163	None	-0.46/0.27	P	-0.14
SS & behavioral	9	287	None	-1.78/-0.24	10-12,P	-1.22*
SS & cognitive-behavioral	5	139	None	-1.48/0.29	9-12,P	-0.83*
Testwiseness (TW)						
TW training	6	350	None	-0.88/-0.11	5,6,8-12,P	-0.55*
TW & SS training	3	72	None	-0.71/-0.29	P	-0.52
Pseudotherapy	18	611	None	-1.17/0.65	5,6,10-12,P	-0.18
Worry component						
Behavioral	20	533	None	-1.95/0.05	P	-0.65*
Cognitive-behavioral	16	483	None	-1.54/-0.12	P	-0.82*
Emotionality						
Behavioral	18	513	None	-1.65/0	P	-0.60*
Cognitive-behavioral	18	524	None	-1.64/0.10	P	-0.73*
Facilitating (AAT+)						
Behavioral	23	746	-1.41	-0.31/1.10	9-12,P	0.35*
Cognitive-behavioral	17	598	None	-0.66/1.52	P	0.45*
SS & cognitive-behavioral	4	82	None	-0.04/0.78	P	0.40
Pseudotherapy	3	89	None	-0.37/0.36	P	0.00

reinforcement, extinction, and hypnosis. SD programs were administered in a broad assortment of conditions: group or individual treatment, direct-contact therapy or a use of audio/video tapes, direct or vicarious participation by the subjects, and accelerated treatment versus a leisurely spread of treatment sessions. The TA scores of elementary and high school students treated by SD were significantly lower (mean effect of -0.54) than the scores of untreated students. Similar results were found for college students treated individually by taped procedures. However, college students in other program arrangements seemed to profit the most from SD treatment (mean effect of -1.08). The next most common behavioral treatment was relaxation training, whose variations included cue-controlled relaxation (using a psychological trigger to induce relaxation) and training augmented with biofeedback. The 32 relaxation effects were homogeneous with a significant mean of -0.68. For the other behavioral treatments combined, the 14 effects displayed a significant mean of -1.10. Hence, all the behavioral treatments resulted in TA reduction.

The cognitive treatment, group counseling, did not appear effective in reducing test anxiety.

Cognitive-behavioral treatments included cognitive modification, attentional training, insight therapy, anxiety management training, and stress inoculation. For elementary and high school students, the combined effects for those treatments were homogeneous with a significant mean of -0.53, about the same as the SD effect. The mean for college students was -0.87, not significantly different from the behavioral treatments (except relaxation).

Treatments by study skills training were not effective in TA reduction. Training combined with other treatment styles reduced TA to about the same levels as the other treatments alone. Testwiseness training for students low in test-taking skills produced a moderate TA reduction. For treatments combining study skills training and testwiseness training, a nonsignificant mean was observed.

The effect of pseudotherapy on TA reduction was not significant.

Worry and emotionality. Behavioral treatments were directed toward emotionality, but he effects seemed to generalize to worry as well. Both components were significantly reduced, with mean effects of -0.65 for worry and -0.60 for emotionality. Cognitive-behavioral treatments also reduced both components, with respective mean effects of -0.82 and -0.73. The two effects for worry were not significantly different, nor were the effects for emotionality.

Facilitating test anxiety. The effects of TA treatment generalized with respect to AAT+, displaying higher levels from both behavioral and cognitive-behavioral programs. Study skills training was not effective in improving AAT+. The mean effect of pseudotherapy neared zero.

Effects on test performance and GPA. Table 12 gives mean effects comparing the performance of treated and untreated students. Two performance variables were examined--(a) results of IQ, aptitude, and achievement posttests and (b) GPA.

Test performance. SD treatments provided a significant mean effects of 0.32 across grade levels. Effects of relaxation training displayed a significant mean of 0.13, whereas hypnosis and modeling showed a combined mean effect of 0.60. Effects of cognitive modification, attentional training, insight therapy, and anxiety management training displayed a common significant mean of 0.52. All these treatments were effective in improving test performance and

TABLE 12 Mean effects of treatment on test performance and GPA

Result by treatment	Number of studies	n	Outliers	End values	Grade levels	Mean *p < .01
Test performance						
Systematic desensitization	38	1,274	None	-0.37/1.52	6-8,10-12,P	0.32*
Relaxation training	21	3,109	None	-0.20/0.71	5,9-12,P	0.13*
Hypnosis & modeling	4	95	None	0.29/0.87	P	0.60*
Cognitive-behavioral	32	1,132	None	-0.11/2.07	3,5,6,8-12,P	0.52*
Study skills (SS)	3	106	None	-0.05/0.72	P	0.39
SS & systematic desensitization	4	123	3.08	0.11/1.71	P	0.76*
Testwiseness training	6	314	None	0.02/0.57	5,6,8-12,P	0.26
Testwiseness & others	3	148	None	0.09/0.58	5,6,P	0.35
Pseudotherapy	5	187	None	-0.05/0.39	10-12,P	0.21
GPA						
Systematic desensitization	20	657	None	-0.13/1.08	6-9,P	0.40*
Relaxation training	8	236	None	-0.10/0.54	7-12,P	0.09
Cognitive-behavioral	8	190	None	0.13/1.70	P	0.72*
SS & others	9	220	None	0.17/0.95	10-12,P	0.73*
Change-score effects						
Systematic desensitization	10	260	None	-0.09/1.72	7,8,P	0.78*
Other behavioral	8	166	-2.00	0.06/1.47	P	0.64*
Cognitive-behavioral	6	150	None	0.19/2.55	7,8,P	0.55*
SS & others	7	164	None	0.55/2.14	P	0.98*

y (except for relaxation) were not significantly different from each other. For all the treatments but relaxation, a collective mean improvement in posttest performance was computed. The resulting value of 0.42 compared the performance of treated (and thus newly LTA) groups and HTA control groups. Previous comparisons for HTA and LTA students had displayed a mean effect of -0.48 (see the first item of Table 9). Thus, the reductions, in test anxiety seemed to be joined with improved performance near the level of untreated LTA students.

Study skills training provided a nonsignificant effect on posttest performance. Training combined with SD provided a significant effect for subjects who were high in test anxiety and low in study skills before the treatment. The effects of testwiseness training and pseudotherapy were not significant with respect to test performance.

GPA. SD treatments were effective in improving the GPA of treated subjects. Relaxation training did not appear to affect GPA. Cognitive-behavioral treatments and study counseling combined with other styles

TABLE 13 Mean effects of treatment on related anxieties and conditions

Variable affected	Number of studies	n	Outliers	End values	Grade levels	Mean *p < .01
General anxiety						
Systematic desensitization	19	667	None	-1.05/0.18	5,6,10,P	-0.40*
Other behavioral	9	356	None	-1.20/0.09	9-12,P	-0.44*
Cognitive-behavioral	7	225	None	-1.20/0.02	3,5,7,P	-0.31
Pseudotherapy	6	249	None	-0.56/0.25	5,6,10-12,P	-0.28
A-Trait						
Behavioral	9	266	None	-1.15/-0.06	P	-0.48*
Cognitive-behavioral	6	132	None	-0.56/0.16	P	-0.34
Study skills (SS) & systematic desensitization	7	205	None	-1.09/0.09	P	-0.47*
A-State						
Behavioral	16	322	None	-2.21/0.04	10,P	-0.73*
Cognitive-behavioral	12	258	None	-2.03/0.32	10,P	-1.00*
SS & relaxation	6	177	None	-0.53/0.15	P	-0.22
Physiological reactions						
Heart rate	11	322	None	-1.30/0.45	P	-0.45*
Muscle tension	5	95	None	-0.49/0.30	P	-0.05
Psychological						
Fear of negative evaluation	7	162	None	-1.43/-0.16	P	-0.65*
Cognitive interference	3	74	None	-1.19/-0.06	P	-0.58

produced significant positive effects for GPA. The collective mean improvement for all these treatments (but relaxation) was 0.52, a value that compared very well with the GPA difference of -0.46 previously found between HTA and LTA subjects (see Table 9).

All the foregoing effects were based on posttreatment measures. Pre- to post-treatment *change* results were also examined with regard to test performance and GPA. Mean effects were significant and positive for systematic desensitization, modeling, covert positive reinforcement, extinction, hypnosis, cognitive modification, attentional training, and study skills training combined with other treatments. Thus, the treatments provided gains in test performance and GPA on the bases of both posttreatment and change scoring.

Effects on related variables. TA treatments generalized to reductions in general anxiety, A-Trait, A-State, physiological reactions to the test situation, fear of negative evaluation, and cognitive interference during tests. Table 13 gives mean effects related to these variables.

General anxiety and A-Trait. Behavioral treatments provided a reduction in general anxiety and A-Trait (anxiety proneness). No corresponding effects on these variables resulted from cognitive-behavioral treatments or pseudotherapy. Study skills training combined with SD reduced A-Trait anxiety.

A-State and physiological reactions. A-State, the transitory emotional condition of tension and nervous reaction, decreased in test situations after either behavioral or cognitive-behavioral treatments. The mean effect on A-State for study skills with relaxation training was not significant. Reductions in A-State seemed accompanied by moderate reductions in heart rate, but the effects for muscle tension were not significant.

Psychological and cognitive conditions. Students' fear of negative evaluation was significantly reduced after TA treatment. In limited studies, the mean reduction of -0.58 for cognitive interference during tests was not significant.

Follow-up effects. Posttreatment follow-up scores were gathered after retention periods of 3 to 60 weeks (with median 6). Table 14 displays the follow-up mean effects. Compared with those of untreated students, the TA scores of treated subjects had declined below the end-of-treatment levels; even the subjects of pseudotherapy experienced a delayed TA reduction. The AAT+ of behavioral subjects increased above the end-of-treatment measures, but a corresponding effect for anxiety management training was not significant. During the retention period, test performance and GPA remained stable near the end-of-treatment levels. General anxiety and A-State were further reduced in treated subjects during retention.

TABLE 14 Mean effects in follow-up studies

Variable affected	Number of studies	n	End values	Grade levels	Mean $^*p < .01$
Debilitating TA					
Behavioral treatment	20	558	-2.22/-0.33	P	-1.21*
Cognitive-behavioral	15	386	-1.89/-0.23	P	-0.96*
Pseudotherapy	5	130	-1.15/-0.14	P	-0.57*
Facilitating (AAT+)					
Systematic desensitization	6	208	0.44/1.79	P	0.89*
Anxiety management	3	93	-0.15/0.39	P	0.10
Test performance & GPA	8	268	-0.29/1.94	P	0.45*
General anxiety	3	96	-1.24/-0.98	P	-1.16*
A-State anxiety	8	196	-2.28/-0.01	P	-1.17*

Note. No outliers were found.

Conclusions and Discussion

This study determined relationships and effects for test anxiety through the synthesis of 562 reports of research. Because this body of studies was exhaustively collected, it was considered a representative sample for meta-analysis. Thus, the sample findings have been generalized to populations as conclusions. (Where variables had been studied within limited conditions, care should be applied respecting how far their data will generalize.)

1. The first three areas of study--correlates, causes, and TA effects--concern relationships rather than experimental findings. Hence, conclusions in their regard have been collapsed to a common discussion.

Test anxiety and performance are significantly related at grade 3 and above. The relationships are inverse and tend to be stronger for worry than emotionality. No differences appear between male and female students, but the relationship is stronger for average students than for those with low or high abilities. The relationship seems significant only for tests perceived as difficult; where a test is thought to be easy, no performance differences occur among TA levels. Conditions that seem to enhance the performance of HTA students include low-stress instructions (at the college level), provision of memory support, minimal distractions, and background music. LTA students function best under ego-involving instruction, an easy-to-hard test item arrangement, and no music during tests. Performance incentives benefit students at all TA levels.

Across grade levels, females exhibit higher test anxiety than males. (However, the females' higher TA does not appear to translate into a performance differential.) Pupils in the early grades have little test anxiety, but its prevalence rises sharply in grades 3 to 5, stays fairly constant through high school, and is lower in college. Black students in elementary school report more TA than white students, a difference that declines to nonsignificance in high school. Hispanic students across grade levels show more TA than white students. Later-born children seem more test-anxious than only children and firstborns. The higher the student's ability level, the lower the test anxiety.

TA is directly related to fears of negative evaluation, dislike of tests, and less effective study skills. Its link with need for achievement seems to change across grade levels, from inverse in elementary school to direct in high school and to nonsignificance in college. HTA students hold themselves in lower esteem than do LTA students. They tend to feel unprotected and controlled by outside forces and are prone to negative qualities, such as other forms of anxiety. They experience more encoding difficulty when learning, more cognitive interference when tested, and more A-State reactions to the testing situation.

2. Test anxiety can be effectively reduced by a variety of behavioral and cognitive-behavioral treatments delivered in a broad assortment of conditions

(e.g., groups of individual subjects). Such treatments reduce both worry and emotionality, and they generalize to increases in facilitating test anxiety. For students low in test-taking skills, testwiseness training offers moderate TA relief. Group counseling to cope with worry does not seem effective in TA reduction. Study skills training is also not effective unless another treatment style is also present.

Improved test performance and GPA consistently accompany TA reduction. This finding differs with the conclusions of prior reviews (e.g., Allen, Elias, & Zlotlow, 1980). Their findings issued from the dearth of studies that showed significant performance differences between treated and untreated subjects. *Significant* is the critical word; the treatment studies need to be probed for their ability to *detect* performance differences usually found between TA levels. In Table 9, the mean effect of -0.48 reflects a test performance difference of about 6 points on a 100-point scale between HTA and LTA students. Thus, an improvement of about 6 points should be expected as a result of TA treatment. For $\alpha = 0.05$ and a pooled standard deviation of 12, a 6-point difference requires experimental and control group sample sizes in the neighborhood of 30 before significance can be observed. Of 137 treatment studies, only 16% had samples larger than 20; one third used samples of 10, 9, or 8. Apparently, these small samples could not detect the significance of performance differences near 6 points. Of 120 performance comparisons, 107 showed higher test scores for the treated subjects. In the aggregate, these effects possess a highly significant mean.

Treatment effects seem to generalize to areas other than test anxiety and performance. Behavioral treatments act to reduce the levels of general and A-Trait anxieties. Behavioral and cognitive-behavioral treatments each reduce the levels of A-State during testing.

No treatment effect appears to decline with the passage of time after treatment.

Theoretical Issues

Nature of test anxiety. TA is considered to possess two primary factors: worry (cognitive concern about one's performance) and emotionality (automatic reactions to the test situation). If it should be the case that both components occur at once with neither needing prompting from the other, then TA would appear to be both cognitive (for worry) and behavioral (for emotionality). However, if there is cause-effect between the two components, TA would appear to be essentially unidimensional. Cause and effect may be examined in terms of treatment results on TA reduction (Table 11). The purely cognitive treatment, group counseling, did not seem effective in TA reduction. The purely behavioral treatments were considerably more effective. Moreover, these treatments reduced not only emotionality; they generalized to reduce the worry component. These findings suggest that emotionality triggers worry. Thus, TA seems to be a behavioral construct.

Debilitating and facilitating test anxieties. Table 5 records a mean correlation of -0.49 between the AAT- and AAT+ subscales of the Anxiety Achievement Test. This moderate value of r implies that these two forms of test anxiety may be relatively independent. However, their distinctiveness blurs beneath the observation that the treatments for reducing AAT- generalized to significant increases in AAT+ both at the end of treatment and after the follow-up (see Tables 11 and 14). The kinship of the two forms was studied further at the college level, where the bulk of research on AAT+ has been conducted. From the data underlying Tables 1 and 6, a display was made of the mean correlations between performance and both forms of test anxiety (AAT- and AAT+, respectively):

IQ	-0.30, 0.30
Aptitude/achievement	-0.29, 0.30
GPA	-0.29, 0.32

The mean rs for debilitating and facilitating forms are almost mirror images. Thus, the forms seem inverse, and distinguishing between them may not be productive, at least in the arena of performance.

Causality in the TA/performance relationship. Test anxiety causes poor performance. This conclusion follows from the finding that better performance accompanies TA reduction.

Comparison of TA models. Behavioral and cognitive-behavioral treatments were effective in TA reduction. Both styles operate within the interference model. Study skills training did not seem effective. Hence, the evidence supports an interference rather than a deficits model of test anxiety.

TA research appears to have prospered because test situations occur so frequently and assume so much importance in the lives of so many people (Sarason, 1980). The process of testing in particular applies to students--to monitor progress, diagnose problems, measure aptitudes and intelligence, screen for admission to schools after high school, and place admitted students in their classes. In all these circumstances, the performance of test-anxious students stands to be depressed, not from a lack of ability but from a dysfunction in trying to show it. Test-anxious students comprise a sizable number. Hill and Wigfield (1984) projected their incidence near 10 million at precollege levels, and the condition seems "pervasive" in college as well (Spielberger, Anton, & Bedell, 1976, p. 13). Three implications follow from these observations.

1. On an individual basis, the IQs, aptitudes, and progress of test-anxious students are consistently misinterpreted and undervalued.
2. Average scores for IQ, aptitude, and scholastic achievement are systematically biased at local, state and national levels.
3. The validity of the entire testing process is challenged.

These implications appear to demand that TA be confronted. In past times, it has seemed to be a topic "like the weather," much discussed but with not much done about it (Sarason, 1980, p. 5). The reason for inaction seems clear; although TA and performance were conceded to be related, the causal direction remained at issue, largely from the perception that better performance could not be expected to accompany TA reduction. That issue now seems resolved, the perception denied; test anxiety harms performance; TA reduction in anxious students can help their performance approach an LTA level. These findings may offer a basis for educational institutions to review the TA problem and seek its solution.

An array of interventions seems to offer effective relief. Under circumstances where performance interacts with ego-involvement (for example, during college placement testing), TA effects may be compensated by grouping the students for separate tests according to the TA levels, with the test instructions adjusted to accommodate each grouping.

These techniques serve to cope with TA. Better methods would try to prevent it. TA seems to be a learned condition, small to nonexistent in the very early grades but firmly in place by grade 5. A primary task for future research thus seems defined: Investigate ways to avert the condition before it matures.

References

Allen, G. (1972). The behavioral treatment of test anxiety: Recent research and future trends. *Behavior Therapy, 3*, 253-262.

Allen, G., Elias, M., & Zlotlow, S. (1980). Behavioral interventions for alleviating test anxiety: A methodological overview of current therapeutic practices. In I. G. Sarason (Ed.), *Test anxiety: Theory, research, and applications* (pp. 155-185). Hillsdale, NJ: Erlbaum.

Alpert, R., & Haber, R. (1960). Anxiety in academic achievement situations. *Journal of Abnormal and Social Psychology, 61*, 207-215.

Denney, D. (1980). Self-control approaches to the treatment of test anxiety. In I. G. Sarason (Ed.), *Test anxiety: Theory, research and applications* (pp. 209-243). Hillsdale, NJ: Erlbaum.

Ferguson, G. (1981). *Statistical analysis in psychology and education.* New York: McGraw-Hill.

Glass, G., McGaw, B., & Smith, M. (1981). *Meta-analysis in social research.* Beverly Hills, CA: Sage.

Hedges, L., & Olkin, I. (1985). *Statistical methods for meta-analysis.* Orlando, FL: Academic Press.

Hembree, R. (1987). *A bibliography of research on academic test anxiety.* Adrian, MI: Adrian College, Department of Mathematics. (ERIC Document Reproduction Service No. ED 281 779).

Hembree, R., & Dessart, D. (1986). Effects of hand-held calculators in precollege mathematics education: A meta-analysis. *Journal for Research in Mathematics Education, 17*, 83-99.

Hill, K. (1972). Anxiety in the evaluative context. In W. W. Hartup (Ed.) *The young child* (Vol. 2, pp. 225-263). Washington, DC: National Association for the Education of Young Children.

Hill, K., & Wigfield, A. (1984). Test anxiety: A major educational problem and what can be done about it. *Elementary School Journal, 85*, 105-126.

Liebert, R., & Morris, L. (1967). Cognitive and emotional components of test anxiety: A distinction and some initial data. *Psychological Reports, 20*, 975-978.

Mandler, G., & Sarason, S. (1952). A study of anxiety and learning. *Journal of Abnormal and Social Psychology, 47*, 166-173.

Morris, L., & Liebert, R. (1969). Effects of anxiety on time and untimed intelligence tests. *Journal of Consulting and Clinical Psychology, 33*, 240-244.

Ribordy, S., & Billingham, K. (1980). *Test anxiety: An annotated bibliography.* (ERIC Document Reproduction Service No. ED 201 901).

Sarason, I. (1958). Interrelationships among individual difference variables, behavior in psychotherapy, and verbal conditioning. *Journal of Abnormal and Social Psychology, 56*, 339-344.

Sarason, I. (1961). Test anxiety and the intellectual performance of college students. *Journal of Educational Psychology, 52,* 201-206.
Sarason, I. (1980). Introduction to the study of test anxiety. In I. G. Sarason (Ed.), *Test anxiety: Theory, research, and applications* (pp. 3-14), Hillsdale, NJ: Erlbaum.
Sarason, S., Davidson, K., Lighthall, F., Waite, R., & Ruebush, B. (1960). *Anxiety in elementary school children.* New York: Wiley.
Sarason, S., & Mandler, G. (1952). Some correlates of test anxiety. *Journal of Abnormal and Social Psychology, 47,* 810-817.
Sarason, S., Mandler, G., & Craighill, P. (1952). The effect of differential instruction on anxiety and learning. *Journal of Abnormal and Social Psychology, 47,* 561-565.
Spielberger, C. (1972). Anxiety as an emotional state. In C. D. Spielberger (Ed.), *Anxiety: Current trends in theory and research* (Vol. 1, pp. 23-49). New York: Academic Press.
Spielberger, C., Anton, W., & Bedell, J. (1976). The nature and treatment of test anxiety. In M. Zuckerman & C. D. Spielberger (Eds.), *Emotion and anxiety: New concepts, methods, and applications* (pp. 317-345). Hillsdale, NJ: Erlbaum.
Tobias, S. (1979). Anxiety research in educational psychology. *Journal of Educational Psychology, 71,* 573-582.
Tobias, S. (1985). Test anxiety: Interference, defective skills, and cognitive capacity. *Educational Psychologist, 20,* 135-142.
Tryon, G. (1980). The measurement and treatment of test anxiety. *Review of Educational Research, 50,* 353-372.
Wildemuth, B. (1977). *Test anxiety: An extensive bibliography.* (ERIC/TM Report 64). Princeton, NJ: ERIC Clearinghouse on Tests, Measurement & Evaluation.
Wine, J. (1971). Test anxiety and direction of attention. *Psychological Bulletin, 76,* 92-104.

SECTION V

Computerized Testing

ON-LINE COMPUTER TESTING: IMPLEMENTATION AND ENDORSEMENT

John F. Gwinn, PH.D.
Biology Department
Loretta F. Beal, M.S.
Center for Computer-Based Education

The University of Akron

ABSTRACT. An interactive computer testing and record keeping system was implemented for a large self-paced anatomy and physiology course. This system including security procedures, is described and results of exploratory research are presented on student preference for on-line testing, test anxiety, attitude and achievement. This required testing program included immediate feedback, second attempts, and retests. When correlates of achievement, test anxiety, and computer attitudes were investigated, we found that over time there was a slight reduction in realistic computer attitudes and a slight increase in general test anxiety. Students reported more facilitating anxiety with computer administered tests and more debilitating anxiety with paper and pencil tests. Strengths and weaknesses of such testing for faculty and for students is discussed. Suggestions are presented for properly integrating a computer testing program into a course.

INTRODUCTION

Computers have been used for well over a decade in the generation of tests. The off-line or batch mode appears to be more frequently used [1] and some universities have established campus-wide testing centers [2]. Other than repeatable testing and flexible scheduling (which do not necessarily require a computer), such off-line testing offers little advantage to the student unless some type of diagnostic prescription for study is also provided.

On-line or interactive computer testing appears to have received little attention. Earlier drawbacks to its development, such as the high cost of computing, lack of availability of terminals, and poor reliability, have been largely overcome.

Concerns about possible adverse effects on student attitudes and performance may have discouraged development, especially where the testing was required as a major portion of the course grade [3,4]. On the other hand, on-line testing can offer advantages such as immediate knowledge of results, corrective feedback, and comprehensive records management. Our goal was

---

Reprinted by permission of Baywood Publishing Co., inc. from the Journal of Educational Technology Systems, Vol. 16(3), (1987-88): 239-251.

to implement an on-line computer testing program which was relatively low in cost, well accepted by students and faculty, and which provided opportunity for students to learn form mistakes during testing.

Background

Nine years ago a traditionally taught, two semester anatomy and physiology course with an enrollment of about 400 was converted to individualized instruction to better serve the diverse academic backgrounds of nursing, allied health, education, and biology students. Postlethwait's audio-tutorial format was adapted for the presentation of course content [5]. An integrated on-line computer testing and records management program was developed to complement the flexibility of the self-pacing. This program is named ATAP for Audio-Tutorial Anatomy and Physiology.

ATAP was originally written in the IBM IIS mainframe programming language. It was replaced by Goal Systems PHOENIX authoring language three years later to improve efficiency. The number of students and complexity of the program dictated that it reside on the IBM mainframe. The details of the development of ATAP, including an analysis of costs, have been presented previously [6-8]. The procedures, problems, and approaches presented here may be of general interest in furthering on-line computer testing.

Registration onto the ATAP Program

On the first day of class students are introduced to the functions of the terminal and instructed in the procedures to be used with the mainframe by a short interactive demonstration program developed by Computer-Based Education (CBE).

Prior to this demonstration the students have been assigned an ATAP computer number. The Registrar provides a tape with ATAP enrollment data and a utility program batch registers the students. Printed labels containing name, social security number, and ATAP sign-on number are affixed to a sheet of instructions given to each student.

Testing Security

The integrity and security of any required on-line computer testing program is of paramount importance to the faculty member who must be convinced there is minimal opportunity for cheating or misrepresentation. Cheating is a potential problem in any testing situation. Development of a secure computer testing procedure requires advance planning, assessment of procedures, and revision.

Although students report that actual knowledge of cheating is about the same on computer tests as on paper and pencil tests, they perceive the opportunities for computer cheating to be greater [9]. The newness of computer testing coupled with their lack of knowledge of some security procedures (such as randomization of items) may contribute to this perception. At present, multipurpose terminal clusters must be used which do not provide an ideal environment for testing.

The sign-on procedure requires a student to tell the monitor his/her ATAP number and to present a photo-identification each time the student wants to take a test. The monitor enters the number on a secure terminal and compares the screen response of the individual's name to the photo-identification.

The student must sign-on within two minutes after the monitor's approval to prevent another student from signing-on under that number at later time without going through the monitor. The monitor randomly assigns the specific terminal at which the student signs-on to prevent students from choosing where they sit during a test, thus reducing the opportunity for collaborative effort. Before each test is presented, the student is reminded on the screen of the required procedures: no talking, no looking at another screen, and no books, papers, or notes at the terminal. The student acknowledges and accepts these procedures by continuing, otherwise he/she is instructed to sign-off. A "test in progress" sign is placed on top of the terminal to remind others not to approach.

Testing Procedure

After sign-on, the student selects the desired test. The management control permits the students to request only those tests for which he/she is eligible. A multiple choice question is presented with five alternatives and the student's response is followed by immediate knowledge of results plus corrective feedback. If the answer is correct, another sentence is presented to reinforce that answer, but an incorrect is explained and a second chance at the same question is offered. If this corrective feedback enables the student to choose correctly the second time, he receives half credit for that item.

Questions are randomly selected from the test item bank where they are stratified according to knowledge level required for a successful response. More difficult items are worth more points.

If a student does not meet the set criterion on a unit, additional tests over that material must be completed until mastery is demonstrated. After three unsuccessful attempts, the student is required to see a tutor before continuing. All students are permitted one optional retest after meeting criterion. The higher score is retained.

After demonstrating mastery on the thirty-point criterion test, the student takes a fifty-point review test covering the previous two units. This counteracts the tendency for students in self-paced course to "cram" for the many small tests and to neglect review and integration of previous material [10]. Since the review test has greater weight and can be taken only once, this encourages a more thorough review of the previous material. The typical student now spends approximately one-half hour per week at the terminal to answer about fifty-five multiple-choice items. Students wishing to challenge a test item may write the question number on a provided colored scrap of paper. Later, the instructor can display that item and discuss it.

Punctuality Points

Procrastination is a human failing observable in traditional classes, but especially evident in self-paced courses where deadlines seem less ominous. An especially effective solution to this problem is to award "punctuality points" [7,10]. In the form of "bonus" points, these motivate students to keep current. It is amazing the self-discipline students will demonstrate to earn this positive reinforcement!

If all of the punctuality points were earned, it could make as much as a grade difference (e.g., A- to A). Four punctuality points are now awarded to students who complete the unit and review tests by Wednesday of the week following the class presentation and who meet criterion on the first attempt of the unit test. (This encourages well-prepared first attempts.) In addition, the student must also submit an essay and attend the oral quiz. The typical student earns about 60 percent of the available punctuality points. This appears sufficient to keep over 90 percent of the class up to date on the testing. If a student gets more than a week behind, the computer program will not allow the student to continue until he/she has had a conference with the instructor.

Management System

A comprehensive management system supports the ATAP program. It sets the testing parameters (objectives to be tested, number and level of questions, criterion, dates available, etc.) and it provides for entry of oral and essay scores. It also supplies names of students who have not met criterion or who are behind in their work and the number of those having completed a given unit. In addition, analysis can be made off-line of grade distributions among different instructors, analysis of responses to test items, average response time per question, and connect time. The student report is a detailed list of all computer test scores, oral quiz and essay scores, punctuality points, laboratory practicals, and total points. It provides a clear indication of the extent and level of performance. A student may call up his/her report at any time, confirm the accuracy of all scores, and obtain a hard copy. The percentage of points earned can be easily extrapolated to the final course grade. At semester's end a print-out of all student reports, total points, and letter grade becomes the permanent record.

EXPLORATORY RESEARCH

The program designers anticipated that the large number of smaller tests, corrective feedback, second attempts at a question, and opportunity to retest would reduce general test anxiety since no one test would have a significant effect on the course grade. Although surveys of students in the program indicated great preference for on-line testing, occasional comments by students suggested that anxiety may not be different from traditional testing situations. The nature and origin of any anxiety, however, had not been investigated in a systematic manner. The research reported here attempted to assess whether on-line computer testing affects test anxiety, attitudes toward computers, and in turn achievement.

METHOD

The target population was composed of 755 ATAP students enrolled in nursing, allied health, medical assisting, dietetics, and physical education programs during the 1985-1986 academic year. Seventy-five percent of these students ranged in age from seventeen to twenty-two years and 47 percent were classified as sophomores; 85 percent were female.

Students were given a series of surveys to investigate several possible correlates of achievement: students' prior experience with computers, students' attitudes toward computers, general test anxiety, and format-specific test anxiety. Only data from students completing all three surveys is presented here ($N = 445$).

The first survey, completed the first day of class, assessed the extent of prior computer experience, computer attitudes, and general test anxiety. Prior computer experience was measured by four 'yes/no' questions, computer attitude by eight statements rated on a 5-point Likert-type scale, and general test anxiety was determined by the Mandler and Sarason "Test Anxiety Questionnaire" [11].

After fourteen weeks of computer testing, i.e., end of fall semester, students repeated the computer experience survey, the computer attitude survey, and the general test anxiety questionnaire. In addition, they completed Alpert and Haber's *Facilitating/Debilitating Test Anxiety Scale* [12] modified to measure format-specific, (computer administered versus paper and pencil

Table 1. Computer Experience Means and t-Values.

	N	Mean	S.D.	Male N	Male t	Male P	Female N	Female t	Female P
Survey 1	445	5.1	1.24	68	3.27	.0022	377	7.13	.0001
Survey 2	445	5.6	1.25						

administered) induced anxiety. At the end of spring semester the students completed the adaption of the Alpert and Haber questionnaire a second time.

RESULTS

Prior Computer Experience

Students came to this anatomy course with very little computer experience. A score of four on the computer experience survey represented no computer experience (other than games) and a score of eight represented some programming ability. The computer experience survey was given a second time to see if students considered on-line computer testing to be a significant computer experience. The mean increased slightly on the second administration of the computer experience test (see Table 1). A t-test of paired comparisons of mean change between the first and second administration produced a t-value significant at the 0.05 level for both male and female students.

Although the increased computer experience in the second survey is statistically significant, the actual scores have little practical significance except to reflect the in-class experience with computer testing.

Computer Attitudes

The computer attitude survey measured students' expectations of computers. Students expressed agreement or disagreement for each of several statements regarding capability of computers. Whether a given statement represented a realistic attitude was determined by the authors. The mean on the second administration decreased slightly indicating less realistic expectations after more experience with the computer! (See Table 2.)

A t-test of paired comparisons of mean change in attitude also produced significant t-values. Although the differences are significant, again the practical differences are small. Scores on this survey ranged from 17 to 39 on the first administration and 14 to 39 on the second.

Table 2. Computer Attitude Means and t-Values.

	N	Mean	S.D.	Male N	Male t	Male P	Female N	Female t	Female P
Survey 1	445	29.1	3.6	68	-2.75	.0078	377	-5.21	.0001
Survey 2	445	28.0	4.3						

General Test Anxiety

General test anxiety increased slightly from the first administration to the second administration of the test. The mean on the second testing is slightly higher than that of the first administration (see Table 3). Although the range on the second administration shifted toward the upper end. The shift seems slight, however, a *t*-test of paired comparisons of mean change indicates a significant increase in test anxiety for females at the 0.001 level and for males at the 0.05 level.

Seventy-eight students who withdrew from the course during the first semester had completed the first survey. Their mean computer experience scores and mean computer attitude scores were nearly the same as the mean of the group completing the course. However, the mean general test anxiety score for this group on the first survey was above the mean on the first survey for the group completing the course (see Table 4).

Correlations with Achievement

Correlation coefficients significant at the 0.001 level or greater indicated that increased computer experience was positively related to more realistic computer attitudes ($r = .24$) and that realistic computer attitudes were negatively related to test anxiety ($r = -.20$), i.e., the more realistic the attitude, the lower the test anxiety. Realistic computer attitudes correlated positively with grade, while test anxiety was negatively related with achievement ($r = -.13$). Also the amount of computer connect time was negatively related to

Table 3. General Test Anxiety Means and t-Values.

	N	Mean	S.D.	Range	Male t	Male P	Female t	Female P
Survey 1	445	28	6.8	12-51	1.99	.05	3.29	.001
Survey 2	445	29.7	7.5	11-46				

Table 4. Comparisons of Means of Students Withdrawing vs. Students Completing the Course

	Withdrawals			Completions		
	N	Mean	S.D.	N	Mean	S.D.
Computer Experience	77	5.0	1.28	445	5.1	1.24
Computer Attitude	78	29.87	3.57	445	29.1	3.60
Test Anxiety	76	30.22	6.9	445	28.0	6.80

achievement ($r = -.19$) but positively related to anxiety ($r = .15$). Students who receive high scores responded to test items more quickly and were less anxious than students receiving low scores. It has been suggested that test anxious students do not attend to the task before them. They are easily distracted and often engage in covert verbal mediation of a self-depreciating nature [12]. This may add to the amount of time it takes to complete a test.

Test Format and Test Anxiety

Not all test anxiety is detrimental to achievement. Alpert and Haber found both debilitating and facilitating effects of test anxiety [13]. The relationship between test anxiety and achievement forms an inverted U-shaped curve [14].

A major part of this study was to determine whether the test format (on-line computer versus paper and pencil) influenced the type (facilitating versus debilitating) and amount of anxiety reported by the students. The questionnaire items were modified from Alpert and Haber and for each statement, which expressed an aspect of either debilitating or facilitating anxiety, the student indicated whether the statement was more true of on-line computer tests or of paper and pencil tests.

The first administration of the format-specific, test anxiety questionnaire indicated that computer administered tests engendered more debilitating anxiety and that paper and pencil tests created more facilitating anxiety. The same survey was administered a second time at the end of the spring semester. This time the results were reversed. During spring semester, the students were given two paper and pencil tests in place of four computer tests. The reversal of attitude may have resulted from actual in-class experience with both paper and pencil and computer tests.

Using a difference score (e.g. the difference between computer facilitating anxiety and paper and pencil facilitating anxiety scores, etc.), a *t*-test of paired comparisons of mean difference score was computed. The *t*-tests produced the values displayed in Table 5.

Table 5. Paired Comparisons of Facilitating/Debilitating Test Anxiety by Format

	First Semester		Second Semester	
	t	pr > t	t	pr > t
Debilitating difference	1.99	.047	-4.36[a]	.0001
Facilitating difference	-3.47	.0006	7.08	.0001

[a]Notice that the sign of the numbers are reversed on the second semester t-value. A negative t-value indicates that the paper and pencil value was greater than the computer value since the paper and pencil score was subtracted from the computer score.

Prediction of Achievement

Two measures of achievement were used: final grades in the course and total points earned on the computer-administered tests which represented 70 percent of the final course grade. Stepwise multiple regression equations were computed to determine which variables were related to course grades, computer test scores, and anxiety. Predictors used included overall GPA, computer test scores, academic program, rank of the student (freshman - sophomore), test anxiety scores and time spent in the learning center.

Forty-two percent of the variance in final course grades could be accounted for by a combination of each of these predictors except test anxiety. General test anxiety was not a significant predictor of final course grade. Fifty-six percent of the variance in computer test scores could be accounted for by a combination of all six predictors. Test anxiety was significant for predicting computer test scores and ranked fourth among the predictors. This may indicate that the type of anxiety we are measuring is *state* anxiety rather than *trait* anxiety since test anxiety was not a significant predictor for final course grade but was for computer administered test scores [15].

Student Acceptance of Required Computer Testing

During the planning stages of ATAP, computer-based education experts [4] cautioned against putting a typical multiple-choice test on-line for two reasons. One, there is no educational or financial advantage when computer are used in a manner similar to paper and pencil testing, and two, students may direct the frustration and anxiety that arises in any testing situation toward the computer, adversely affecting other computer-based education programs. At that time, few students had had any computer experience and many regarded computers as intimidating. Today our students are more familiar with computers, yet fewer than 20 percent actually have had any computer experience with the exception of playing games.

Students in ATAP overwhelmingly approve of computer testing. Results of our surveys consistently indicate that about 70 percent of the students have a decided preference for computer testing over paper and pencil, about 7 percent dislike it, and the remainder find it makes little difference [6, 10, 16]. This acceptance was accomplished by appropriately integrating the testing into the structure of the course and by designing a program which offered the student advantages impossible with traditional testing methods.

After implementation of the ATAP program, there was an increase in the average class grade. There were indications that students were devoting much more time to mastery of the objectives than when the course was traditionally taught. The course itself is regarded as very demanding since 97 percent of all points (excluding punctuality points) are required for an "A," 94 percent for "A-," etc. Approximately half of the class earn an A or B and about 25 percent earn D, F, or withdraw.

There is overwhelming student preference for ATAP computer interactive testing compared with traditional paper and pencil tests (including optical scan sheets). The major advantages of this program, as determined by surveys and interviews have remained consistent over the years [10, 16]:

- being tested over only one week's material at a time
- being able to take the test whenever desired
- receiving immediate feedback
- having a second attempt to answer a question
- being able to retest to raise a score.

With the exception of immediate feedback and a second attempt, which are possible only with interactive computer testing, the other advantages are those characteristic of master oriented, self-paced courses which are generally valued by students [17]. Students clearly view the computer as a means of providing flexibility and information for them and feel that a basic concern, course grade, is not going to be jeopardized by computer testing.

In a variety of surveys students have been asked to identify major problems associated with computer testing:

- computer or program down-time
- long response time
- noise and distraction at computer terminal clusters
- vague or unclear questions
- long waits when all the terminals are busy
- errors in test scoring
- opportunity for cheating.

Computer down-time is always considered a major problem by the students even though the actual down-time presently averages less than two hours out of eighty hours per week. The other problems diminished in their relative importance as remedies were applied. The long response times were drastically reduced by a larger mainframe and a more efficient language. Noise in the multi-purpose terminal clusters was somewhat reduced by cooperative efforts. Vague and unclear questions were culled by editing. Additional terminals decreased waiting time. The opportunities for cheating were reduced through added security provisions.

DISCUSSION

It was hypothesized that more computer experience would lead to more realistic attitudes toward computers and that these two factors in combination, would reduce general test anxiety. Thus far our explorations have indicated a minor decrease in realistic computer attitudes and an increase in test anxiety over time. This might have been expected if there had been many system or programming errors throughout the two semesters, however, this was not the case. (Students are very sensitive to this type of problem.) Therefore ambiguity of the program or instability of the computer system would not appear to be responsible for these changes. Students did indicate, however, that they viewed the material included during the second semester to be more difficult than the material in the first semester. Level of difficulty of the material may contribute to the increase in test anxiety.

Computer attitudes and test anxiety are both related to performance in this course. Our results suggest that enhancing realistic computer attitudes and reducing general test anxiety may have a beneficial effect on student achievement. We are currently exploring possible interventions which may accomplish this.

The reversal from viewing computer-administered tests as engendering more debilitating to engendering more facilitating anxiety was a positive outcome. This switch may have occurred due to the administration of two paper and pencil tests in the second semester. This experience with a paper and pencil test may have introduced a point of comparison which had been lacking on the previous administration of the format-specific debilitating/facilitating anxiety test. This may also account for the change of attitude and may reflect the more accurate perspective.

CONCLUSIONS

Testing in an academic setting has traditionally been accomplished by a written exam marked with a pencil. Thus far, computers have been used primarily for off-line generation of tests which are then presented in a traditional paper and pencil format, including optical scan sheets. An interactive computer testing program has been successfully implemented in a large self-paced course. The scheduling flexibility, testing to mastery, and the feedback capabilities of on-line computer testing are especially compatible with individualized instruction. Student acceptance of the ATAP testing program has been overwhelming.

On-line computer testing offers advantages of immediate scoring with no paper handling, as well as corrective feedback and second attempts at an item. Although students have clearly demonstrated a strong preference for on-line testing, this exploratory research attempted to determine whether there were underlying factors that detracted from an optimal testing situation. Attitudes toward the computer became slightly less realistic and general test anxiety increased slightly as students gained more experience with on-line testing. Although the large sample size made these changes statistically significant, they were relatively so small as to have little practical value.

This on-line computer testing program was reported by students to promote more facilitating and less debilitating anxiety than do paper and pencil tests. The corrective feedback and second attempt at a question plus the administration of many small tests may have contributed to this desirable improvement in testing. All computer testing formats may not necessarily be perceived in this way. Details of implementation are important.

General test anxiety is a significant predictor of computer administered test scores but not of the final grade in the course. Since test anxiety is negatively correlated with realistic computer attitudes, this suggests that class presentations designed to promote better understanding of computers may reduce test anxiety.

Overall we found no major educational or economic drawbacks in the use of on-line computer testing where it comprises a significant portion of the course grade. Advantages to faculty included much less paperwork and fewer grading errors, more class time, and greater uniformity of testing in a multiple-sectioned course. In view of the strong approval and acceptance by students, it appears that on-line computer testing is an appropriate testing format.

Success of this educational innovation has been dependent upon the students' perception that they are being treated fairly. Student complaints have been carefully considered and flexibility demonstrated whenever students are inconvenienced or wronged. (For example, computer down-time in excess of four hours in a week extends the punctuality deadline three days.) Computer test items are not regarded as infallible measures of achievement, and students may receive credit for a missed item when they persuade their instructor they really knew the material being asked.

Although ATAP uses a high degree of educational technology (audio-cassettes and computers), students report that it is less impersonal than other large courses. This has been reinforced by viewing technology as an aid to learning--not as a substitute for human contact. On-line computer testing has been demonstrated to be an efficient and fair method of evaluation in large classes as well as an accepted method. The benefits for both faculty and students indicate it is likely to become much more widely used.

References

1. G. E. Dunkleberger and H. Heikkinen, A Review of Computer-generated Repeatable Testing, *AEDS Journal*, pp. 218-225. Summer 1982.
2. A. C. Oosterhof and D. F. Salisbury, Some Management and Instruction Related Considerations Regarding Computer-assisted Testing, *Educational Management: Issues and Practice*, pp. 18-23, Spring 1985.
3. M. D. Roblyer, The Greening of Educational Computing: A Proposal for a More Research-based Approach to Computers in Instruction, *Educational Technology, 25:*1, pp. 40-44, 1985.
4. Dr. J. Hirschbuhl, Director of Computer-based Education and Dr. G. Blumenfeld, Educational Foundations, University of Akron, personal communication.
5. S. N. Postlethwait, J. Novak, and H. Murray, *An Integrated Experience Approach to Learning, with Emphasis on Independent Study*, Burgess Publishing Company, Minneapolis, Minnesota, 1964.
6. J. F. Gwinn, Development of an Audio-Tutorial Anatomy and Physiology Course (abstract), in *Proceedings of the Eleventh Annual Conference of the International Congress for Individualized Instruction*, Athens, Georgia, November 1979.
7. J. F. Gwinn and J. Sentieri, ATAP: A Model for Interactive Computerized Testing and Records Management as an Integral Part of a Self-paced Anatomy and Physiology Course, *Proceedings of the 1980 Annual Meeting of ADCIS*, Washington, D. C., pp. 87-93, March 1980.
8. J. F. Gwinn, Can You Afford to Not Individualize/Computerize? *Journal of College Science Teaching, 12:*1, pp. 27-28, 1982.
9. ___, Problems (with Solutions) in the Design of a Comprehensive Computer Testing Program, paper presented to the Mideastern Chapter of ADCIS, Akron, Ohio, October 1982.
10. ___, An evaluation of Audio-Tutorial Anatomy and Physiology (ATAP) (abstract) *Proceedings of the Thirteenth Annual Conference of the International Congress for Individualized Instruction*, Tucson, Arizona, October 1981.
11. G. Mandler and S. B. Sarason, A Study of Anxiety and Learning, *Journal of Abnormal and Social Psychology, 47:*2, pp. 166-173, 1952.
12. I. G. Sarason, *Anxiety: Current Trends in Theory and Research*, C. D. Spielberger (ed.), Academic Press, New York, p. 383, 1972.
13. R. Alpert and R. M. Haber, Anxiety in Academic Achievement Situations, *Journal of Abnormal and Social Psychology, 61,* pp. 207-215, 1960.
14. J. E. Sieber, et al., *Anxiety, Learning and Instruction*, Erlbaum Associates, Publishers, Hillsdale, New Jersey, pp. 31-32, 1977.

15. C. D. Spielberger, *Anxiety: Current Trends in Theory and Research, II*, Academic Press, New York, Pp. 481-486, 1972.
16. J. F. Gwinn and J. Sentieri, Factors Important to Student Acceptance of Computerized Testing (abstract), Ohio Academy of Science, Vol. 80, 1980.
17. J. R. Hinton, Individualized Learning--A summary of Recent Research, *National Society for Performance and Instruction Journal*, May 1978.